# IDENTITY AND FREEDOM

"Leonidas Donskis' book challenges both western specialists on post-Soviet nationalisms and Lithuanian readers ... Donskis' background and training provide him with unique qualifications to carry out this sort of study ... Moreover, [he] does not limit himself to narrow considerations of the identity of just one nation ... There is ample material in this book for controversy and discussion."

From the Foreword, Alfred E Senn, Professor Emeritus, *University of Wisconsin-Madison, USA*

Nationalism is not necessarily an evil phenomenon; nor is it about to fade away in our globalised world. According to Leonidas Donskis, general theorists of nationalism have so far paid insufficient attention to the ethic of nationalism as a resource for critique of society and culture. Donskis argues that this critical potential is, in fact, a key aspect of the symbolic organisation of nationalism.

In Central and Eastern Europe, liberal nationalism has become a crucial framework for modernising critique, not to mention its merits in the struggle against totalitarianism. The ethic of liberal nationalism should not be confused with the blood-and-soil ethnic cleansing brand of nationalism. Nor can nationalism be reduced solely to the rise of the industrial, standardised world. As an identity-building phenomenon, this book asserts that nationalism has sustained the modern intellectual and grounded moral sensibilities.

*Identity and Freedom* provides a discursive map of Lithuanian liberal nationalism by focusing on the work of three eminent Lithuanian émigré scholars – Vytautas Kavolis, Aleksandras Shtromas and Tomas Venclova. Presenting these critics of society – and also analysing the significant impact of such writers as George Orwell and Czesław Miłosz on Lithuanian political and cultural dissent – this book elaborates on their three models of liberal nationalism as social criticism. Incorporating material that has so far only been available in Lithuanian, Polish and Russian sources, this book will be invaluable for anyone interested in Central and East European politics, culture and society.

**Leonidas Donskis** is Paschal P. Vacca Visiting Professor of Liberal Arts at the University of Montevallo, Alabama, USA. He is the author of *The End of Ideology and Utopia? Moral Imagination and Cultural Criticism in the Twentieth Century*.

# ROUTLEDGE STUDIES OF SOCIETIES IN TRANSITION

1 THE ECONOMICS OF SOVIET BREAK-UP
*Bert van Selm*

2 INSTITUTIONAL BARRIERS TO ECONOMIC DEVELOPMENT: Poland's incomplete transition
*Edited by Jan Winiecki*

3 THE POLISH SOLIDARITY MOVEMENT: Revolution, democracy and natural rights
*Arista Maria Cirtautas*

4 SURVIVING POST-SOCIALISM: Local strategies and regional response in Eastern Europe and the former Soviet Union
*Edited by Sue Bridger and Frances Pine*

5 LAND REFORM IN THE FORMER SOVIET UNION AND EASTERN EUROPE
*Edited by Stephen Wegren*

6 FINANCIAL REFORMS IN EASTERN EUROPE: A policy model for Poland
*Kanhaya L. Gupta and Robert Lensink*

7 THE POLITICAL ECONOMY OF TRANSITION: Opportunities and limits of transformation
*Jozef van Brabant*

8 PRIVATIZING THE LAND: Rural political economy in post-communist socialist societies
*Edited by Ivan Szelenyi*

9 UKRAINE: State and nation building
*Taras Kuzio*

10 GREEN POST-COMMUNISM?: Environmental aid, innovation and evolutionary political economics
*Mikael Sandberg*

11 ORGANISATIONAL CHANGE IN POST-COMUNIST EUROPE: Management and transformation in the Czech Republic
*Ed Clark and Anna Soulsby*

12 POLITICS AND SOCIETY IN POLAND
*Frances Millard*

13 EXPERIMENTING WITH DEMOCRACY: Regime change in the Balkans
*Geoffrey Pridham and Tom Gallagher*

14 POVERTY IN TRANSITION ECONOMIES
*Edited by Sandra Hutton and Gerry Redmond*

15 WORK, EMPLOYMENT AND TRANSITION
*Adrian Smith, Al Rainnie and Adam Swain*

16 ENVIRONMENTAL PROBLEMS OF EAST CENRAL EUROPE: 2ND EDITION
*Edited by F W Carter and David Turnock*

17 TRANSITION ECONOMIES AND FOREIGN TRADE
*Jan Winiecki*

18 IDENTITY AND FREEDOM: Mapping nationalism and social criticism in twentieth-century Lithuania
*Leonidas Donskis*

# IDENTITY AND FREEDOM

Mapping Nationalism and Social Criticism in
Twentieth-Century Lithuania

*Leonidas Donskis*

London and New York

First published 2002
by Routledge
11 New Fetter Lane, London EC4P 4EE

Simultaneously published in the USA and Canada
by Routledge
29 West 35th Street, New York, NY 10001

*Routledge is an imprint of the Taylor & Francis Group*

© 2002 Leonidas Donskis

Printed and bound in Great Britain by
St Edmundsbury Press, Bury St Edmunds, Suffolk

All rights reserved. No part of this book may be reprinted or reproduced or utilised in any form or by any electronic, mechanical, or other means, now known or hereafter invented, including photocopying and recording, or in any information storage or retrieval system, without permission in writing from the publishers.

*British Library Cataloguing in Publication Data*
A catalogue record for this book is available from the British Library

*Library of Congress Cataloging in Publication Data*
A catalogue record for this book has been requested

ISBN 0-415-27086-3

To the memory of Aleksandras Shtromas

If the choice is between the nation and truth, between the nation and freedom, my decision is perfectly clear: I choose truth and freedom. Many people will reply, "Such a choice is unthinkable. The nation is precisely what constitutes truth and freedom." Alas, such a response is nothing but demagogy. However sad it may be, we often find ourselves in a situation where we have to choose. For me the prosperity and even the simple survival of the nation are dubious joys if they have to be bought at the price of hatred of others, of suppression of "elements harmful for the nation," at the price of conformity and lies. The nation is dear to me to the extent that its customs, history, and contemporaneity embody truth and freedom—values that are higher than the nation itself. And, insofar as by birth and upbringing I happen to belong to this nation and not a different one, my duty is to contribute to its everyday life the small part of those values that is within my personal power.

Tomas Venclova, *Forms of Hope*

# Contents

| | |
|---|---|
| *Foreword by Alfred Erich Senn* | ix |
| *Preface* | xi |
| *Acknowledgements* | xiii |
| Introduction | 1 |
|     Notes | 12 |
| Chapter One  Between Identity and Freedom: Mapping Nationalism in Twentieth-Century Lithuania | 13 |
|     Notes | 35 |
| Chapter Two  Vytautas Kavolis: Liberalism, Nationalism, and the Polylogue of Civilisations | 39 |
|     Notes | 71 |
| Chapter Three  Aleksandras Shtromas: Liberal Nationalism and the Politics of Dissent | 73 |
|     Notes | 118 |
| Chapter Four  Tomas Venclova: Ethical Universalism and the Discovery of the Other | 121 |
|     Notes | 161 |
| *Bibliography* | 163 |
| *Index* | 173 |

# Foreword

Leonidas Donskis's book challenges both western specialists on post-Soviet nationalisms and Lithuanian readers. Using the Lithuanian example, he argues that many commentators have oversimplified East European nationalisms—just as in earlier times they underestimated the significance of national feelings in the former Soviet Union. He does not deny the existence of "blood-and-soil" nationalisms, but he declares that "nationalism" has more than one definition. He insists that there are manifestations of national feeling that contribute positively to human ideals of peace and freedom.

At the same time, Donskis calls upon Lithuanians to look beyond the traditional beliefs of what he calls "mainstream" Lithuanian nationalism. He builds these arguments into a detailed discussion of three Lithuanian intellectuals, all of whom spent a good part of their lives in the emigration. Vytautas Kavolis (1930–1996), a former professor at Dickinson College in Pennsylvania, was a part of the flood of Lithuanian displaced persons fleeing Soviet rule in their homeland after World War II. Aleksandras Shtromas and Tomas Venclova, both of whom came to maturity in privileged Soviet households, emigrated to the West in the 1970s. Shtromas, who died in 1999, was a professor at Hillsdale College, Michigan, while Venclova is a professor at Yale University. While distinguishing the style and nature of the work of each, Donskis concludes that the thoughts of the three authors combine to offer a workable pattern for a liberal and democratic nationalism.

Leonidas Donskis's background and training provide him with unique qualifications to carry out this sort of study. A native Lithuanian, he has taken advantage of the opportunities offered by a decade of Lithuanian independence to study and work in the West. One could describe this book as a synthesis of his own experiences in diverse educational systems. His presentation makes clear his own western orientation, and he therefore offers the reader the rare opportunity of looking at Lithuanian national identity through the eyes of an insider but with western interpretations.

In exploring the ramifications of his subjects' thoughts, Donskis, moreover, does not limit himself to narrow considerations of the identity of just one nation. In discussing the works of his three main writers, he offers penetrating and challenging thoughts on a number of other issues, ranging from Jewish writings on the Holocaust to the thoughts of Romania's "1927 Generation." There is ample material in this book for controversy and discussion.

A few words yet on the *Santara-Šviesa* federation in which all three of Donskis's subjects participated. There is little written in English about this group that became controversial in the 1960s after the Soviet authorities had opened up the Baltic to foreign tourists. At the time, the major Lithuanian émigré organisations opposed travel to the Baltic, insisting that the act of obtaining a visa not only indicated acceptance of Soviet rule in the region but also contributed money to Communist causes. Participants in *Santara-Šviesa*, to the contrary, argued that there was in fact only one Lithuania and that travellers could actually influence Lithuanian thought and culture. As Donskis points out, *Santara-Šviesa* maintained no formal membership rolls, and therefore, in the style of the Russian Serapion Brothers, each member could paint his or her hut in any colour.

After the establishment of Lithuanian independence, *Santara-Šviesa* found new support in the homeland, and since 1993, the group has held annual meetings in Lithuania in addition to the annual meetings it has held in the United States since the 1950s. After the election of Valdas Adamkus, one of *Santara-Šviesa's* early leaders, as president of Lithuania in 1998, some Lithuanian nationalists have called *Santara-Šviesa* a sinister organisation that is bringing western ways in to undermine traditional Lithuanian values. Ideas and thoughts expressed originally at *Santara-Šviesa* gatherings in Michigan and Illinois may undergo considerable change in being transplanted onto Lithuanian soil, but Donskis's book nevertheless constitutes essential reading for anyone wanting to examine fundamental issues in contemporary Lithuanian politics.

Alfred Erich Senn
Professor Emeritus
University of Wisconsin-Madison

# Preface

I am happy to have been able to research and lecture at the colleges and universities where my friends and mentors started, or reached the heights of, their academic careers. Having spent the 1993–1994 academic year and the fall 1994 semester at Dickinson College in Pennsylvania, USA, I became a friend and disciple of Dr Vytautas Kavolis (1930–1996), Professor of Sociology and Charles A. Dana Professor of Comparative Civilisations at Dickinson College. I returned to Dickinson for the 1998–1999 academic year as an International Visiting Scholar. Kavolis was not there any more, but I felt his presence all the time.

Then I was fortunate to spend the 1999–2000 academic year in the United Kingdom as a Leverhulme Trust Visiting Fellow of the Department of European Studies at the University of Bradford, the University where Dr Aleksandras Shtromas (1931–1999) began his second career. My meetings and conversations with Shtromas's colleagues and friends at Bradford evoked in me a strong feeling of being back in time. Before I became a Visiting Fellow at the University of Bradford where Shtromas started his academic odyssey in 1974, I visited him twice in 1995 and 1998 at Hillsdale College in Michigan, USA, where, having achieved international recognition, he was Professor of Political Science. I would never have suspected that I was, in a way, to repeat his path, making friends with his friends and experiencing what he told me about his life and work in Britain.

Dr Tomas Venclova and I made friends in the United States, although we knew each other before I met him at the annual conference of *Santara-Šviesa* in Lemont, Illinois, 1994. Long before he rose to international prominence as a poet and literary scholar, and long before he was promoted to the title of Professor of Slavic Literatures at Yale University, Tomas Venclova served as a lecturer in literature, linguistics, and semiotics at his *alma mater*, the University of Vilnius. And I am delighted to remember that I earned my first doctorate in philosophy from that same university where I also served as a visiting lecturer in philosophy. At the same time, I cannot help searching for some elusive trajectories of human biographies: Tomas Venclova was born in Klaipėda, Lithuania, which is my hometown too. Mapping the company of critics, every single detail acquires its significance.

Therefore, this book is an account of friendship. For me, it was a blessing to become a colleague and friend of three eminent Lithuanian émigré scholars. Looking back, I can only describe my friendship with the heroes of this study as the high point of my life. Passionate and iconoclastic intellectuals, mavericks and dissenters, they might best be described as men of remarkable political, intellectual and moral biographies who richly deserve to join the gallery of great Central and East Europeans.

May this book—which I wrote as a continuation of my previous book, *The End of Ideology and Utopia? Moral Imagination and Cultural Criticism in the Twentieth Century*—be regarded as a token of my intellectual and moral fidelity to all of them. I dedicate the book to the memory of Aleksandras Shtromas, a recently deceased friend of mine, who was able to bridge ideas, cultures, and human hearts.

Uppsala, Sweden<br>
October 2000

# Acknowledgements

I owe a great debt to Dr Alfred Erich Senn, Emeritus Professor of History at the University of Wisconsin-Madison, USA, who guided me in the original concept of this book, and without whose generous support and expertise I would never have accomplished my work. In this case, I wish to express my deepest gratitude to a colleague for whose brilliant scholarship I have much admiration and whose work I would be happy to emulate.

I am indebted to several colleagues at the Department of European Studies of the University of Bradford whose benevolence, encouragement, and criticism helped me in preparing the manuscript for publication. My warm thanks are due to: Dr John Hiden, Professor of Modern European History and Head of the Baltic Research Unit, Mr Thomas Lane, Senior Lecturer in History, Dr David Smith, Lecturer in Contemporary History, Dr Martyn Housden, Lecturer in History, and Dr Gábor Bátonyi, Lecturer in History.

It has been a pleasure and a privilege to consult Aleksandras Shtromas's family members and friends both in the United Kingdom and in Lithuania. I am indebted to Lady Margaret Kagan for valuable information and warm conversations. I thank Dr Irena Veisaitė, Lithuania, for her encouragement, long-lasting support, and friendship. I am grateful to Dr Peter van den Dungen, Lecturer in Peace Studies at the Department of Peace Studies of the University of Bradford, for his important suggestions and illuminating remarks.

I thank the Leverhulme Trust for a research grant for the 1999–2000 academic year at the University of Bradford, which has enabled me to write this book.

I owe a great debt to Dr Kristian Gerner, Professor of East European Culture and History, Head of the Department of East European Studies at the University of Uppsala, Sweden, for graciously inviting me to Uppsala as a Guest Professor at his Department, and also for his valuable suggestions concerning my research. This appointment has enabled me to complete my book. It was my good fortune to be able to present and try out the crucial points of the book in interesting and thought-provoking discussions with my colleagues at Uppsala. I am grateful to Mr Claes Levinsson, a colleague and friend of mine at that same Department, for making my stay at Uppsala productive and rewarding. For generous institutional support, I thank the entire Department of East European Studies at the University of Uppsala.

I thank Ms Liana Ruokytė, Cultural Counsellor at the Lithuanian Embassy in Stockholm, Sweden, for her support and friendship.

I am indebted to Mr Vladas Straupas, Lithuania, for his kindness and benevolence in providing me with a setting in which to put the finishing touches to the book.

I thank the following journal for its gracious permission to include my work:

Leonidas Donskis, "Between Identity and Freedom: Mapping Nationalism in Twentieth-Century Lithuania," *East European Politics and Societies*, Vol. 13, No. 3 (1999). At the same time, I thank the American Council of Learned Societies, the copyright holder of this issue of the journal, and also the University of California Press for this copyright permission. © The American Council of Learned Societies. All rights reserved.

I thank the following institutions for their gracious permissions to reprint from the following works:

Aleksandras Shtromas, "Ideological Politics and the Contemporary World: Have We Seen the Last of 'Isms'?", in Aleksandras Shtromas, ed., *The End of "Isms"? Reflections on the Fate of Ideological Politics after Communism's Collapse* (Oxford & Cambridge, MA: Blackwell, 1994). Reprinted by permission of the publisher. I also thank the Political Studies Association, the copyright holder of this special issue of *Political Studies*, for graciously granting permission to reprint from the aforementioned article. © The Political Studies Association. All rights reserved.

Vytautas Kavolis, *Civilization Analysis as a Sociology of Culture* (Lewiston, NY: The Edwin Mellen Press, 1995). Reprinted by permission of the publisher. All rights reserved.

Tomas Venclova, *Forms of Hope: Essays* (Riverdale-on-Hudson, NY: The Sheep Meadow Press, 1999). Reprinted by permission of the publisher. All rights reserved.

Much of my creative inspiration came from my wife Jolanta, whose long-lasting support, understanding, and friendship made my book possible. May she regard this book as a token of our shared belief in friendship as a joint devotion.

Visby, Sweden<br>
November 2000

# Introduction

> The modern project promised to free the individual from inherited identity. Yet it did not take a stand against identity as such, against having identity, against having a solid, resilient and immutable identity. It only transformed the identity from a matter of ascription into one of achievement, thus making it an individual task and the individual's responsibility.
> 
> Zygmunt Bauman, "Making and Unmaking of Strangers"[1]

This book attempts to construct an interpretative and historical framework within which the traits and dynamics of nationalism and identity politics in twentieth-century Lithuania can be traced. In mapping Lithuanian nationalism, it also employs a comparative perspective from which we can view processes that are deeply inherent in Central/East European politics and cultures. As a phenomenon of the conjunction of thought and action, nationalism can never be located within a single political ideology or moral culture; nor can it be solely represented by ideological or cultural movements. Throughout the eighteenth and nineteenth centuries, nationalism manifested itself first in the philosophies of history and culture, literature and literary criticism—thus becoming an important part of the European intellectual and moral sensibilities—and then in various popular currents. Nationalism proved to be capable of equally attaching itself to liberalism, conservatism, and socialism.

One of the most puzzling traits of nationalism is its radical change in the second half of the nineteenth century and in the first half of the twentieth. Having started as a phenomenon of the Romantic ethic of compassion and of the sympathetic understanding of the Other, it became increasingly mass-oriented, anonymous, ideological, and doctrinal. Another feature of nationalism is its ability to transform social reality beyond recognition. As a thought-and-action system, nationalism, from this point of view, far surpasses any other phenomena of consciousness. Nationalism is not only part of social reality; it *makes* social reality. The twentieth century was supposed to have been the age of nationalism. Nationalism destroyed empires. Its explosive and reshaping potential deeply affected and hastened the break-up of the former Soviet Union.

Lithuania may well exemplify this process. On the one hand, it cherishes its memory and reputation as one of the multi-ethnic, multi-religious, and multi-cultural models of Renaissance and Baroque Europe. It also cherishes the most generous and noble-spirited traditions of the Romantic ethos of liberal nationalism, and quite justifiably so. In the late 1980s, Lithuania's national rebirth movement, *Sąjūdis*, and its "singing revolution" not only revived the spirit of the epoch of the springtime of the peoples (whose slogan—"For your and our freedom!"—was raised as the banner), but also became a litmus test of the Soviet policy of glasnost and perestroika. The first breakaway republic in the former Soviet Union, Lithuania came to embody the historic triumph of nationalism over forced internationalism, which is the high point of modern Lithuania's history.

On the other hand, twentieth-century Lithuania, in more than one way, departed from the noble-spirited ethic of liberal nationalism, which may be said to have been the initial phase of Lithuanian nationalism. Lithuania also departed from its multi-ethnic, multi-religious and multi-cultural past. The country became a typical homogenous actor of contemporary history. Indeed, already in inter-war Lithuania, the "one nation, one language, one culture, one state" principle had become predominant. The questions thus arise: What happened in Lithuanian history? Is Lithuania unique in the aforementioned breakaway from its historical past? To what extent can the small nation's nationalism be both liberal and inclusive? Does it now allow room for the discovery of the Other? (The Other may refer to an other social group or an other society or an other culture or simply another human individual.)

To answer these questions, it is first necessary to analyse the clash of conservative and liberal facets of nationalism in twentieth-century Lithuania. Such an analysis brings us not only to a proper understanding of why and how the most militant, exclusionary, and anti-modernist forms of nationalism prevailed, from time to time, in Central/East European countries, but also to a comparative perspective in studying the origins and dynamics of social criticism and cultural dissent in Central and Eastern Europe. This analysis adopts a multi- and interdisciplinary approach, bridging social and moral philosophy, sociology, politics, and intellectual history.

Interestingly enough, the difference between conservative nationalism and liberal nationalism is still overlooked by the current social sciences and critical scholarship in general. Liberal nationalism allows room for cosmopolitan stances and multiculturalism in politics and public discourse, as well as the modernising critique of politics and culture it employs. However insightful, the authors of general theories of nationalism—Ernest Gellner, Eric Hobsbawm, Anthony Smith, and Benedict Anderson, among others—failed to take into account the enormous modernising potential of Central/East European nationalism, in particular, the ethic of liberal nationalism and its implications for public discourse and social criticism. At this point, it suffices to recall Czesław Miłosz, Václav Havel, Milan Kundera, Adam Michnik, Tomas Venclova, and other eminent Central European critics of totalitarianism, ideocracy, xenophobia, and manipulative exchanges.

In this book, I am portraying three Lithuanian social and cultural critics of world stature whose insights into the nature of identity, freedom, individual and collective moral responsibility, morality and politics, and the discovery of the Other have become an inescapable part of what has been described by Milan Kundera as "yet another Europe," i.e., Central Europe. The critics are: Vytautas Kavolis (1930–1996), an internationally recognised sociologist who taught sociology and comparative civilisations at Dickinson College in Carlisle, Pennsylvania, USA—a major figure in influencing critical thought in Lithuania after 1990; Aleksandras Shtromas (1931–1999), a British-American political scientist who lectured and researched at several British universities and at Hillsdale College in Michigan, USA, a political dissident who was expelled from the former Soviet Union; and Tomas Venclova (born 1937), a poet and literary scholar teaching literature at Yale, who in the 1970s became a prominent figure of cultural dissent in Soviet Lithuania.

All of them are émigré intellectuals who greatly contributed to the debates on the politics of identity and freedom in their native Lithuania, which had long sought and eventually regained independence and liberty. It was they who anticipated the downfall of the Soviet Union. A scholar who should be particularly credited for this was Aleksandras Shtromas. He clearly foresaw and even was theoretically modelling the break-up of the USSR. In this, Shtromas remains unique in the political science world. They had also predicted the challenges and dangers of xenophobia, ethnic and religious intolerance, ideological zeal, and the resurgence of exclusionary nationalism in some of the post-Soviet republics and countries of "people's democracy." At this point, Tomas Venclova was a leading figure in Lithuanian political and cultural dissent. It was they, too, who drew a dividing line between the humane facet of liberal/modernising nationalism and the sinister, murderous philosophical anthropology of the blood-and-soil, ethnic-cleansing nationalism. This distinction was made and plausibly interpreted by Vytautas Kavolis.

They were all close friends. Kavolis and Venclova, although they had much mutual respect and admiration, remained relatively more remote with regard to each other than, respectively, Kavolis and Shtromas or Shtromas and Venclova—perhaps due to the fact that Venclova, as the youngest of them, was less rooted in inter-war Lithuania's reality, and, consequently, less affected by that period of Lithuanian history than Kavolis and Shtromas, who grew up in inter-war Lithuania, and who were classmates in an inter-war Kaunas gymnasium. Shtromas and Venclova, who were more linked to Russian literature and intellectual culture—let alone the domain of Russian and Soviet political and cultural dissent—than anybody else amongst Lithuanian émigrés, developed a life-long friendship. Shtromas may well be regarded as a unique figure bridging the worlds of Kavolis and Venclova—Kavolis's world of Anglo-American sensibilities, refracted through his Lithuanian experience and through his silent dedication to Lithuania, and Venclova's cosmopolitan and universalistic world of Russian, Polish, and Lithuanian sensibilities that also includes a deep knowledge of, and a great sensitivity to, the fate of Central and East European Jews. In his article on Lithuanian émigrés in the social sciences, Kavolis described Shtromas in the following way:

> Aleksandras Shtromas is modelling, within the frame of the Soviet dissidents' intellectual movement, East European political processes in a deductive manner close to the way of theorising of seventeenth- and eighteenth-century British political philosophers. The difference, however, is that individual actors are replaced in his works by acting social forces. Shtromas easily surpasses any other émigré political scientist due to the incisiveness of his insights into the dynamic implications of his premises, as well as due to the spell of his rhetoric. He is the only Lithuanian who would be capable of fighting Trotsky in the debate at the city gates, before a crowd of soldiers who had not yet decided which side they were on. Yet a representative of the empirical social sciences, i.e., the "American" school, may remain puzzled about the relationship, in his research, between the analytical models and the distributions of empirical evidence.[2]

In that same article, Kavolis presents his own research programmes and major contributions to several social science and humanist disciplines. He writes of himself:

> Vytautas Kavolis... can barely be placed in the domain of sociology alone. His early research programme systematised the data of anthropology, art history, psychology, and sociology concerning the relationship between, on the one hand, the expression traits of visual arts and, on the other hand, social structure and value orientations; this programme was also focused on the historical contexts of artistic creativity. The use of the data of many academic disciplines, as well as the taking of the entire history of humanity as his field of studies, was also present in the second research programme at

which he later arrived along with his colleagues from other disciplines, the colleagues who co-operated with him in elaborating the methodology of "civilisation analysis." The latter was developed as a framework for in-depth study, in a comparative historical perspective, of the broadest spectrum of issues in the social sciences and humanities. So far, this perspective was extended to the study of such issues as the history and typology of the modes of self-comprehension; the symbolism of order and disorder; and the comparative analyses of the models of evil, of moral cultures, and of the structures of consciousness. The results of the first programme, in the literature of the sociology of art, are considered to have constituted an alternative—which acquired the form of a new kind of empirical social psychology—to the phenomenological and semiotic schools that dominate the current sociology of art. Those results have also been compared with the works of Karl Mannheim and of structuralists. The second research programme had just begun showing its offspring in scholarly literature. [Kavolis] also wrote on social pathology, and interpreted cultural psychology of the nineteenth and twentieth centuries.[3]

Venclova comes from a different intellectual milieu. Unlike Kavolis and Shtromas who had always been academics, Venclova had arrived at his academic career rather late. A poet, literary scholar, and translator, he might best be described as a major figure of cultural dissent in the 1970s who joined the human rights movement and the Soviet political dissidents' movement through his broad humanist and liberal-democratic concerns, rather than plain patriotism and nationalism. As Anatol Lieven observes,

[a]lthough... he was critical of many aspects of the Soviet Union from an early age, Venclova by contrast only became completely disillusioned with the Soviet Union and Communism at the time of the invasion and subjugation of Hungary in 1956. In this, he was a good deal closer to much of the Russian (or indeed Ukrainian) reformist intelligentsia than to the Lithuanian nationalists. His first real move towards what became the dissident movement was not via Lithuanian nationalism, but in protesting against the Soviet state's treatment of Pasternak.[4]

Yet it makes sense to stress the emergence of what might be described as post-modern nationalism which, according to Kavolis, "would allow for and recognise the human quality of *openness* and the cultural characteristic of translucence...—a Miłosz-like commitment to one's own nation permeated with a responsiveness to others, a sense of multiple, communicating identities."[5] Indeed, Shtromas, Venclova, and Kavolis himself perfectly fall into this category of liberal and inclusive nationalism. In their case, such term as "cosmopolitan and universalistic nationalism" ceases to sound as a contradiction in terms. Moreover, they came to transform the theory of nationalism into a means of the critical questioning of their society and culture. Small wonder, then, that of Gellner and Hobsbawm Kavolis wrote: "The general theories of nationalism... fail to take into account the importance of national cultures in producing different kinds, or symbolic designs, of nationalism. This has the unjustifiable practical consequence that all nationalisms are treated alike—usually, by most social scientists, either with some hostility or with anticipations of their demise."[6]

Hence, the main foci of this book. It attempts to map the discourse of Lithuanian identity and freedom, combining social and moral philosophy, sociology, social theory, politics, modern European history, and intellectual history. Within a broad historical and political context of the dynamics of nationalism in twentieth-century Lithuania, it concentrates on the politics of identity and freedom, on the one hand, and the culture of dissent on the other. In doing so, it describes three modes of social and cultural critique originating in liberal and modernising nationalism. Liberal nationalism itself is conceived of here as a social and cultural criticism.

Nobody has yet attempted a critical and thorough analysis of how the Lithuanian intelligentsia, media, and politicians have reacted to Kavolis and Venclova's severe critiques of antisemitism in post-war Lithuania. This book may be seen as a modest effort to fill this gap. The first chapter of the book is focused, among other things, on some controversies that took place around the Holocaust, its assessment, and antisemitism in present-day Lithuania. All chapters of the book are devoted to the analysis of the Holocaust discourse, i.e., the modes of thinking and speaking about the Holocaust, and antisemitism in Lithuania. The assessment of the Holocaust has become, in Lithuania and beyond, a political and moral watershed in distinguishing between liberal democracy and radical nationalism, the latter being far beyond the liberal-democratic intellectual and moral sensibilities. Therefore, a study of the Holocaust discourse and of antisemitism sheds new light generally on the attitude towards minorities in Lithuania. In addition, a study of minority issues may be seen as a major contribution to the establishing of critical social theory. This is particularly true of the restored Baltic states, where the research or discussing nationality issues is often seen as an act of social criticism.

Since 1990 Lithuanian political culture has demonstrated a new political willingness and ability to accommodate minorities, their languages and cultures. Lithuanian mainstream politics has had much success in embracing, or at least not alienating, the Russian, the Ukrainian, and the Belorussian minorities. Lithuania has even become a refuge against censorship and political persecution in neighbouring lands. The existence of small groups, such as Karaites and Roma, is not, for example, causing conflicts.

Things are, however, far more complicated with regard to the Jewish and Polish minorities. The problem for Lithuanian Jews is that quite a large sector of Lithuanian society—including not a few representatives of the intelligentsia—is still inclined to consider the Jews as collectively responsible for the mass killings and deportations of civilians, as well as for other atrocities committed during the Soviet occupation on the eve of the Second World War. This represents the disgraceful adoption of the Nazi rhetoric that equated Communism with the Jews. In an effort to modify the charges that Lithuanians participated in the mass killings of Jews in 1941 and after, some Lithuanians have spoken of "two genocides," or—as some Jewish writers have called it—"symmetry" in the suffering of both peoples.

The notorious theory of the historic guilt of Lithuanian Jews for the nation's disaster, which up to now has been deeply embedded in Lithuanian political discourse and popular consciousness, deals with a Jewish segment of the Soviet regime as decisive. At the same time, this theory includes considerations on the allegedly subversive and treacherous activities, on the eve of the Second World War, of local Jewry, the latter perceived as lacking in loyalty, patriotism, and civic-mindedness. Hence, its derivative theory of two genocides, which provides an assessment of the Holocaust and of local collaborators of the Nazis in terms of the revenge for the Soviet genocide of local population. It is little wonder, then, that the theory of two genocides, which is just another term for the theory of the collective guilt of the Jews, has been qualified by Venclova as "troglodytic," thus characterising people who are still inclined to practise it as moral troglodytes. Regrettably, Lithuania has failed to bring war criminals to justice and provide an unambiguous legal assessment of those Lithuanians who were active in the Holocaust.

Also problematic is the parallel existence of Lithuanian and Jewish cultures, and it has been so for centuries. Antisemitism is by no means the only attitude to the Jews that can be accurately ascribed to Lithuanians. The predominant attitude may better be described as insensitivity to, and defensiveness about, inconvenient aspects of the past. The alienation of the Jews from their host countries and their cultures is more likely to have been a tragedy for the whole of Central and Eastern Europe, and should not be seen as confined to Lithuania. Yet a tiny minority of young Lithuanian intellectuals have shown, in recent years, a genuine interest in the history of, and a great sensitivity toward, their Jewish fellow citizens. The establishing, in the year 2000, of the House of Memory in Lithuania, which is a non-government institution inspired by the Beth Shalom Holocaust Memorial Centre in Britain and which includes quite a few Lithuanian intellectuals, is therefore a sign of hope for the future. There are many reasons to believe that Kavolis, Shtromas, and Venclova effected and stood behind a relatively new process of the moral reflection on, and theoretical reinterpretation of, Lithuanian modern history.

The Polish minority, although it is well accommodated in Lithuania in terms of Polish education and institutional settings for Polish culture, is still pursued by the shadow of pointless debates, often initiated even by renowned linguists and historians from the Lithuanian establishment, about whether they are "authentic" Poles or merely Polonised Belorussians and Lithuanians. However, the historically unprecedented improvement, in recent times, in the relations between the nation-states of Poland and Lithuania was a result of a realistic and sound foreign policy for the region pursued on both sides. This gives hope that the destructive ethnic debates will sooner or later be exhausted, at least as far as the Poles are concerned.

In spite of the quest for adjustment to new global realities and, above all, the pressure from the European Union—Lithuania is applying for membership—there can be no miraculous recapture of Lithuania's multicultural past. Political and legal frameworks for minorities cannot easily displace the authentic cultural or even metaphysical need for the Other; nor should they be too rashly taken as a sign of mature political and cultural tolerance. There is still important ground to cover if the defensive nationalist culture is to be replaced by Lithuania being seen as one of the big family of modern democracies: this requires the recognition of otherness as a positive asset.

Hence, the crucial importance of the liberal social critique pursued by Kavolis, Shtromas, and Venclova. Such political essays by Venclova as, for instance, "Jews and Lithuanians," "Poles and Lithuanians," "Russians and Lithuanians," and "A Dialogue about a City" (his dialogue with Czesław Miłosz on Vilnius) revealed a huge gap between the need for the Other—still a vague category in Lithuanian politics and culture—and a time-honoured tradition of self-centredness, self-righteousness, and self-victimisation. The gap remains a major problem of Lithuanian consciousness and culture.

Yet these great Lithuanian émigrés achieved intellectually what their country has yet to achieve politically, namely, the accommodation of Lithuanian consciousness and culture in an increasingly global and interrelated world of today and tomorrow. If culture precedes and anticipates politics—the reverse is true only of totalitarian countries—then the three Lithuanian critics of society and culture have demonstrated this better than anybody else in the twentieth-century world. At this point, Kavolis, Shtromas, and Venclova richly deserve to reach a wider audience and to be placed beside such phenomena of the contemporary critical intellectual discourse as Group 47 in Germany, and beside the great critics of society and culture of the twentieth century in general, such as Karl Jaspers, Hannah Arendt, Raymond Aron, George Orwell, Arthur Koestler, Ernest Gellner, Czesław Miłosz, and Zygmunt Bauman.

However respected and cherished in their native country, Kavolis, Shtromas, and Venclova are far from being properly understood and placed in an appropriate intellectual context. Kavolis, who is the most frequently cited writer on the humanities in Lithuania today, was rediscovered there in 1992 when he began visiting Lithuania and lecturing at Lithuanian universities. Yet Kavolis's critical and interdisciplinary scholarship is appreciated there only to the extent it has influenced Lithuanian cultural history and literary scholarship, thus failing to take into account—most probably because of the weakness of the social sciences in Lithuania, particularly in their theoretical and interpretative aspects—his major international contributions to civilisation theory and sociology of culture.

In contrast to Kavolis, who was never fully understood in Lithuania and, in particular, amongst émigrés, Shtromas established his reputation as a legendary and prophetic political analyst who foresaw the decline and fall of the Soviet Union. A mesmerising orator, Shtromas was capable of captivating even those who were sceptical or hostile to him. However, as a profound political thinker and as an essayist of great humanity and sensitivity, Shtromas has yet to be discovered. His political fame in Lithuania and amongst émigrés somehow failed to reveal the substance of his rich and iconoclastic personality, as well as his thought-provoking and passionate scholarship.

Venclova still remains a maverick and dissenter both in his country and the Lithuanian diaspora. His essays and public statements may be said to have become a litmus test of Lithuanian liberal-democratic sensibilities. A Soviet political dissident, Venclova is also an inner cultural dissenter. Although he is recognised in Lithuania as a national poet and as an eminent literary scholar, he remains alienated from the Lithuanian intelligentsia. Highly regarded abroad and also amongst Lithuanian Jews and Lithuanian Poles, Venclova represents the double dissent. The dissent which originated in his fight against the regime inimical to humanity and, subsequently, to his country—the reverse formulation would be in principle incorrect, and this is precisely why he has always been at odds with Lithuanian mainstream nationalism—and which continues in his protests against what he perceives as a deviation not only from the universally valid human values, but also from the historically formed and, therefore, characteristically Lithuanian intellectual and moral sensibilities.

Yet they all represent an important current of political thought in Lithuanian culture, namely, liberal nationalism which was and continues to be not a deviation, but the model of the historically formed and multidimensional Lithuanian sensibilities. On the contrary, it is the mainstream version of conservative and backward-looking nationalism, tinged with moral provincialism, which can be qualified as a deviation from the original and paradigmatic form of Lithuanian nationalism.

Much of the symbolic design of liberal nationalism, its ethics, and its moral implications for social criticism comes from Czesław Miłosz, the great Polish poet and one of the greatest intellectuals of the contemporary world, whose *The Captive Mind* may quite justifiably be said to have achieved a breakthrough in drawing the world's attention to the tragedy of the Baltic countries. This masterpiece of twentieth-century literature still stands as a landmark in social criticism capable of unmasking totalitarian evil, hate, and manipulations through the means of a faultlessly perceptive political essay. One of the chapters of *The Captive Mind*, namely, "The Lesson of the Baltics," in more than one way anticipated the best writings of Shtromas and Venclova. Following the path of George Orwell, Arthur Koestler, and Czesław Miłosz, Lithuanian émigré critics of society and culture have contributed greatly to this characteristically Central and East European attempt to disclose the cynical nature of ideocracy, regardless of how it masquerades and in what philosophical or political disguise it appears.

The first chapter of this book shows how the traditional Western concepts of arrant East European nationalism can indeed find the material they want. Yet the other chapters put forth the cases for understanding the democratic qualities that liberal nationalism nurtures in Lithuanian culture. And this constitutes the message of the book: if we fail to penetrate the identity and freedom discourse in culture, we will never understand nationalism—in all its diversity—in politics. And the reasons behind so frequent misinterpretations and misrepresentations of nationalism are likely to lie in the absence of the dialogue among cultures, rather than inefficient scholarship or politics.

Despite the propensity of the authors of general theories of nationalism to depict nationalism as a passing phenomenon, there are no indications that nationalism is about to pass away from the stage of history. Contrary to those who have predicted the imminent demise of the nation-state, nationalism is alive and well. Indeed, it is too early to play funeral music for nationalism, for nationalism may last as long as the human need for making history—as far as the need to symbolically repeat history is concerned—and for symbolic participation in the community of historical memory. An identity-building phenomenon, nationalism has always been and continues to be instrumental in sustaining the modern intellectual and moral sensibilities. As a social and moral philosophy, nationalism constitutes a separate modern moral culture. Like utopias and ideologies, nationalism comes to establish, within moral imagination, the tension between truth and value. At the same time, nationalism may well be identified as a driving force behind the proliferation of the social science and humanities disciplines, as well as the emergence of new boundary disciplines.

Most importantly, modern moral imagination would be unthinkable without nationalism as a social and cultural criticism. A modern phenomenon *par excellence*, nationalism stands between or attempts to bridge what has been separated by modernity: truth and value, tradition and innovation, community and individual, community and humankind. By unconditionally endorsing or passionately denying nationalism, moral imagination examines the modern individual's identity and freedom either as a great threat or as a great promise of modernity.

Like the nineteenth and twentieth centuries that were pronounced to have been the centuries of nationalism, the twenty-first century, in all likelihood, will be a century of nationalism as well. Contrary to the mirages of ideological consciousness, nationalism is deeply grounded in this-worldly reality and also in all recognisable modern idioms of human connection, loyalty, and attachment. Last but not least, nationalism is a litmus test of modernity itself. Therefore, to blame the dark side of the modern world solely on nationalism makes as much sense as to fight the modern moral imagination for inspiring the modern human individual to uphold his/her identity and freedom.

## Notes

1. Zygmunt Bauman, "Making and Unmaking of Strangers," in Sandro Fridlizius and Abby Peterson, eds., *Stranger or Guest? Racism and Nationalism in Contemporary Europe* (Stockholm: Almqvist & Wiksell International, 1996), p.62.
2. Vytautas Kavolis, "Išeivijos lietuviai socialiniuose moksluose" [Lithuanian Émigrés in the Social Sciences], *Mokykla* [The School], 10–11 (557–558) (1992), p.51.
3. Ibid., p.49.
4. Anatol Lieven, "Tomas Venclova: The Essential Lithuanian," in Tomas Venclova, *Forms of Hope: Essays* (Riverdale-on-Hudson, NY: The Sheep Meadow Press, 1999), p.x.
5. Vytautas Kavolis, "Nationalism, Modernization, and the Polylogue of Civilizations," *Comparative Civilizations Review*, 25 (1991), p.136.
6. Ibid., p.142.

# *Chapter One*

## Between Identity and Freedom: Mapping Nationalism in Twentieth-Century Lithuania

> It is easy to detect nationalism behind the official facade of prevarication in Eastern Europe. It is an ambivalent force, and a dangerous one. The whole value of world culture is in its variety of traditions and languages, but when language and ancestry become a fetish for salvation at the moment of slaughter, then I prefer to be one of the slaughtered. The humanisation of national sentiment is a matter of utmost importance and we must apply ourselves with great energy to this goal.
>
> Tomas Venclova, *Forms of Hope*

A phenomenon of the conjunction of thought and action, nationalism can never be located within a single political ideology or moral culture; nor can it be solely represented by social or cultural movements. Throughout the eighteenth and nineteenth centuries, it manifested itself first in the philosophies of history and culture, poetry and prose (thus anchoring itself in aristocratic culture), and only later in various popular currents. Nationalism proved adaptable to liberalism, conservatism, and socialism: this is precisely why it makes no sense to over-generalise nationalism either as part and parcel of the principle of collective identity or as the embodiment of social evil. In fact, nationalism—nearly from its inception—had been an inescapable part of liberalism. In the long run, however, their paths diverged.

One of the most puzzling aspects of nationalism is its radical change in the second half of the nineteenth century and in the first half of the twentieth. Having started as a phenomenon of the Romantic ethics of compassion and of the sympathetic understanding of the Other, it grew increasingly mass-oriented, anonymous, ideological and doctrinal. More enigmatic still is nationalism's immense ability to transfigure social reality till it is nearly unrecognisable. As a thought-and-action system, nationalism, at this point, far surpasses any other phenomenon of consciousness—not only a part of social reality, nationalism *makes* social reality.

Lithuania may well exemplify this phenomenon: it cherishes its memory and reputation as one of the multi-ethnic, multi-religious, and multi-cultural models of Renaissance Europe. At the same time, it has been transfigured into a typical homogenous actor of contemporary history. Already in inter-war Lithuania, the "one nation, one language, one culture, one state" principle had become predominant, prompting the following questions: What happened in Lithuanian history? Is Lithuania unique in this rupture with its historical past? Does it make sense to search for answers to those questions in the Central/East European understanding of culture?

## The Central/East European Understanding of Culture

Vincas Trumpa, an émigré Lithuanian historian who spent much of his life in the United States, once noted that during the inter-war period Lithuania transformed its will-to-power into a will-to-culture, and thus transformed itself from a *Naturvolk* into a *Kulturvolk*.[1] Trumpa stresses that this might help to explain why and how the philosophy of culture, developed by such Lithuanian philosophers as Stasys Šalkauskis and Antanas Maceina, flourished in inter-war Lithuania. In fact, the philosophy of culture of the first half of the twentieth century can be considered a specifically Central/East European—in particular a Russian, Romanian, Polish, and Lithuanian—phenomenon, for it sprang from "German subculture," which was related to European culture as a national variant relates to a general cultural model.[2]

However, Trumpa might have added that the principle of culture, and numerous projects for promoting the rise of national culture (and providing it with a theoretical or interpretative framework), was as empirically disconnected from mundane reality in Lithuania as was the nineteenth-century Russian intelligentsia from the common people, or the eighteenth-century German middle-class intelligentsia from the court aristocracy.[3]

Norbert Elias's *Über den Prozess der Zivilisation* and Louis Dumont's *Essays on Individualism: Modern Ideology in Anthropological Perspective* might explain and demonstrate how Central/East European intellectuals were bewitched by *Geschichtsphilosophie* and *Kulturphilosophie*, the German philosophies of history and culture. While Elias reveals the sociogenesis and psychogenesis of the concepts culture and civilisation, Dumont traces the history of the specifically German split between the realm of culture/ideas and that of politics/social reality.

Elias demonstrates how the German middle-class intelligentsia identified *Zivilisation* with politeness, delicate manners, and behaviour, i.e., the superficiality, artificiality, and even banality, of the court nobility and their life-style, while *Kultur/Bildung* was identified with the realm of *das rein Geistige* (the purely spiritual), which in turn was understood as signifying—as symbolically referring to—the realm of depth, genius, creativity, honesty, and true virtue. Dumont, for his part, shows how culture becomes detached from social reality. In his view, this tendency in German consciousness reached its apex in the German formula for freedom, "self-dedication + *Bildung*." My working hypothesis is that, like Italy, which historically and politically resembled Germany in the nineteenth century, the countries of Central and Eastern Europe became attached to a German variant, or subculture, of European culture, rather than to, in Dumontian terms, French or Anglo-American variants of modern ideology.

The following two implications for the Lithuanian understanding of culture might be pointed out:

(1) Lithuanian social philosophy inherited, from its German counterpart/predecessor, a hypostatised model of cultural individualism, which treats national culture as a collective individual. This type of individualism leads culture to orient itself and refer to identity, rather than to multidimensional human reality. In order to demonstrate how deeply this sort of hypostatised cultural individualism is grounded in German philosophies of history and culture, it suffices to recall Herder's treatises in the philosophy of history, *Ideen zur Philosophie der Geschichte der Menschheit* and *Auch eine Philosophie der Geschichte*.[4]

(2) The gap between culture/ideas and politics/social reality is deeply rooted in Lithuanian consciousness: it springs from the endorsement of "axial ideas"—a term nearly simultaneously employed by Karl Jaspers and Lewis Mumford—drawn from Germany's history of consciousness and ideas, rather than having developed from Lithuania's cultural resistance to Soviet domination, ideological and political practices, use of power, brainwashing, and so on. It must, however, be noted that the Lithuanian intelligentsia's tendency toward escapism, which developed as a reaction to Soviet ideological and political oppression, undoubtedly deepened the gap between culture and politics.

Vincas Trumpa, then, must have been right—culture (or, in his terms, the "will-to-culture") was the principal driving force behind the politics of inter-war Lithuania. However, while Trumpa must be credited for many interesting insights, he failed to stress that, because it was based on religious thinking, the concept of culture wielded by inter-war Lithuanian philosophers could not be effectively applied to either modern, secularised—in both religious and ideological terms—society, or multidimensional reality in general. Moreover, this concept understood culture as pure spirituality or as the conscious renunciation of social reality, and, thus, offered no way to process the complex, diverse, and multifaceted nature of human reality.

The history of consciousness, in contrast, can be considered one of the most appropriate research strategies for examining questions of ethnicity and nationalism in post-Communist societies. Both as an interdisciplinary perspective and methodological approach, the history of consciousness has been developed by Philippe Ariès, Michel Foucault, Louis Dumont, Vytautas Kavolis, and Hayden White. This approach enables in-depth exploration of the historical and cultural imaginations and of the flux of symbolic meanings in history. Moreover, it introduces a comparative framework within which sub-cultural versions of nationalism—as a general model for the conjunction of, and relationship between, the nation and body politic—can be traced.

Analysis, in terms of the history of consciousness, of the understanding of culture predominant in Central/East European countries, allows us to explicate the tendency to reduce culture to ethnic identity. Foremost among the methodological and epistemological advantages of this research strategy in the context of the history of ideas is that, on the one hand, it is possible to locate the origins of the aforementioned cultural reductionism and, on the other hand, to show how European identity as a whole relates to each of its national variants.

## Messianic Nationalism and its Overtones in Central and Eastern Europe

The American historian and political scientist Alfred Erich Senn once pointed out that one of the most characteristic features of Central/East European consciousness is a sense of vulnerability and fragility. This results, in his terms, in a "comparative martyrology," best expressed by the question, "Who is suffering the most?" One working hypothesis might be that feelings of innocence and victimisation—also very widespread in post-Communist countries—are nothing but an inversion of what J. L. Talmon has described as political messianism.[5]

Experiences of depression and despair usually call for symbolic compensation. For example, the new and allegedly vulnerable nations of Central and Eastern Europe appear to be determined by a kind of inadequacy of self-consciousness and collective identity, and as a result tend to look backward in—though this is not exclusively the case—an obviously messianic manner. For example, the Third Rome of the Russian Slavophiles or the Athens of the North extolled by Lithuanian neo-Romantics—among them the French poet of Lithuanian-Polish origin, Oscar Miłosz—are both symbolic constructs that seem grounded in a fundamental denial of modern Western civilisation and an emphasis on personal heritage. This was evident in the ideological disputes that took place, from the time of Peter the Great, between the anti-Western, anti-modern Russian Slavophiles and the Hegelian *Zapadniks* (Westerners), who were sympathetic to Western reforms.

This sort of Central/East European messianism has common roots in purist, ethnocentric ideology that is inherently wary of modern, and in particular Western, conventions. The messianic tendency undoubtedly penetrated Lithuanian consciousness and culture through the works of Adam Mickiewicz—whose poetic vision of Poland as crucified nation and redeemer of other nations can be considered the climax of messianic thought—and Polish Romanticism in general, not to mention Jules Michelet's revolutionary messianism and Giuseppe Mazzini's vision of *Roma Terza*, which, in turn, grew out of the *Risorgimento*.

The Russian pan-Slavist Nikolai Danilevsky's enormously influential comparative study of civilisations, *Rossia i Evropa* [Russia and Europe] (1869), not only anticipated the morphological conception of culture later elaborated in Leo Frobenius's *Ursprung der Afrikanischen Kulturen und Naturwissenschaftliche Kulturlehre* (1898) and *Paideuma* (1921), and Oswald Spengler's *Der Untergang des Abendlandes* (1918–1922), but also conceived of the development of a completely independent Russian culture, which would replace Western civilisation after its inevitable collapse. Instead of using such terms as "culture" and "civilisation," Danilevsky proposed a new vocabulary and a new theory of cultural-historical types based on a cyclical theory of history. Unwilling to claim full credit for this new perspective, he acknowledged his debt to Heinrich Rückert's *Lehrbuch der Weltgeschichte in organischer Darstellung* (1857).

From the perspective of Danilevsky's historical analysis and model for the future, the case of modern Lithuania is provocative. Throughout the twentieth century, Lithuania's self-image as the Athens of the North has peacefully coexisted with a moderate messianic construct, casting this small nation as an important bridge between East and West (the former often reduced to Slavic civilisation or Russia). This concept of a synthesis of civilisations—East and West—was elaborated and promoted by the Lithuanian philosopher Stasys Šalkauskis, particularly in *Sur les confins de deux mondes*, a book on Lithuania written in French in Switzerland. Later it was severely criticised by other Lithuanian philosophers and essayists, including Šalkauskis's disciple Antanas Maceina. Still more negative views of this thesis were expressed by such inter-war Lithuanian nationalists as Vytautas Alantas, in his militant nationalist manifesto, *Žygiuojanti tauta* [The People Marching On].

An examination of several inter-war Lithuanian philosophical texts reveals just how strongly modern Lithuanian philosophy was affected by nineteenth- and twentieth-century Russian philosophy. Two key Lithuanian intellectuals—Stasys Šalkauskis and Vincas Mykolaitis-Putinas—wrote their doctoral dissertations at the University of Fribourg in Switzerland (both written in French), focusing on the prominent Russian religious thinker and social philosopher Vladimir Solovyov. Šalkauskis studied Solovyov's philosophy of religion, while Putinas analysed the Russian thinker's aesthetics. During that period, in addition to Solovyov, other Russian thinkers—Berdyaev, Dostoevsky, Leontyev, Rozanov, the Russian nihilists, among others, influenced many Lithuanian academics and public intellectuals. In addition to other influences of Russian culture on Lithuania, these thinkers' ideas can in part be seen as a principal source of Lithuanian messianism.

Roughly speaking, Šalkauskis's vision of Lithuania as a bridge between the civilisations of East and West is nothing but another term for the specifically Russian notion of Eurasia, though this concept is usually reserved exclusively for Russia and its historic mission. Šalkauskis's concept of a synthesis of civilisations is merely a Lithuanian variation on a classic theme in nineteenth- and twentieth-century Russian social philosophy. "Eurasianism," both as a philosophical tendency and model of cultural/civilisational identity, was a central concept in Lev Karsavin's work and writing—he spent several decades lecturing in Lithuania, and fundamentally influenced the development of Lithuanian philosophy of culture and cultural history. In 1928, he was offered professorship at the then newly founded University of Lithuania in Kaunas where he arrived from Paris. An eminent Russian religious thinker and an erudite cultural historian, Karsavin soon became a fluent speaker of Lithuanian and established his reputation as one of the most brilliant lectors at the University of Lithuania. His five-volume magnum opus, *Europos kultūros istorija* [The Cultural History of Europe], written in Lithuanian and published in inter-war Lithuania, is a work of European significance and has yet to be surpassed among Lithuanian contributions of this sort. When the Soviet Union occupied Lithuania, Karsavin was exiled to the Komi ASSR, where he died in 1952.

Essentially, the same things can be said about Šalkauskis's disciple—in terms of their mutual commitment to the elaboration and promotion of the philosophy of culture—and critic Antanas Maceina, who, it appears, was deeply influenced by Nikolai Berdyaev's apocalyptic philosophy of history. It suffices to recall how Berdyaev, in *Smysl istorii* [The Meaning of History] (1923), defines the genesis of the philosophy of history as a painful reflection upon history, rather than in terms of how *Geschichtsphilosophie*, as a philosophical discipline, comes *sui generis* into existence.

> The historic catastrophes and turning points that lead to the crucial moments of world history have always contributed the development of the philosophy of history, efforts to reflect upon historical process, the creation of the philosophy of history, regardless of its logic or what direction it might have taken… The first substantial philosophy of history created in the Christian era—that of the Blessed Augustine,[6] which fundamentally influenced the further development of the philosophy of history, coincided with one of the most catastrophic moments in world history—the decline of the Ancient world and the fall of Rome. Another original philosophy of history (it was created in the pre-Christian era, with the first philosophy of history to enlighten humanity) was the Prophet Daniel's Book, which deals solely with the catastrophic events characteristic of the fate of the Jews. After the Great French Revolution and the Napoleonic wars, human thought once again turned to the philosophy of history and its constructions, and attempted to grasp and reflect upon the process of history. In Joseph de Maistre's and Bonald's visions of the world, the philosophy of history is accorded an important role. I do not believe that anyone could radically oppose the statement that not only Russia, but also all of Europe and perhaps the entire world have recently entered a catastrophic period in their development. We live in a time of grand historical collapse. A new epoch of history has certainly begun.[7]

The catastrophic concept of history elaborated in Russian philosophy was eventually adopted by various thinkers representing the speculative approach to the philosophy of history in the first half of the twentieth century. Popular throughout Central and Eastern Europe, it did not bypass Lithuania. In *Asmuo ir istorija* [The Individual and History] (1981), Maceina virtually repeats Berdyaev's principal thesis, agreeing with him that the philosophy of history is a product of historical crises and breakdowns:

> During such historical crises or turning points the philosophy of history emerges as a form of cognitive historical consciousness: the Prophet Daniel in Israel, St Augustine in Antiquity, Joachim de Fiore in the Middle Ages,

Giambattista Vico and Joseph de Maistre in the modern era, Oswald Spengler and Nikolai Berdyaev in our times—all of them theorised in times of historical catastrophe, and all of their theories are related to the painful and frightening shifts of history. The philosophy of history is a product of neither wonder nor doubt, but of suffering—both personal and national.[8]

An apocalyptic understanding of history thus led Maceina and other Lithuanian philosophers who followed him, or who continue to follow him in this respect, to conclude that learning—including the acquisition of historical knowledge—occurs through suffering. The philosophies of history and culture are, therefore, inevitably employed as the only appropriate framework within which the genesis and historic mission of the people can be traced. The people (interpreted in historical and cultural terms) and the nation (understood as a socio-cultural phenomenon, though with obvious political implications) accede to a meta-discursive level and in that context the proliferation of the humanities and/or social sciences is explicated. Unlike inter-war Romanian literary and academic intellectuals, who succeeded in promoting not only the humanities but also the social sciences, their Lithuanian counterparts remained locked within the philosophies of history and culture as the only relevant way of dealing with the question of where *We* came from.

It was Vytautas Kavolis who urged current Lithuanian scholars to make an analytic comparison of Maceina's ideas with those of Romania's "1927 Generation." First of all, the thinking of the 1927 Generation—including Nae Ionescu, Emil Cioran, Mircea Vulcănescu, Constantin Noica, Mircea Eliade, and Eugène Ionesco—can be seen as a model of Central/East European intellectual movements in general. They provided numerous explanations for the origins of the Romanian nation. They wrote and spoke in the context of never-ending intellectual debates about how to contextualise the nation historically and culturally: while attempting, desperately, to choose between East and West, Romanian intellectuals developed Western, Oriental, i.e., based on Greek Orthodox theological traditions, Roman, and Dacian, or indigenous, versions and interpretations of the origins of their nation. The 1927 Generation's members conceived their theories, doctrines, myths, and even their poetry, in terms of the ideological tension between East and West. Thus, it is possible to identify streams of consciousness that are paradigmatic of Central/East European nationalist movements—structural isomorphisms or, in Raymond Williams's terms, the structures of sentiments inherent in Central/East European consciousness.[9]

Second, the 1927 Generation dedicated itself to the search for the most appropriate ideological framework for the Romanian nation's pursuit of its historic mission. However, ethnocracy, messianism, rigid and militant antisemitism, conscious indoctrination of society, the creation of an ideocratic community and a theocratic state, and so on, do not accurately describe the reactionary attitudes shared, even promoted by, the Generation. They, not others, were the leading intellectuals who welcomed Ion Antonescu's regime. In this respect, the 1927 Generation can be legitimately compared with its counterpart in France, the *Action Française* movement headed by the Generation's French alter egos, Léon Daudet and Charles Maurras, and profoundly influenced by Maurice Barrès.

Notwithstanding obvious structural isomorphisms and almost identical structures of sentiments, inter-war Lithuania's nationalist movement differed in various ways from its counterparts in Romania, Poland, and other Central/East European countries. Although, as a meta-discourse, the nation in Lithuania emerged from the system of dominant ideas and values, intellectual strategies, moral stances, keywords and even frameworks for self-interpretation, the development of the humanities and social sciences in Lithuania at that time hardly compares with that in, say, Romania. Recall the debate between two influential inter-war Romanian scholars—Lucian Blaga, the philosopher of culture, and Henri Stahl, one of the founders of Romanian sociology.[10]

In short, for a long time the philosophy of culture was the only theoretical framework for the interpretation of the self; the historical essence of the nation; the nation's past, present, and future; and the nation's cultural achievements. No surprise that, in addition to the academic philosophers who developed the Lithuanian version of the philosophy of culture—Šalkauskis, Maceina, Juozas Girnius, Vosylius Sezemanas, Bronius Stočkus—a number of Lithuanian writers, journalists, critics, and lay intellectuals also contributed to the philosophy of culture by raising problems and questions related to the vision/project of Lithuanian national culture.[11]

Various explanations might be offered for why, during this inter-war period in Central/Eastern Europe, essentialist philosophies of history and culture so clearly prevailed over nominalism-oriented social science. First of all, neither Anglo-American nor French social and political philosophy had any significant influence in inter-war Lithuania. The weakness, if not the absence, of the social sciences in Lithuania might explain why and how, in inter-war Lithuania, entire epistemological/discursive dimensions did not open up—why an appropriate interpretative vocabulary for understanding society and culture failed to develop, and how, as a result, modernity and liberal democracy were fundamentally misinterpreted.[12] It was therefore not only the widespread influence of ideological discourse, but also the absence of an appropriate conceptual and explanatory framework that led to widespread misinterpretations and misconceptions of social reality.

This is not to say, however, that theoretical fallacies may have resulted from the incongruity between, on the one hand, social reality and the ineffective tools for social analysis, and, on the other hand, the lack of an appropriate analytical language. Lithuanian academics of that period were quite enthusiastic about Oswald Spengler, Leo Frobenius, Ludwig Klages, Eduard Spranger, Anton Hilckman, and Martin Heidegger, as well as, needless to say, the most prominent representatives of *Lebensphilosophie*, *Geschichtsphilosophie*, and *Kulturphilosophie*. Unfortunately, however, none were very concerned with the thought of John Stuart Mill, let alone of Émile Durkheim or Max Weber. As a result, the messianic nationalism that characterised inter-war Lithuanian intellectual culture sprang from peripheral models of consciousness deeply rooted in Central/East European linguistic and cultural politics and from what might be called the fear of modernity.[13]

## The Fear of Modernity

Among inter-war Lithuanian intellectuals insightful enough to be aware of the dangers presented by the spread of radical nationalism and Fascism in Europe, Mykolas Römeris and Valentinas Gustainis were most prominent. They represented an important—and very liberal—tendency in Lithuanian nationalism that also included Jonas Basanavičius and Jonas Šliūpas, the founders of the *Aušra* [The Dawn] movement, and Vincas Kudirka, founder of the *Varpas* [The Bell] movement and the author of the Lithuanian national anthem. Although quite unpleasant antisemitic innuendoes can easily be found in Kudirka's satires and pamphlets, his use of such rhetoric can be explained: in early twentieth-century Lithuania, antisemitism was related to anti-urbanism, which was deeply rooted in the collective consciousness of the Lithuanian intelligentsia, itself descended from the peasantry.

Needless to say, these movements were inscribed with linguistic and cultural nationalism. This sort of nationalism, though sometimes exaggerated, was rather inclusive and liberal. The *Aušra* movement leaders, for example, described a Lithuanian as anyone who had once breathed Lithuania's air. It is no wonder, then, that *national identity became another way of conceiving of freedom*. Such a positive notion of freedom—in contrast with a negative one, which might be characterised, following John Locke, as freedom from constraint—is evident in the political and cultural formula used to describe Lithuanian national identity: "native/national language and self-dedication." Inasmuch as freedom coincided with identity, the *Bildung* principle—in terms of a sense of self-dedication and self-cultivation—is seen as constituting the only path to political freedom. Linguistic/cultural nationalism and political nationalism thus become intertwined.

This specifically Lithuanian formula for freedom/identity might be the clue to some puzzling questions. One of them is the parallel existence of Lithuanian and Jewish cultures. These two cultures may never have achieved mutual understanding, to say nothing of achieving an interpretative framework within which to embrace or critically question one another. Prior to the Second World War, Lithuania was famous for its very large Jewish community (about 250,000 Jews lived in Lithuania; only 20,000 survived the Holocaust). The Lithuanian capital, Vilnius—occupied by Poland from 1920 to 1939—was known around the world as the Jerusalem of the North, and many internationally eminent Jews lived in or were from Lithuania, among them the philosophers Emmanuel Lévinas and Aron Gurwitsch, the painters Chaïm Soutine (a close friend of Amedeo Modigliani in Paris) and Neemija Arbitblatas, the sculptor Jacques Lipchitz, the violinist Jascha Heifetz, and the art critic Bernard Berenson, one of the most sophisticated twentieth-century students of the Italian Renaissance.

Yet none of these individuals was ever considered a significant actor in Lithuanian culture—despite the fact that it was they who inscribed Lithuania's name on the intellectual and cultural map of the twentieth-century world. Why? The answer is very simple: the Russian-speaking and Yiddish-speaking Jewish community in Lithuania was always alienated from the Lithuanian inter-war intelligentsia, which, for its part, cultivated linguistic and cultural nationalism both as a means of self-definition, and as a way of distinguishing rurally oriented Lithuanian compatriots (that is, the organic community; in Ferdinand Tönnies's terms, *Gemeinschaft*) from "rootless," cosmopolitan urban professionals (the mechanised, fragmented, diversified society, i.e., *Gesellschaft*). Despite the fact that many Lithuanian intellectuals—among whom, Jonas Basanavičius, Vincas Krėvė-Mickevičius and Juozas Tumas-Vaižgantas should be mentioned first—and common people were sympathetic to them, Jews and other aliens were excluded from the Lithuanian cultural/intellectual mainstream. The specifically Lithuanian intelligentsia decided who belonged to the nation, which they perceived as the embodiment of a historical-cultural project, rather than as empirically identifiable social reality.

The portrait of Lithuanian nationalism discussed till this point is a more or less liberal facet of Lithuanian nationalism that recognises all nations' equal right to self-determination and that conceives of the nation as a self-asserting, self-sufficient, and historically/culturally unique collective individual. This tendency, marked by a commitment to constant social and cultural critique in addition to the values of liberal democracy, thrives to this day in the West, where, following the Second World War, it was continued and developed by Lithuanian liberal émigré intellectuals. It is exemplified by the *Santara-Šviesa* [Concord-Light] movement in the United States. This liberal nationalism—representing the most inclusive, sophisticated, and humane facet of nationalism in general, by no means prevailed over conservative nationalism, without a doubt the principal form of nationalism in contemporary Lithuania.

The point is that, even in Lithuania today, the *Santara-Šviesa* movement only attracts an alternative creative and intellectual community consisting mainly of young academics and literary intellectuals. Speaking *in medias res*, sophisticated and insightful social/cultural critiques by Vytautas Kavolis and Tomas Venclova are still capable of aggravating the mainstream— conservative and populist—Lithuanian intelligentsia, whose members react with anger and bitterness, and often interpret these critiques in terms of conspiracy theories (one of the main ones equates liberalism either with moral indifference and ethical relativism, the alleged products of agnosticism, or with Communism and KGB networks), thus adding insult to injury.[14] Liberal nationalism, which calls for critical questioning of one's society and country in terms of universal intellectual and moral criteria, is condemned in present-day Lithuania to be relegated to the margins of societal consciousness and culture.

Lithuanian mainstream nationalism, founded upon the alliance and ideological kinship between conservative nationalism and the ecclesiastical power structure, i.e., the Roman Catholic Church and its ideological and political network, formed during the inter-war period. It was enormously influential during the 1930s, when it reshaped Lithuanian nationalism— transforming it from a nation-building process into an authoritarian identity politics discourse. This is the origin and the formula for Lithuanian identity, according to which being Lithuanian is equated with being Roman Catholic—to be Lithuanian means to be Roman Catholic. This identity formula and stance was decisively important during the Soviet occupation, when remnants of pre-war Lithuanian nationalism were transfigured—through religious resistance—to become an essentially defensive phenomenon of consciousness, thus establishing continuity in the collective/historical memory and, in effect, keeping Lithuanian identity alive.

Notwithstanding the positive role played by mainstream/conservative nationalism during the Soviet occupation, in inter-war Lithuania this facet of Lithuanian nationalism had dangerous implications for the country's politics and culture. In the first place, conservative Catholic nationalism was the official and exclusive ideology of then Lithuanian President Antanas Smetona's authoritarian regime (established by a coup in 1926). Second, it was principally responsible for the development of a new political discourse that had nothing to do with Renaissance and Baroque Lithuania's discursive strategies and practices—its multi-ethnic, multi-religious and multi-cultural identity. Lithuania, which had the historical and cultural inheritance of having once been a multi-ethnic, multi-religious, and multi-cultural society, was suddenly brainwashed by a new ideology whose consequences and impact on contemporary Lithuania are too obvious to need emphasising.

To this day the clash between these two facets of Lithuanian nationalism is marked by what can metaphorically be called the struggle for historical memory. Liberal nationalists, who, in the Lithuanian humanities, are represented by young literary scholars and cultural historians, generally lean toward study of Renaissance and Baroque Lithuania. Conservative nationalists, on the other hand, are represented by the post-war generation of writers, literary critics, and historians, who generally agree with the prominent inter-war Lithuanian historian Adolfas Šapoka's claim that "a true historian should reveal the importance of Lithuanians in Lithuanian history." This group has a shorter historical memory, and generally limits its attention to the second half of the nineteenth century and, particularly, to the first half of the twentieth. Needless to say, when the "one nation, one language, one culture, one state" principle is employed as a research strategy, it is always related to, and implemented through, a specific disciplinary choice. Thus, raising the concept of the nation to a meta-discursive level encourages, in the framework of the humanities and social sciences, the proliferation of disciplines, approaches, perspectives, discourses, and strategies. This is precisely how nationalism functions as a driving force behind many modern, and anti-modern, discourses.

Last but not least, inter-war conservative Lithuanian nationalism began to use an anti-Western and anti-modern rhetoric regarding the West and its derivative phenomena—capitalism, the bourgeoisie, liberal democracy, secularisation of consciousness, pluralism—as a threat to and incompatible with Christian values, national culture, and Lithuanian spirituality. In this way the Catholic Church-oriented journals *Židinys* [The Hearth] and *Naujoji Romuva* [The New Sanctuary] contributed significantly to the spread of anti-Western attitudes and rhetoric, which are usually accompanied by embarrassingly inaccurate comments about the modern Western world and modernity in general. Fuelled by translations, into Lithuanian, of texts by reactionary and second-rate Western writers, confusion regarding terminology, misconceptions, misinterpretations, and misrepresentations of the West and modernity provided a basis for what might be termed the fear of modernity.

The most striking and interesting example of the fear of modernity is Maceina. In the late 1930s and beginning of the 1940s, Maceina published several social philosophy essays betraying that he was simultaneously sympathetic to Bolshevism and National Socialism (which he termed "the new paganism"). This seemingly incomprehensible stance can easily be explained by Maceina's intense contempt for the bourgeoisie, to which he accorded the status of eternal metaphysical principle. Inasmuch as Maceina felt deep contempt for Western liberal democracy, capitalism, the bourgeoisie, and simultaneously remained consistently loyal to the Catholic Church, which he saw as essential to society's infrastructure and as an agent of political power, he quite naturally drew inspiration from Maurice Barrès's radical nationalism, and Charles Maurras's integral nationalism, which stressed the importance of the alliance between the Catholic Church and the proletariat in the struggle against the bourgeoisie, capitalism, Jews, and Protestants, as well as from Georges Sorel's ideas about syndicalism and social poetry, i.e., social mythology. In *Socialinis teisingumas* [Social Justice], *Buržuazijos žlugimas* [The Downfall of the Bourgeoisie], and *Prometėjizmo problema* [The Prometheanism Problem], Maceina's social philosophy reveals itself to be inscribed with one of the most reactionary collections of opinions to have been expressed in either the nineteenth or twentieth centuries:

(1) Hero-worship, almost equal to Thomas Carlyle's in *On Heroes, Hero-Worship, and the Heroic in History*;

(2) The cult of the dead inherent in the blood-and-soil nationalism;

(3) Prescriptive identity discourse, bordering with a kind of historical-cultural determinism, reminiscent of such conservative nationalists of the nineteenth century as Heinrich von Treitschke;

(4) The *Action Française* movement and its sinister ideas of clerical Fascism;

(5) Demonisation of and contempt for capitalism and the bourgeoisie, which Maceina apparently inherited from nineteenth-century Russian philosophy of history, Werner Sombart, *Lebensphilosophie*, and French social ideas—from Lamennais's Christian socialism to twentieth-century mystical revolutionaries; and

(6) Irrationalist thinking in general, resulting from a denial of empiricist approaches and of Anglo-American traditions of political philosophy.

On the eve of the Second World War, Maceina simultaneously leaned toward Bolshevism and National Socialism, which both, in his terms, embodied the spirit of Prometheanism that was incompatible with that of the bourgeoisie. What lay behind such an intellectual and moral stance is unclear, though Maceina's conscious acceptance of Nazi ideological idioms and propaganda was surely pivotal. Maceina himself was the architect of the Lithuanian Activist Front's ideological programme, which inspired the provisional government of Lithuania and stood behind the June 1941 anti-Soviet uprising. Indeed, this contribution to the LAF's ideological platform was acknowledged by Kazys Škirpa, the Lithuanian ambassador to Nazi Germany before the Second World War, under whose supervision the LAF was established.[15]

In the 1941 LAF's programme for the liberation of Lithuania from the Soviet Union, Maceina identified the following priorities:

(1) The preservation of the Lithuanian nation's racial purity;

(2) The encouragement of Lithuanian women in the accomplishment of their paramount mission—to provide the nation with as many healthy new-borns as possible;

(3) The promotion of Lithuanian ethnic domination in the country's largest cities; and

(4) The strict and uncompromising battle against trends within Lithuanian culture that are insufficiently loyal to and respectful of Lithuanian-ness, or that do not hold the nation and national cohesion to be the first priority in all matters.[16]

Maceina was most explicit on this issue in his article, "Tauta ir valstybė" [The Nation and the State], which appeared in the journal *Naujoji romuva* [The New Sanctuary] (March 19, 1939):

> The most important feature of the state is its cohesion... The existence of the new state is founded not on the citizen, but on the Lithuanian compatriot... The state, being the reification of the nation, cannot treat foreigners, or so-called ethnic minorities, in the same way that it treats Lithuanian compatriots.[17]

In terms of his doctrinaire stance and the spread of reactionary ideas, Maceina was far from unique in the context of inter-war Europe. We might recall developments in Europe prior to the Second World War, when such forms of ideological influence and mass indoctrination were widespread throughout Western and Central/Eastern Europe. The more distant a particular intellectual, or even an entire intellectual movement as in the case of the 1927 Generation, was from Anglo-American epistemological and intellectual traditions—common-sense philosophy, scepticism, and the critical assessment of ideological constructions in all aspects of life—the less immune to ideological brainwashing and indoctrination of him/herself and others he/she tended to become.

However, to caricature or demonise Maceina is the last thing I would do. Maceina should be credited for admitting his fallacies. Having established himself as professor of philosophy in Germany after the Second World War, Maceina critically reconsidered his mystically revolutionary prophecies regarding the inexorable downfall of the bourgeoisie and of liberal democracy. He summed up his former propensity to prophesy as a total failure.

It is hardly surprising that Maceina, who did not read English and was therefore unable to follow or critically question Anglo-American social and political philosophy, expressed naïve, knee-jerk reactions—or even spread pure nonsense—about liberal democracy, the bourgeoisie, capitalism, cosmopolitanism, and the like. How is it possible to say or write anything reasonable about liberalism without taking into account John Locke, Thomas Paine, Jeremy Bentham, and John Stuart Mill; or about capitalism, without reference to Bernard Mandeville, David Ricardo, Adam Smith, Max Weber, and R. H. Tawney?

What is surprising and embarrassing is that Maceina's ideological idioms are alive and well in present-day Lithuania. For the vast majority of Lithuanian intellectuals, nationality is merely another term for ethnicity. This confusion of political and cultural terms reaches its climax in the inability—or conscious refusal—to equate Lithuanian-ness with Lithuanian citizenship. By implication, if someone is an ethnic Pole or Russian or is Jewish, then he/she cannot be a true Lithuanian. The tendency to conceive of Lithuanian-ness in strictly ethno-cultural, rather than political, terms betrays the very narrow, rigid and exclusionary concepts of loyalty and identity that determine Lithuanian consciousness.

Without a doubt, the source of this tendency is an obvious misinterpretation of identity. Identity, in Lithuania, is often defined in terms of ever-presence, rather than in terms of activity. However, even well-established identities tend to be, in effect, empty. This might help to explain why and how Lithuanian intellectuals and even government officials still believe that they have the right to decide, on the one hand, where a man/woman—or an entire ethnic group—belongs,[18] and, on the other hand, why and how conservative Lithuanian nationalists perpetuate a phenomenon that might be termed "negatively determined identity"—an identity that can function only with the existence of an enemy. Needless to say, negatively determined identity—or simply negative identity—is always founded upon a conspiracy theory (such as "a Jewish-Masonic plot against our country," or the continuing influence and omnipotence of the KGB).

The fear of modernity is inconceivable without the struggle against cosmopolitanism. As in the former Soviet Union, in present-day Lithuania "cosmopolitan" and "cosmopolitanism" are pejoratives. Even the explicitly West-oriented and Eurocentric upholders of Lithuanian political liberalism and civic virtue—such as Romualdas Ozolas and Arvydas Juozaitis (both were among the founders and leaders of the independence movement *Sajūdis*)—suddenly appear to see cosmopolitanism as a threat to both societal cohesion and civic-mindedness and to the very foundations of national culture.

Liberal and conservative nationalism can be distinguished in terms of different attitudes towards the past. The evaluation of the country's historical past remains the only distinguishable watershed between the left- and right-wing political parties of Lithuania, too. Another criterion for distinguishing between liberal and conservative nationalism would be attitudes toward cosmopolitanism. Liberal nationalism allows room for the cosmopolitan stance—which can be seen as simply a way of embracing otherness, i.e., other identities and cultures—while conservative nationalism tends to exclude the possibility of a cosmopolitan stance from its political and cultural discourses. More explicitly, we might say that the struggle of Lithuanian conservative nationalists and populists against cosmopolitanism is but one aspect of a failed modernisation and a subsequent anti-modernist stance—both within a particular individual and within an entire nation.[19]

My working hypothesis would be as follows: these anti-modernist, anti-liberal, anti-cosmopolitan, and antisemitic stances are merely different names for the same thing. Within the framework of Lithuanian conservative or radical nationalism and populism, these phenomena and the terms referring to them—"capitalism," "the bourgeoisie," "secularisation," "liberalism," "liberal democracy," "cosmopolitanism," "the Jews," "the West"—are all combined under the same rubric of self-and-civilisation. George Schöpflin explains how deeply this anti-Western idiom of self-and-civilisation is entrenched in Central/East European consciousness:

> Anti-Semitism is not an automatic corollary of this set of attitudes, but the Jewish question inevitably became linked with the role of the populists because, as a result of the very particular patterns of Central European history, Jews were among the primary modernisers in the nineteenth century and came to be seen as the bearers of the alien values of modernity, albeit this was least true of the Czech lands. Some, though not by any manner of means all, of the populists brought anti-Semitism back to the political agenda, by in effect arguing that Jews could not become members of the nation, inasmuch as their ideas in politics were suspect and alien... Thus there were unmistakable hints in some of these ideas that the establishment of a liberal democracy was tantamount to an attempt by Jewish liberals "to 'assimilate' the nation to its style and thinking."[20]

It would be appropriate, at this point, to recall a thought recently expressed by John Lukacs: that the principal conflict at play in the twentieth century was between radical nationalism and liberal democracy,[21] that is, between, on the one hand, ethnic homogeneity and the goals of tribal subordination, and, on the other hand, a political-legal system based on morally committed individualism.

## Defining Nationalism: Ideology or Identity?

Nationalists, as a rule, tend to take nationalism for granted. Most Lithuanian scholars define nationalism as merely a phenomenon of collective identity related to neither a universally valid system of values and ideas, nor a prescriptive political discourse. It suffices to examine several examples of writings about nationalism—these vary considerably in their degrees of analytic accuracy and theoretical sophistication—to confirm how widespread this stance is among Central/East European scholars. This can be demonstrated by referring to Eugene Kamenka, the political theorist and historian of ideas, and Aleksandras Shtromas. In his analytical study, "Ideological Politics and the Contemporary World: Have We Seen the Last of 'Isms'?", Shtromas notes:

The topic of nationalism is dealt with in this book [*The End of "Isms"? Reflections on the Fate of Ideological Politics after Communism's Collapse*] by Professor Eugene Kamenka. Basically, I agree with the main thrust of his argument that single nations' nationalisms are not real ideologies but rather neutral forms of collective consciousness dictating certain common attitudes, preferences, values, orientations and goals. Indeed, a nation is a self-defined and unique organic entity bound together by what it deems to be its common origin and fate, but what in fact expresses itself in a specific set of values and goals shared exclusively by those who identify themselves and are reciprocally identified by others as members of that particular nation. According to Joseph-Ernest Renan, the nation is an everyday plebiscite, and I believe that a subjective definition of the nation, first put forward by Johann Gottfried Herder and then accepted and put into wider philosophical circulation by Immanuel Kant, is the only one that makes sense. To this definition I would only add one qualification, that of territorial identity. A nation which is not identifying itself with a certain homeland, is not a nation but a nationality which, by living in another nation's land without claiming for itself any different status, constitutes itself within that other nation's territorial realm as a national minority.[22]

At this point, I would like to make at least three critical remarks. First of all, nationalism is too complex a phenomenon to be reduced to collective identity alone. As for nationalism's relationship to different ideological frameworks, it is worth taking into account the following remark by Brian Barry:

> If an ideology is a general way of thinking about the world that has prescriptive implications for politics, then nationalism is an ideology—and by far the most potent ideology in the world. As a way of thinking about the world it emphasises the importance of nations in explaining historical developments and analysing contemporary politics, and also typically claims that "national character" is a pervasive factor in differentiating human beings. Prescriptively, nationalism carries the implication that all human beings should have one and only one nationality, which should be their primary focus of identity and loyalty.[23]

Moreover, nationalism—even if it is qualified as a para-ideology, rather as a *par excellence* ideology—historically succeeded in equally attaching itself to all three principal political ideologies: namely, liberalism, conservatism, and socialism. Secondly, one should distinguish, following Louis Dumont, between the ethnic theory of nationalism (put forward by Herder) and the elective one (elaborated by Renan).[24] These two theories of nationalism cannot be assumed to be identical; some distinction, if not a very sharp one, must be made between them.

Exactly the same thing can be said about Herder and Kant, who represent two different lineages in German social philosophy. Herder initiated the historicist-monadic lineage in the German philosophies of history and culture (Herder, Rückert, Frobenius, Spengler, and Hilckman), while Kantian political philosophy represents the universalist tendency in German social philosophy (including, in addition to Kant, Fichte, Hegel, and Marx). Notwithstanding their considerable affinity in what Shtromas takes as subjective definition of the nation, the Herderian discourse, based on Herder's *Geschichtsphilosophie* and *Kulturphilosophie*, and Kantian philosophy—universalist philosophy *par excellence*—are hardly compatible.[25] It should not be forgotten that Kant was the first modern Western philosopher to adopt the cosmopolitan perspective, and thus significantly transcended the limits of nationalist discourses that developed later. Finally, a definition of the nation that claims to be subjective even as it suggests (as in Shtromas's case) that territorial identity is a necessary aspect of national self-identification, ceases to be subjective and must be considered objective.

In short, within the interpretative framework of Central/East European nationalism, the Herderian discourse prevails over all other discursive strategies and practices. Although Shtromas was by far more analytically incisive and theoretically sophisticated than his Lithuanian counterparts, he did occasionally make pigeonholing points regarding nationalism as the only framework of consciousness that makes sense in the contemporary world. Even Herder, Kant, and Renan—who, in Shtromas's analysis, are obviously refracted through the theory of political change and its analytical/linguistic paraphernalia—do not provide theoretical justification for such a pigeonholing nationalism; as he demonstrates:

> Insofar as a nation tries to establish itself in the world as an entity independent from another nation's rule and recognisable as a separate and equal partner by other nations and the world at large, that nation's nationalism is justified in the same way in which is justified the demand of the individual for the recognition and guarantee of his right not only to liberty but to life itself—*for a nation is a kind of collective personality which, differently from an individual human being, cannot survive without liberty even in sheer physical terms; it will, in the end, either get assimilated by the nation-state in which it lives… or it is going to be otherwise annihilated. In all other respects the rights of nations as collective personalities are akin to the human rights of individuals, too.* In today's world of nation-states, this translates itself, in the first place, into each nation's equal right to self-determination and sovereign statehood.

Therefore, as long as nationalism is understood as "primarily a political principle which holds that the political and the national unit should be congruent" [this is Ernest Gellner's definition.—L.D.], as long as it demands for each nation the equality of political condition, it is a healthy nationalism deserving in my view the wholehearted support of every fair-minded person and every free and democratic nation. (My emphasis.—L.D.)[26]

Although, behind its modern political-science framework, Shtromas's notion of nationalism betrays the vulnerability of the Herderian discourse, it remains a potent alternative to the implicitly exclusionary and defensive nationalism so deeply rooted in contemporary Lithuanian politics and culture. However, no positive dialogue between Shtromas, who paradigmatically represented liberal nationalism, and his counterparts in Lithuania, whether liberal or conservative, was possible because of the weakness, if not the virtual absence, of the social sciences in Lithuania.

Aggressively defensive, exclusionist, victimised, and constantly searching for internal and external enemies, Lithuanian nationalism is not yet capable of theoretically reflecting upon itself. In present-day Lithuania, nationalism is either perceived as merely the cultivation of the collective self, or is described pejoratively as another term for xenophobia and the cultivation of hatred. This is a *coincidentia oppositorum*—neither attitude has anything to do with theoretical articulation and critical analysis of Lithuanian nationalism. Lithuanian nationalism lacks an introspective component. The absence of theoretical reflection and analytical articulation is betrayed in numerous angry reactions and *ad hominem* writings directed at various attempts at social and cultural critique.[27]

Another extreme that undermines any ideologically neutral approach to the study of nationalism is the tendency to describe nationalism in pejorative terms. Alexander J. Motyl accurately describes this extreme:

> Further complicating the definitional problem is that users of the term often ascribe to it an exclusively pejorative connotation. The adjectives that are frequently appended to the word—such as suicidal, irrational, hyper and emotional—reveal that nationalism is merely a code word for exaggerated national sentiment… Indeed, Conor Cruise O'Brien explicitly defines nationalism as "a conglomerate of emotions…" (So, too, I add, are love, hate and, alas, virtually everything else!)[28]

Nationalism is frequently described in pejorative terms not only by Americans—for example, the adjective "suicidal" was appended to the word by President George Bush—but also by Central/East European scholars, though an obvious difference in emphasis and assessment remains between American and European scholars. In fact, neither a highly enthusiastic point of view nor the demonisation of nationalism can lead to in-depth interpretation and analysis of the origins of this nineteenth- and twentieth-century phenomenon. Instead of attacking or attempting to justify nationalism, one should explore how it influences the social structure and symbolic organisation of a given society or even civilisation. For, in fact, nationalism has been and continues to be instrumental in the (re)shaping of modern consciousness and social reality. Such a fundamental change is worthy not of the reduction to which it is so often subjected, but of serious analytical attention and theoretical exploration. This is more than true with regard to Lithuanian nationalism.

Nationalism is the key concept of modern Lithuanian emancipation. At the same time, the older historical ideal of a multicultural Lithuania meets the criteria for a contemporary European democracy. Is it possible to reconcile, within the framework of the current nation-state's institutional settings and discursive practices, the ideals of nationalism and multiculturalism? Where within this dichotomy does Lithuania lie today? If Lithuania, as well as the other Baltic nations, remains at the nationalist pole, how will it reconcile democratic ideals with those of an increasingly multicultural Europe? How does a small-state East European nationalism relate to civil society? To what extent can this nationalism be inclusive and liberal?

Those questions come not only as a theoretical examination of Lithuanian nationalism, but also as an examination of the maturity of Lithuanian political existence and of Lithuanian civil society in the beginning of the twenty-first century.

# Notes

1. See Vincas Trumpa, "Kultūros filosofijos suklestėjimas Lietuvoje" [The Flourishing of the Philosophy of Culture in Lithuania], *Metmenys* [Patterns], 51 (1986), pp.165–166.
2. See Louis Dumont, *Essays on Individualism: Modern Ideology in Anthropological Perspective* (Chicago, IL: University of Chicago Press, 1986); Louis Dumont, *From Mandeville to Marx: The Genesis and Triumph of Economic Ideology* (Chicago, IL: University of Chicago Press, 1983).
3. For more on this issue, see Isaiah Berlin, *Russian Thinkers* (Harmondsworth, Middlesex: Penguin, 1979), pp.114–135; Norbert Elias, *The Civilizing Process* (Oxford & Cambridge, MA: Blackwell, 1994), pp.1–24.
4. For more on this issue, see Dumont, *Essays on Individualism*, op. cit., pp.116–118.
5. For more on this issue, see J. L. Talmon, *Political Messianism: The Romantic Phase* (New York: Frederic A. Praeger, 1960), pp.242–277.
6. The point here is that St Augustine is treated by the Greek Orthodox Church as merely Blessed.
7. Nikolai Berdyaev, *Smysl istorii* [The Meaning of History] (Moscow: Mysl, 1990), p.4.
8. Antanas Maceina, *Asmuo ir istorija* [The Individual and History] (Chicago, IL: Ateitis, 1981), p.4.
9. For more on this issue, see Vytautas Kavolis, "Centrai ir apytakos kultūros dirbtuvėse" [Centres and Exchanges in the Workshops of Culture], *Metmenys*, 68 (1995), pp.36–37; Katherine Verdery, "The Production and Defense of 'the Romanian Nation,' 1900 to World War II," in Richard G. Fox, ed., *Nationalist Ideologies and the Production of National Cultures* (Washington, D.C.: American Ethnological Society Monograph Series, No. 2, 1990), pp.81–111; Vladimir Tismaneanu and Dan Pavel, "Romania's Mystical Revolutionaries: The Generation of Angst and Adventure Revisited," *East European Politics and Societies*, Vol. 8, No. 3 (1994): pp.402–438.
10. See Verdery, "The Production and Defense," op. cit., pp.103–104.
11. For more on this issue, see Arūnas Sverdiolas, *Kultūros filosofija Lietuvoje* [The Philosophy of Culture in Lithuania] (Vilnius: Mintis, 1983), pp.148–189.
12. In inter-war Lithuania, not a single serious sociology monograph or even textbook was published, with the relative exception of vaguely sociological theses in the writings of Mykolas Römeris, a professor of law at Vytautas Magnus University, and an amateurish introduction to sociology text written by Petras Leonas, a professor of law at the same university.
13. For more on the time-honoured Romanian "flight from modernity," and the Central/East European tradition of self-centredness and lack of concern with political and moral dilemmas, traumas, and even dreams—what Milan Kundera once called "the tragedy of Central Europe,"—see Tismaneanu and Pavel, "Romania's Mystical Revolutionaries," op. cit., p.409. For more on this issue,

see Milan Kundera, "The Tragedy of Central Europe," *The New York Review of Books*, Vol. XXXI, No. 7 (April 26, 1984): pp.33–38.
14. The nature of this kind of ghost-chasing is very well expressed in an introductory passage of an issue of the journal of cultural resistance *Į laisvę* [To Freedom], No. 121 (158) (September 1995), p.2: "A spiritual gap is growing between the sincere Lithuanian intellectual, for whom Lithuanian-ness, Lithuanian culture and the nation's interests are of the first order, and that new creature—probably a product of the Soviet period—the super-cultural-activist-intellectual, who, supposedly in the name of Western culture, offers obscene trash to television programmes, books and theatre festivals of a questionable nature. Unfortunately, together with these self-named intellectuals comes another threat to the Lithuanian nation—cosmopolitanism."
15. See Kazys Škirpa, *Sukilimas Lietuvos suverenumui atstatyti* [The Uprising for the Restoration of Lithuania's Sovereignty] (Washington, D.C.: Franciscan Fathers Press, 1973), p.573.
16. See ibid., pp.567–572.
17. Cited from Kavolis, "Centrai ir apytakos kultūros dirbtuvėse," op. cit., pp.36–37.
18. According to Professor Zigmas Zinkevičius, the former minister of education and science of Lithuania, Lithuanian Poles living in the Vilnius region are, in fact, Polonised Lithuanians. In his opinion, they can have no awareness of who they are because, once assimilated, these Lithuanian Poles/Polonised Lithuanians lost their original identity. The minister concludes that it is every dedicated Lithuanian's duty to educate and re-Lithuanianise those people who are incapable of understanding where they truly belong.
19. The essence of the populist struggle against cosmopolitanism is perfectly expressed by Romualdas Ozolas, leader of the Centre Union, in "Įžvalgos: filosofo užrašai" [Insights: A Philosopher's Diary], *Varpai* [The Bells], 10 (1996), p.211: "I am a nationalist. Nationalism is the sole source of my strength. Each, according to the level of his stupidity, is free to decide what that means." The following maxim is a unique pearl of nationalist wisdom: "The cosmopolitan cannot be moral. The cosmopolitan is a-subjective; for that reason, he is incapable of imperative self-questioning."
20. George Schöpflin, *Politics in Eastern Europe, 1945–1992* (Oxford & Cambridge, MA: Blackwell, 1993), p.296.
21. See Tismaneanu and Pavel, "Romania's Mystical Revolutionaries," op. cit., p.438.
22. Aleksandras Shtromas, "Ideological Politics and the Contemporary World: Have We Seen the Last of 'Isms'?", in Aleksandras Shtromas, ed., *The End of 'Isms'? Reflections on the Fate of Ideological Politics after Communism's Collapse* (Oxford & Cambridge, MA: Blackwell, 1994), p.201.
23. Brian Barry, "Nationalism," in David Miller, ed., *The Blackwell Encyclopaedia of Political Thought* (Oxford & Cambridge, MA: Blackwell, 1991), p.352.

24. See Dumont, *Essays on Individualism*, op. cit., p.118.
25. On the misinterpretations of Kantian political philosophy that are widespread among nationalist thinkers and writers (especially regarding the Kantian notion of self-determination), see Ernest Gellner, *Nations and Nationalism* (Ithaca, NY: Cornell University Press, 1994), pp.130–134.
26. Shtromas, "Ideological Politics and the Contemporary World," op. cit., pp.201–202.
27. The thoughts of Donatas Sauka, a Lithuanian literary critic and scholar, are symptomatic of this hotbed of problems. In "Ideologija, kultūra ir absurdo karuselė" [Ideology, Culture, and the Carousel of Absurdity], *Metai* [The Years], 10 (October 1995), p.123, Sauka writes: "Who, then, defends society's conservative opinions—who speaks in the name of the injured nation, who describes its historical insults, who mythologises its rural moral reputation? Who, really? What is the point of trying out the sharpness of one's arrows when attacking a monster created by one's own imagination; but please give us a true picture of its traits, give us its first and last names! The liberals of the younger generation and their older colleagues among émigrés, who often hold condemnatory trials, do not have a concrete target, which could embody the essence of such an ideology. And the target of their polemic is not very fresh: faded ideas and moral directives, statements by the current leaders of the nation that were expressed during the euphoria of the Rebirth period [the independence movement.—L.D.]."
28. Alexander J. Motyl, "The Modernity of Nationalism: Nations, States and Nation-States in the Contemporary World," *Journal of International Affairs*, Vol. 45, No. 2 (1992), p.309.

# Chapter Two

## Vytautas Kavolis: Liberalism, Nationalism, and the Polylogue of Civilisations

> Fragmentary writing is, ultimately, democratic writing. Each fragment enjoys an equal distinction. Even the most banal finds its exceptional reader. Each, in turn, has its hour of glory. Of course, each fragment could become a book. But the point is that it will not do so, for the ellipse is superior to the straight line...
> Jean Baudrillard, *Fragments: Cool Memories III, 1990–1995*

Vytautas Kavolis appears as one of those twentieth-century intellectuals whose critical thought was in constant interplay with the subjects chosen by them for analysis, and whose disciplinary choices or methodological preferences were derived from, and suggested by, their existential and social experiences. The ways of looking at society and culture conceptualised and articulated by Kavolis obviously reflect his passionate striving for active participation in, and even symbolic correction of, social reality.

This is borne out by Kavolis's numerous texts dealing with Lithuanian history as well as with present culture, in which he explained where, how, and why his country failed to embrace the norms and values he so passionately advocated: the denial of any kind of collective oppressiveness and *consensus gentium*-type morality—as opposed to the principles of individual responsibility, reason and conscience; critical self-reflexivity of a society and its culture—against any sort of self-centredness and self righteousness; intellectual and moral sensibility towards the Other—against the sense of fatal innocence and victimisation; morally committed individualism—as contrasted to individual and collective forms of anomie. Kavolis's critical insights into the nature of clichés and even reactionary attitudes of Lithuanian immigrants in the United States (ranging from antisemitism, so widespread in twentieth-century Lithuania, to the lack of intellectual and moral sensibility in general), deeply permeated and penetrated by his own experiences, shed new light on sociology itself as a phenomenon bridging thought and action.

Vytautas Kavolis was born on September 8, 1930, in Kaunas, Lithuania. In 1945, the fifteen year-old boy and his parents fled to Germany and joined countless Lithuanian refugees known under the generic term of DP, that is, displaced persons. Having left their country occupied by the Soviet

Union, the family spent four years in various refugee camps. In Tübingen and Hanau, Germany, Kavolis finished his secondary education. Then the family moved to the United States where Kavolis pursued his undergraduate studies at the University of Wisconsin (1950–1952) and at the University of Chicago (summer, 1951). His graduate training took place at Harvard University (MA, 1956; PhD, 1960). His doctoral dissertation was titled "Failures of Totalitarian Socialisation in East Germany: A Theoretically Oriented Case Study." In order to imagine the context of Kavolis's academic relations and personal acquaintances at Harvard, it suffices to note that Pitirim A. Sorokin and Talcott Parsons were among his professors.

The years of Kavolis's youth and maturity are equally marked by his attachment to Lithuania. Yet, as opposed to conservative Lithuanian immigrants in the United States who were nostalgic about inter-war Lithuanian state and identity politics, Kavolis moved the centre of his intellectual and cultural concerns to the future vision of Lithuania and its culture. In his political and moral imagination, Lithuanian culture was projected as West-oriented, liberal, open, critical, self-reflexive, and equally sensible to itself and to the great themes or political/moral issues of the twentieth-century world. Although Kavolis never applied for American citizenship, thus keeping his fidelity both to the idea of Lithuanian statehood and to his own cultural identity, his political and moral stance was far from plain patriotism. Kavolis's stance can only be described in terms of critical and even severe examination of what he passionately identified himself with—Lithuanian modernity, its consciousness and culture. Kavolis always remained an American academic by his professional vocation and theoretical context, but a Lithuanian by virtue of his choice of being social and cultural critic.

Kavolis taught sociology and comparative civilisations at Tufts University (1958–1959), the Defiance College (1960–1964), and Dickinson College (1964–1996). From 1970, he was Professor of Sociology at Dickinson College. In 1975, he was promoted to the title of Charles A. Dana Professor of Comparative Civilisations and Professor of Sociology at Dickinson. Kavolis was Visiting Professor of Sociology at the New School for Social Research in New York (1970–1971).

When his native Lithuania regained its independence in 1990, he was active in numerous academic programmes and research projects at Lithuanian universities. Kavolis was Visiting Professor of Sociology and Cultural History at the University of Vilnius, Vytautas Magnus University in Kaunas, and at the University of Klaipėda (1992–1996). In 1993, Kavolis received Lithuania's National Prize for Culture and Art for his books on the modernity and contrasting models of self-understanding in Lithuanian culture, namely, *Sąmoningumo trajektorijos: lietuvių kultūros modernėjimo aspektai* [Trajectories of Consciousness: Aspects of the Modernisation of Lithuanian Culture] (Chicago, IL: Algimanto Mackaus knygų leidimo fondas, 1986) and *Epochų signatūros* [Epochal Signatures] (Chicago, IL: Algimanto Mackaus knygų leidimo fondas, 1991).[1] In 1995, Kavolis received an honorary doctorate from the University of Klaipėda.

Yet the discursive map of Kavolis's social and cultural criticism, likewise his intellectual portrait in the broader sense, would be missing a main feature if we were to pass by another key aspect of his personality and of his activities. Kavolis seems to have never been a disconnected academic solely locked within a narrow world of academic references and connections. I am referring not only to Kavolis's intellectual and moral commitment to Lithuanian culture but also to his need for active participation in, and symbolic correction of, Lithuanian society and culture.

In other words, he needed not only to construct cultural theory but to symbolically construct dynamic cultural practice as well, such a cultural practice which he could symbolically complement, correct, or at least affect through his explanatory framework, interpretative skill, incisiveness, and impressive power of analysis. After all, Kavolis was always striving not for the formation of his referent group in the strict sense but for the formation of his *Seelengemeinschaft*, that is, the community of souls providing some intellectual and emotional intimacy of human connection. As cultural theorist, Kavolis always tried to transcend the purely theoretical constructs, in order to enter the dynamics and mundane reality of his own culture, and, then, to experience and describe them from within. This is why Kavolis has come to define Lithuanian culture in terms of a cultural workshop, thus bridging the dimensions of cultural theory and cultural practice. In doing so, he was tracing and critically examining, in his own culture and its political/linguistic practices, those forms and models of the universally valid human experience that have been suggested by his comparative studies and theoretical reconstructions of society and culture.

Exactly the same might be said about Kavolis as sociologist. He was quite active in the construction of Lithuania's social and cultural reality, thus transcending the limits of the social analysis and trying to find out whether his imagined—for such a long time—community is constituting itself as the society *par excellence* (i.e., as a common political and legal framework for the self-activating public domain moved by the political and moral commitment and by human trust, rather than as a mere arithmetic totality of atomised and victimised human individuals).

At this point, Kavolis appears to have been nearly the paradigmatic intellectual. His life and intellectual/moral stance may well illustrate the notion of intellectuals as the agency of consciousness. Kavolis was the intellectual by definition, a man of the movement for whom his group was of great importance in experiencing a collective identity/group commitment or cultivating a strong sense of "us" against "them." Indeed, it was the case—without his vigorous journalism, persuasion, political propagandising, polemic passion, and even ruthless irony targeted at the conservative part of the Lithuanian immigrant community in the United States, Kavolis would be unthinkable. His group was of great importance also in disseminating his moral and cultural imaginations/implementing his ideas.

Every intellectual movement comes into existence through a kind of self-legitimising discourse or rather meta-discourse from which result such phenomena as theoretical strategies; methodological preferences and disciplinary choices; the proliferation of the social sciences and/or the humanities; keywords (such as "the people," "freedom," "toleration," "justice," "equality," "liberalism," "human rights"); and the discourse—i.e., the complex of the modes of speaking and thinking—of something that is equally important for all members of a given group or movement.

Such a meta-discourse, or background consciousness, containing the signifying centres of social reality, on the one hand, and the strategies or modes of speaking of them, on the other, calls for a Grand Text. It may well be a programme document, manifesto, encyclopaedia (as in the case of the *Encyclopédie* of the French Enlightenment movement), or journal (as in the case of the *Aušra* and *Varpas* nationalist movements and their journals on the eve of the emergence of modern Lithuania).

For Kavolis, the *Santara-Šviesa* federation—that is, the cultural union of Lithuanian immigrant liberals in the United States headed by Kavolis—virtually became his intellectual/cultural movement and *Seelengemeinschaft*, whereas the vision of modern, liberal and West-oriented Lithuania, accompanied by the search for the new political and cultural discourse capable of contextualising and articulating Lithuanian liberalism, served as the aforementioned meta-discourse. Subsequently, the *Metmenys* [Patterns]—i.e., the cultural journal of the *Santara-Šviesa* movement edited by Kavolis from 1959 to 1996—had become his Grand Text. Sadly and symbolically, Kavolis died on June 24, 1996, immediately after the annual conference of *Santara-Šviesa* in Vilnius, Lithuania.

Existential, cultural, and ideological links between Kavolis and *Santara-Šviesa* reveal Kavolis to have been a man of political and cultural dissent. The pattern of thought that was to be fully developed by Kavolis arose first in the student group *Šviesa*, formed in Germany in 1946, and then in the American student group *Santara*, formed in 1953. An ambitious student movement, *Santara* came to formulate new goals for Lithuanians living abroad. Together, *Santara* and *Šviesa* initiated a new policy whose essence lay in establishing better communications with Lithuania. The purpose of their pragmatic policy was threefold: to learn more about actual conditions in the homeland, to open Lithuania up to modern Western intellectual currents, and to confirm the thought that there was in fact but one, united Lithuanian culture.

*Santara-Šviesa* evoked much controversy in the Lithuanian immigrant community dispersed all over the world. First, in the context of the mainstream of conservative Lithuanian culture dominated by the politically and intellectually influential Catholic Church, liberalism inevitably meant strong opposition to the Catholic Church. It is little wonder that liberalism, in inter-war Lithuania and in the post-war Lithuanian immigrant community, was associated with anti-clericalism, agnosticism, and radicalism, a typical case in a Catholic culture. It was the way in which conservative Lithuanian immigrants started identifying the beginnings of the "suspect and alien ideas," thus implying guilt by association. In fact, *Santara-Šviesa* raised the idea of the Westward-looking, fully emancipated, liberal-democratic, inclusive and cosmopolitan Lithuanian-ness as their banner.

However, there was one more good reason for controversy. Whereas the vast majority of Lithuanian immigrants in the United States were convinced that there should be no ties between their community and occupied Lithuania, *Santara-Šviesa*, in the 1980s, began inviting Lithuanian artists and scholars to participate in its annual conferences in the United States. Moreover, members of this cultural union launched a book- and magazine-smuggling campaign in Lithuania, quite a risky and dangerous undertaking in those days. They took it for granted that Lithuania would sooner or later regain independence and that the lessons of liberal democracy and pluralism were of decisive importance for Lithuanian consciousness and culture. This is how the *Metmenys* and other liberal émigré journals and magazines reached not a few Lithuanian intellectuals.

Those actions had sharply divided the Lithuanian community in the United States. Whilst the mainstream of Lithuanian immigrants held that every single contact with Soviet officials and high-ranking compatriots was, in effect, unacceptable on political and moral grounds (as legitimising the Soviet regime in Lithuania) and that there was no Lithuania any more but the Lithuanian communities in foreign countries, *Santara-Šviesa* proclaimed its slogan, "Face to Lithuania," thus assuming the fact that the Lithuanian communities abroad were all branches of the sole tree which was nowhere else but in Lithuania. Constantly abused and labelled by the conservative immigrant press either as KGB spies or as "a bunch of godless pinkos," Kavolis and his friends from *Santara-Šviesa* had reached a much wider audience among the Lithuanian intelligentsia than all the militant immigrant fighters for Lithuania's independence and freedom combined. The final outcome was that *Santara-Šviesa*, not others, had eventually made a profound impact on the beginnings of the modernising and liberal nationalism in Lithuania, a process that reached its climax after 1990.

*Santara-Šviesa* appears as a *sui generis* phenomenon in the modern political and cultural history of Lithuania. It was a loose organisation. Small wonder, then, that it puzzled not only other émigré organisations, but Soviet Lithuania's officials, too. Soviet authorities had particular misgivings about *Santara-Šviesa*, which, in a concept formulated by the KGB, was "an organisation without an organisation." There was simply no clandestine organisation to penetrate and misinform. Instead, all participants and observers of the *Santara-Šviesa* annual conferences were allowed and even encouraged to discuss every single issue concerning its book-publishing strategy, forthcoming conferences and other cultural events, or overall intellectual stance shared by *Santara-Šviesa*. Moreover, all present there, regardless of their political allegiances and convictions, were encouraged to vote in making decisions. The character and political orientation of *Santara-Šviesa* might best be described by recalling the war cry raised by Kavolis: "Revisionists of the world, unite, you have nothing to lose but your orthodoxy!" Small wonder, then, that the KGB viewed *Santara-Šviesa's* ideas as subversive to the Soviet system; it particularly disliked the group's mocking slogan, "Revisionists of the world, unite!"

It suffices to glance at the way Kavolis had been leading the International Society for the Comparative Study of Civilisations (1977–1983) to prove that he had always been the programme intellectual, a man of the movement *par excellence*. In the United States (and in the Anglo-American world in general), the International Society for the Comparative Study of Civilisations (ISCSC) had become, for Kavolis, his intellectual movement and *Seelengemeinschaft*, while his international meta-discourse might have been defined, in his own terms, as the search for the "multi-civilisational universe of discourse" in the social sciences and the humanities.² The *Comparative Civilizations Review* served, for Kavolis, as the Grand Text, even in the sense of a historical narrative.

The movement of North American civilisationists, initiated by Sorokin and then essentially influenced by Benjamin Nelson and Kavolis, seems to have been perceived by Kavolis as the collective alter ego of the *Santara-Šviesa* movement. Kavolis named the latter the Institute for Multidisciplinary Studies not in vain; thus his intellectual commitment and moral one coincided. Exactly the same may be said about the invisible kinship between the *Metmenys* and the *Comparative Civilizations Review*. Indeed, *Santara-Šviesa* and the ISCSC, in Kavolis's life, were the communities of affinity in terms of his life-long search for the ways of understanding the Other—in the idiom of self-and-civilisation.

Kavolis's social and cultural criticism would be unthinkable without those methodologies that have been elaborated and vitalised by him— civilisation analysis (along with Benjamin Nelson, S. N. Eisenstadt, and Louis Dumont) and the history of consciousness (among his predecessors and co-contributors, in theoretically constructing this interpretative technique and methodology, one could list Philippe Ariès, Michel Foucault, Louis Dumont, and Hayden White). The former provides a framework within which the key components of every sociologically identifiable civilisation—of its social structure and symbolic organisation—can be traced, in order to uncover the flux of symbolic meaning; whereas the latter employs in-depth structural exploration of the dynamics of the tendencies of consciousness and of the predominant ideas in a given society or culture or historical epoch.³ They both bring us to a proper understanding of what has been suppressed in one civilisation but more or less released and developed in other, let alone the models of self-understanding and the ways of the perception of the Other.

## The Concept of Civilisation

Kavolis's intense, thorough, and impeccable scholarship allows us to theoretically reconstruct the discursive map of the concept of civilisation. His theoretical concerns and the frame of reference range from the classical exponents of sociological thought and civilisation theory (Max Weber, Marcel Mauss, Sorokin, and Elias) to the mainstream of the contemporary Anglo-American and European social scientists and humanists. In his contributions, Kavolis names Benjamin Nelson a major contributor to the civilisation-analytic perspective, although it is beyond any doubt that

Kavolis's own name and scholarship have become inseparable from this perspective and from civilisation theory. It is very important to theoretically reconstruct and describe in detail Kavolis's concept of civilisation, since his theory of nationalism can only be properly understood within the framework of his civilisation theory.

The following foci represent the conceptual frame within which Kavolis defined and described civilisations as the largest comprehensible and theoretically identifiable units of socio-cultural study:

(1) Civilisations as the largest comprehensible units of socio-cultural study consisting of social structure and symbolic organisation;

(2) Civilisations as symbolic designs (such as symbolic authority, power, configuration of values and ideas);

(3) Civilisations as mentalities/histories of mentalities;

(4) Civilisations as explanatory or interpretative frameworks within which people search for the concepts and frames of meaning to explain themselves and the world around them;

(5) Civilisations as theories dealing with world history and with the phenomena of consciousness and culture in terms of their interplay and coherence;

(6) Civilisations as the relationships between theory and practice—the working definition of civilisations most favoured by Kavolis; and

(7) The controlling principles of civilisations: among early, or "classical," theorists of civilisations who have contributed substantially to the study of the controlling principles of comparative civilisations, Spengler and Sorokin should be mentioned first; among current theorists of civilisations, we could list Dumont, Francis L. K. Hsu, and Takie Sugiyama Lebra.

In his last book, *Civilization Analysis as a Sociology of Culture*, which may be regarded as his major contribution to civilisation theory, Kavolis defines the civilisational approach in the following way:

> The civilisational approach differs from other schools of thought in sociology in taking as its primary object of study the symbolic designs within which social action is located. These designs are examined in their empirical specificity, in their historical trajectories, and in comparative perspective as frameworks from which human actors derive their conceptions of action, of its purposes, and of themselves... Civilisational sociologists seek to understand how these designs evolve and are put together within a civilisation (the largest comprehensible unit of socio-cultural study)—and how people draw upon them in constituting their actions both in the ordinary circumstances of their lives and in the critical

junctures of their histories. Civilisational sociologists claim that this approach is necessary for an adequate understanding of major sociological processes, such as political transformations, religious and economic "rationalisations of the world" and anti-modernist reactions to them, and shifts in self-comprehension.[4]

Having defined the civilisational approach, Kavolis engages in mapping two modes of being of civilisational sociology. The analysis of Dumont and Eisenstadt's theories of the rise of modern individualism enables Kavolis to make an important distinction between nomothetic and ideographic approaches to the comparative study of civilisations—a pivotal issue in the philosophy of the social sciences since neo-Kantians.

This last major contribution of Kavolis to civilisation analysis raises a number of questions crucial for the social sciences and humanities, ranging from the paradigms of order and the coherence of cultures to the models of collective identity and civilisational processes in contemporary Eastern Europe. In tracing the ancient and modern images of order and disorder, Kavolis comes to reconstruct the symbolic designs, or paradigms of order, within which the historical and cultural imaginations, blueprints for social and moral order, political power structures, and institutional networks operate over time. The paradigms of order are: "the lawful and spontaneous natures," "the order of the factory," and "the order of the work of art."

The concept of "lawful nature" sheds new light not only on the mediaeval practices of exorcism, witch hunts, the struggle against earthly representations and agencies of evil, demons, fiends, and *maleficia*, but also on Freud's dictum, "Biology is destiny," not to mention the dichotomising of the realm of cultural and moral categories into "righteousness" and "transgression," "purity" and "pollution," "sanity" and "madness," "true consciousness" and "illusion." Hence, Kavolis offers a remarkable insight into inversions of structure that occur within lawful nature:

> Where either hierarchy or dichotomy is present, the possibility of inversion—turning the world upside down, sanctification or transgression, Satanisation of an earlier set of deities, the aesthetics of ugliness, resurrection from the dead, the perception of "madness" as a superior kind of "health"—is always a live possibility, whether tempting or threatening... Inversion of structure is possible only within lawful nature. (p.63)

Having started from his illuminating and elegant insights into the nature of the mediaeval feasts of fools, carnivals, and other anti-structural phenomena (in this, Kavolis relies on such scholars as Victor Turner and Mikhail Bakhtin), Kavolis examines the concepts and patterns of chaos and order in Hinduism, in Chinese religions and social thought, in Judaeo-Christian cosmology and theology, and in Marxist social philosophy.

Kavolis's analysis of the order of the factory reveals the roots of magical and technocratic consciousness, of the sociological concepts of "mega-machines," and of the notions of economic and technological efficiency.

> The historical roots of the factory conception of order may be sought in magic, in the sociological "mega-machines" by which the ancient civilisations accomplished the building of pyramids and irrigation works, in Chinese Legalism, and especially in the Christian God's assignment to men of the obligation to transform the face of the earth in accordance with divine specifications… The machine, in much of its earlier history, and in the notion of the *machina mundi*, was used as the explanation of how the universe, or a particular part thereof, operates, not as the instrumentality for changing it… It was a revolutionising of this view of the machine attained under the influence of spiritual presuppositions—of which Puritanism has been in modern times perhaps the most outstanding—that made it the technological foundation of the factory. The early technologists have been interpreting the world, the ideologists first thought of changing it. (p.71)

Thus, an elegant allusion to Marx's 11th thesis on Feuerbach—"Up till now the philosophers have only interpreted the world; the point, however, is to change it"—underlines Kavolis's great theoretical ambition to grasp how the great ideas, concepts, explanatory systems, and interpretative frameworks come to shape social reality transforming themselves into ideological programmes, political doctrines, technological innovations, and finally, into paraphernalia of a mass anonymous society—a world of factories, offices, bureaucracy, and "rationalisation." The question arises: What kind of symbolic design or pattern of civilisation or interpretative framework might be identified behind the rise of capitalism and the genesis of modern bureaucracy?

As Kavolis clearly demonstrates, the efficiency, within the symbolic framework for the order of the factory, is achieved at the expense of other crucial social and moral faculties of human existence. "When social action is oriented to the symbolic framework of the factory, it has an immense capacity of producing specified types of effects (whether victories in sports or in warfare, capitalistic affluence or revolutionary reconstruction of society), but it does so at the cost of destroying the larger natural, social, and moral contexts within which the desired changes are located" (ibid.). By employing the factory metaphor, Kavolis attempts in-depth exploration of the difference between a totalitarian factory and the plural factories of the free market.

Finally, the analysis of the paradigm of the order of the work of art allows Kavolis to present his remarkable insights into the structural isomorphisms and similarities between the modern artistic enterprise and its ideologies—"in which the artist is still dimly perceived as the secularised shadow of the Judaeo-Christian Creator God" (p.80)—on the one hand, and the "aesthetisation of politics" inherent in authoritarian or even totalitarian political images and practices, on the other (p.78). We can recall here the phenomenon of the "aesthetisation of politics" as deeply characteristic of Italian Fascism, the latter having been enthusiastically endorsed by a number of eminent Italian artists of that time.

Kavolis was at his best when he successfully combined his theoretical sophistication, analytical incisiveness, empirical evidence, and existential experience derived from what he recognised as his cultural background. It is little wonder that Kavolis's insights into the models of collective identity, social movements, and civilisational processes in Eastern Europe are, in a way, reminiscent of the brightest examples of the comparative study of Central/East European nationalism and of European studies in general. The way in which Kavolis describes the former Soviet Union as a failed project of modernisation, and Communism as an alternative and rival civilisation, is worthy of the best passages of Raymond Aron, Ernest Gellner, Leszek Kołakowski, and Czesław Miłosz.

> The Soviet Union has for seventy years endeavoured to produce a new civilisation by establishing a secular version of the religion-above-culture paradigm as its centre. The result was a pattern most similar, among contemporary civilisations, to that of the Islamic world, except that (1) a *secular* religion was placed in the position of super-ordination to all culture, and (2) this secular religion was, in contrast to Islam, not deeply embedded in the attitudes of the "masses" or the "intellectual elites." It therefore has remained an artificial entity, not a "genuine civilisation" capable of attracting adherence even without the use of violence; a failed effort in a boundary region of the West to become a civilisational alternative to it... This pattern has now collapsed. But will Eastern Europe move toward the modern West, in which ontological hierarchy has been replaced, beginning in the seventeenth century, by a polymorphous political-moral-aesthetic polylogue as the main integrative device? Or will Eastern Europe remain a culturally distinctive region, with another, perhaps more "traditionalist," ontological hierarchy acquiring hegemony? (pp.153–154)

Every passage from Kavolis's books, every piece of his iconoclastic and critical scholarship stands as his silent intellectual and moral autobiography. Kavolis's theoretical views and insights, methodological preferences and disciplinary choices not only reflect his value orientation, convictions, and individual experience, but also underlines and redefines what is at the core of the civilisational perspective and of the critical study of modern society and culture.

> The sociologists who have taken civilisations rather than nation states, world-systems, communities, or interacting individuals, as their units of analysis have all been deeply concerned with contemporary life. Indeed it was through their efforts to explain the distinctive characteristics of contemporary life that they have been led to the comparative study of civilisations. Without it, in their view, contemporary life could not be sufficiently understood. (p.173)

Not only Kavolis, but also Max Weber, Louis Dumont, Ernest Gellner, S. N. Eisenstadt, and other towering theorists of civilisations subscribed to this point of view. Indeed, the ambition to conceive of the nature of modern life is a major inspiration for the comparative study of civilisations. So, too, I add, are the discontents of one's own milieu, and the striving for the critical questioning of one's own society and culture, in order to reveal where, why and how they failed to embrace the ideals, values, and norms of universal humanity. The search for the intellectual and moral sensibilities capable of discovering the Other is therefore inseparable from the awakening, both in oneself and others, of conscience and self.

## Reconciling Liberalism and Nationalism

One of the tensions experienced and reflected on by Kavolis (particularly, in his Lithuanian essays) is that between self-appointed liberalism and the authentic liberal stance. In his essay, "Šiandieninė pažangumo reikšmė" [The Current Meaning of Being Progressive], Kavolis points out:

> We feel spontaneously that we can never consider as liberal the one who, though he/she appoints him/herself to be liberal, fights for restrictions of the freedom of discussions, and thus contributes to such a societal atmosphere in which one is afraid of expressing one's non-conformist opinion. We consider as *liberal person* the one who, notwithstanding his or her ideological views and political coalition, fights for the diminution of restrictions in his or her milieu and in the world in general. In this sense, John XXIII and Paul VI, by virtue of having done their best to diminish restrictions within their institution, far surpass those who, desperately trying

to become the popes of the struggle for freedom, succeed in turning to mere political propagandists of anti-Communism.[5]

Kavolis also adds that liberalism can in turn have its own limitations. The editor of the *Lietuviškasis liberalizmas* [Lithuanian Liberalism], a unique book in the context of twentieth-century Lithuania, had severely criticised the weak points of liberalism, for he as nobody else was perfectly aware of its ups and downs. "In some cases, liberalism may be unprogressive: when children are given more freedom than they can deal with; when there is more care about criminals and their rights than about the protection of their victims. However, even in those cases when liberalism, in its effects, is unprogressive, it is assessed in terms of the effort at diminishing restrictions, rather than in terms of some abstract principle."[6]

Another tension, which might be considered as the most intense and, in the theoretical sense, the most dramatic in Kavolis's works, is that between liberalism and nationalism. For such a theoretician of responsible, i.e., morally committed, individualism as Kavolis, it was obvious that liberalism and nationalism might be compatible and even complementary phenomena—particularly, in bridging the individual identity and the collective one. However, the elitist and aristocratic nationalism of the first half of the nineteenth century, that is, nationalism of the epoch of the springtime of the peoples which came into being manifesting itself in Adam Mickiewicz and Giuseppe Mazzini's visions and their struggle for peoples' independence and freedom, had eventually transformed itself into a mere exclusive nationalism. The latter, in the second half of the nineteenth century and, particularly, in the first half of the twentieth, was getting more and more mass-oriented, exclusionary, doctrinal, and ideological. So it is not accidental that nationalism of the epoch of the springtime of the peoples, which has come to respect and esteem the Other's freedom in the same way it did with regard to its own people, has been qualified by Kavolis as a liberal nationalism. Liberal nationalism was later replaced by the aforementioned exclusive, doctrinal nationalism permeated by what Kavolis called moral provincialism.

Small wonder, then, that Kavolis, while crediting Vincas Kudirka with paving the way for Lithuanian liberalism and with being paradigmatically liberal and modernising regarding such crucial issues as the national emancipation, education, and secularisation of politics and culture, came to assess Kudirka's antisemitic writings in vigorous terms. According to Kavolis, Kudirka, in his hatred of, and contempt for, the Jews, appears to have been a typical biased Lithuanian incapable of overcoming his moral provincialism.

Indeed, some of the founders of Lithuanian liberalism had much antisemitic prejudice which, most probably, sprang from their wish that ethnic Lithuanians should dominate all urban professions and areas of urban life that were traditionally dominated, in Lithuanian cities and towns, by Jews, Poles, and Russians. In contrast to the fiercely antisemitic Vincas Kudirka, or Jonas Šliūpas tinged with a kind of more moderate antisemitism, the noble-spirited and sensitive Jonas Basanavičius stands as a unique figure in the context of the dawn of Lithuanian liberalism and Lithuanian modernity in general—Basanavičius's intellectual and moral sensibility shows him to have been a man of the epoch of the springtime of the peoples. None of those things went unnoticed by Kavolis.

In his article, "Moralinės kultūros: žemėlapiai, trajektorijos, įtampos" [Moral Cultures: Maps, Trajectories, Tensions], Kavolis put it thus:

> The danger of nationalist [moral] culture lies in its moral provincialism. Nationalism, as John Stuart Mill noted, makes people indifferent to the rights and interests of any part of humankind, except for that which is called the same name as they are, and speaks the same language they do. Not always, however, has nationalist culture been provincial. In the first half of the nineteenth century, Europe was full of liberal nationalists who believed that the struggle for the liberation of all peoples was a common cause: therefore, a patriot of one people must help other peoples as well. Thus, later on, Basanavičius participated in the movement of Bulgarian democrats, and Georg Julius Justus Sauerwein [the nineteenth-century German liberal nationalist, who was equally sympathetic to the Lithuanians and to the Sorbs.—L.D.] wrote "We Were Born Lithuanians" (and another version of the same song which was dedicated to the Sorbs). Yet nationalism in the second half of the nineteenth century—in part, because of the impact of social Darwinism—moved away from the notion of universal brotherhood, enthusiastically shared by all nationalists, and reshaped itself within quite a narrow frame of the exclusive ("zoological") defence of people's interests by all means. This is to say that nationalism became "primitive." (In many non-Western countries—for instance, in India,—the twentieth-century nationalism has repeated this sequence; so we can ask if it might be taken as a natural part of the nationalist movement's evolution, that is, as a consequence of the transformation of nationalism into a mass-oriented phenomenon?) Exclusive nationalism is incompatible with liberal culture, which is, in principle, morally universalistic. (In the rationalist version of liberal morality: *all are equal in their rights*; in the Romantic version of liberal morality: *all are equal in their pain which equally hurts everybody*.)[7]

The question arises: Why and how did such a focus of theoretical and ideological tension appear in Kavolis's discursive universe? The reason seems quite simple: Kavolis was perfectly aware of the total absence and even impossibility of liberalism, in its paradigmatic Anglo-Saxon version, in Lithuania. Obsessive efforts to identify it in, or to impose it on, Lithuanian consciousness and culture would have led only to the coercive falsification of Lithuania's history, politics, and culture.

Some important prerequisites of political liberalism, which may indeed be identified in Lithuania's history, date back to the sixteenth and seventeenth centuries: the aristocratic legacy of liberalism and some manifestations of political and religious tolerance in the sixteenth- and seventeenth-century Lithuania that have been explored by Kavolis through his painstaking study of Renaissance and Baroque Europe. The beginnings of political and religious tolerance in Lithuania—which manifested themselves in Lithuania's historic virtue of once having been a multi-ethnic, multi-religious, and multi-cultural country—fascinated Kavolis; this is why he considered the multi-ethnic, multi-religious, and multi-cultural past of Lithuania its lost golden age.

Kavolis had to search for what have been termed by him the responding tendencies in consciousness and culture. This process was closely related to the invention of the responding traditions of Lithuanian politics and culture. He had to find room, within the framework of Lithuanian consciousness, for the theoretically identifiable beginnings of liberalism—in the form of the responding historical trajectories and tendencies of the thought and of intellectual/moral stances. This is exactly how Kavolis came to construct the concept of cultural liberalism, the latter referring to the priority of individual reason and conscience—whether explicit or implicit in a given society and culture—over collective oppressiveness and *consensus gentium*-type morality.

The concept of cultural liberalism served as a means to culturally and intellectually assimilate liberalism to modern Lithuania's mainstream value-and-idea system, though liberalism, in Lithuania, used to be and still is misinterpreted and misrepresented as just another term for agnosticism or left-wing political stances. The concept of cultural liberalism enabled Kavolis to hypostatise liberalism as such to the autonomous moral culture or even paradigm of consciousness. It sheds new light on the way Kavolis employs a comparison of the nationalist, liberal, and romantic moral cultures. The nationalist moral culture, placed at the level of a broad comparative historical perspective, is assessed by him in the following way:

The moral culture of this type is deeply rooted in history; one may find its early, pre-modern forms in Jewish and Chinese traditions. Yet those traditions were "ethnocentric," i.e., perceiving the entire virtue of the world as represented solely by their own communities. Current nationalism is said to have become, in the brightest manifestations of its maturity, "polycentric," i.e., striving for the equal and normal participation of its own nation in the concert of all nations—consulting their equally valuable cultures and learning from them. The symbolic arena of nationalist culture is the ritual of the repetition of history, be it the never-ending campaign to re-conquer Alsace or Gandhi's demonstrations of non-violent resistance. The addresses of nationalists are just the same—the continual repetition of the same.[8]

Being aware of how problematic is the search for the origins—or at least manifestations—of liberalism in Central and East European political history, Kavolis was trying to identify and analyse both the particular liberal stances and the element of liberality itself in the history of Lithuania's national rebirth (or, to be more precise, of Lithuanian modernity, however failing in the course of history). He had qualified the ideas and stances of the *Aušra* and *Varpas* nationalist movements—along with those of their leaders Jonas Basanavičius, Jonas Šliūpas, and Vincas Kudirka—as liberal, thus drawing a sharp dividing line between a liberal nationalism and a conservative one. In doing so, Kavolis was theoretically and intellectually bridging the nationalist and liberal moral cultures in virtue of employing the perspective of the history of consciousness. Otherwise, he would inevitably have failed to accomplish such a task, for neither political theory nor political practice may provide a sufficient basis for bridging those, one would think, mutually exclusive things. At the same time, Kavolis was consistently trying to overcome the abyss between his own frame of reference, conceptual framework, and analytic/interpretative language, on the one hand, and the mainstream Lithuanian consciousness and culture, on the other.

In his comparative studies, Kavolis impressively contextualised cultural liberalism tracing it back to:

(1) Socrates's ethical intellectualism and, particularly, his idea of the priority of individual reason and conscience over collective decisions;

(2) Some elements of Christian theology stressing the principle of the free will;

(3) Chinese neo-Confucianists' intellectual and moral stances;

(4) The frame of mind of the Heian epoch Japanese aristocratic culture;

(5) The assertion of Hinduism and of the Grand Duke of mediaeval Lithuania Gediminas's that all the ways—regardless of how distinct they can be—lead to that same God; and

(6) Even the early Islam's principle of *ijtihad*, according to which, one is entitled to use one's individual reason in interpreting the religious laws of Islam.[9]

Kavolis seems to have always been convinced that cultural liberalism, in the West and in non-Western civilisations, disseminates as the universal element of human experience, although he had unambiguously taken explicit and developed political liberalism as the solely Western phenomenon of political consciousness. The implication of this thought is that cultural liberalism has its chance even in those societies and cultures where political liberalism, historically speaking, has never had any possibility of coming into being.

The theoretically accurate, flexible, and differentiating attitude toward nationalism has assisted Kavolis in encompassing its grandeur and misery. Without such an attitude it would be impossible to make any clear distinction between the Herderian-Renanian paradigm of nationalism, that is, liberal nationalism *par excellence*, and the *Action Française*-type reactionary, radical and integral nationalism. Without such an attitude the grasp of how the modern Central and East European nations came into political existence would be hardly possible as well.

> For liberals, the principal criterion to evaluate nationalism is that of free self-determination. The nation's rights to political and cultural independence are protected insofar as the nation expresses its members' self-determination to perceive themselves in the way the nation represents itself. Yet the liberals will always raise their voices in defence of the individual's rights and, above all, of the right of self-determination about how to be a human individual in certain cases: if the authorities of a given nation happen to determine who does belong to the nation, and who does not; what should be found in its members' souls, and what can never be found; or if they happen to deny the normal human rights of those who do not belong to that nation/those who do not wish to belong to it. The collective may be respected insofar as it respects both the individuals and the variety of their reason, conscience and life-styles. In a liberal democracy, only pluralist and ethnically unlimited nationalism is acceptable, whereas assimilationist and ethnic-cleansing nationalism can never be accepted.[10]

However, in bridging Lithuanian consciousness, as one of the manifestations and agencies of the nationalist moral culture, and the liberal moral culture, Kavolis kept his fidelity to the principle of critical self-examination. As noted, Kavolis was perfectly aware of the limitations of liberalism itself. This is why he was striving for its integration in the multidimensional, complementary and coherent framework for a more proper interpretation of the world. Both as one of the modern moral cultures and as one of the predominant political ideologies of the modern world, liberalism is one of many ways of reflecting on social reality and the individual, one of many possibilities to describe human consciousness in terms of existential and social experiences. In fact, being the derivative of Western rationalism and individualism (undeniably of the British empiricist tradition and common-sense political philosophy as well), liberalism missed many points of human experience that are deeply grounded in other faculties of human sensibility: the sense of history, collective identity, group commitment, joint devotion, religious and mystical experiences, and the like. Those points, throughout history, have been dealt with and articulated by other moral cultures.

One of the paradoxes of liberal social philosophy and of liberal moral culture would be that the classic British version of liberalism, i.e., Millian liberalism of the nineteenth century, remained surprisingly insensitive to the process of the formation of the new national entities, and particularly to the cultural and moral dimensions of this process. One wonders why and how it could be the case, since nothing else but liberalism came to construct the concept of political nation, thus lifting it to the rank of the key ideas of modernity. The concept of political nation came into being through French social philosophers of the Enlightenment, especially such theoreticians of equality and tolerance as Voltaire, Montesquieu, Condorcet, Helvétius, and Bayle, and Anglo-American political philosophy of the eighteenth and nineteenth centuries.

This is the reason why the disconnectedness of nineteenth-century liberalism (with regard to those dramas and passions that captivated half of Europe) is surprising. Most probably because of this kind of disconnectedness, Kavolis, in his works, mentions—from time to time—the inability of liberalism to conceive of several structures of sentiment and the nuances of emotion that are of decisive importance for moral stances of individuals and for social connection as well.

Notwithstanding its limitations, Kavolis considered liberalism as the only moral culture, the essence of which lies in advocating the principles of individual reason and individual conscience. Nowhere else but in liberal moral culture, and its historical prototypes that anticipated and shaped cultural liberalism, has there emerged the free human being capable of determining him/herself by his/her own reason and individual conscience, and critically questioning him/herself and his/her society and culture.

However, nationalist moral culture has also made its substantial contribution to social criticism, for the nationalist type of moralisation promoted the connected and committed social criticism. Through the notions of the universal brotherhood/sisterhood and moral egalitarianism immanent to, and deeply inherent in, nationalism, nationalist moral culture promoted the historically unprecedented social intimacy between a particular individual and his/her imagined or real community.[11]

By stating the insufficiency and limitations of liberal moral culture in embracing the variety of the forms of modern consciousness and culture, Kavolis notes:

> Liberal culture itself insufficiently embraces the totality of human essence and of the human being's relationship with his/her milieu. The nineteenth-century liberal culture took seriously neither nature, nor radical evil, nor the distinctiveness of national cultures, nor the subconscious sphere of human experiences and its demands. It failed somehow to identify the emotional reciprocities and emergent, though never verbalised, human solidarities—*Seelengemeinschaften*.[12]

At the same time, Kavolis had never had any doubts about the liberal moral culture's ability to provide a serious alternative to those negative tendencies of other moral cultures that have been termed by him moral provincialism, ecclesiastic imperialism, ascetic revolutionism, and irresponsible determinism. Kavolis had no doubt that "liberal culture underlines one of the basic human elements which is suppressed in other moral cultures, namely, the individual's ability to judge everything by his/her own reason and conscience, while recognising others' right to arrive at conclusions different from his/her own, and his/her duty to perfect the ability of his/her judgement all the time. The problems we encounter in the course of human and civilisational development tend to become more and more complex" (pp.191–192).

Although Kavolis always subscribed to the liberal standpoint, the liberal moral culture, in his theoretical vision, can only acquire its real theoretical and moral value by entering the space of dialogue or even polylogue with other—both classic and modern—moral cultures. The same interpretative principle of polylogue, translated from his moral stance into the explanatory framework, has been applied by Kavolis to the comparative study of civilisations. There are no (and there cannot in principle be) self-sufficient civilisations, since some of them come to release and develop something that is inevitably suppressed, or neglected, in others. Thus, the comparative study of civilisations coincides with social and cultural criticism while tracing the models of self-understanding and of the perception of the Other.

This is precisely the theoretical context and moral focus where the idea of the bridging of moral cultures, that is, the idea of one's free participation in several moral cultures, which implies the critical questioning and symbolic correction of one's own culture from a comparative perspective, comes from. The scholar's participation in, and critical examination of, several moral cultures becomes part of the scholar's moral biography. One's ability to reflect on one's own participation in several models of cultural logic, thus theoretically attaching oneself to, and contextualising in, their interplay, makes social and cultural critique possible. In so doing, he/she places him/herself in the imagined gallery of other individuals and in the symbolic archives of their moral biographies as well.

Modernity with a human face—this term, coined by Kavolis, refers to the necessity of sensibility in social analysis and interpretation of culture. Both coincide with social and cultural criticism, since they are constantly accompanied by the tension between the *is* and the *ought to be*. On the other side, truth and value can never be located in a single culture or civilisation. Truth and value disseminate insofar as a comparison of the complementary, though distinct, models of self-understanding is employed.

An exponent of the modern sociological disciplines—indeed, a major contributor to such boundary social science and humanities disciplines as the sociology of literature and the sociology of fine arts—civilisation theorist, and sociologist of culture, Kavolis seems to have never been tempted to exaggerate the significance of Western scholarship or of Western intellectual culture in general. He was interested not only in Western civilisation's "conquest and exodus" (to use Eric Voegelin's term), that is, not only in its political and cultural accomplishments, crises and cul-de-sacs, but in the possibility to theoretically contextualise Western civilisation itself by conceiving it within, in Kavolis's terms, the idiom of self-and-civilisation, too. Hence, Kavolis's idea of creating what he terms a multi-civilisational universe of discourse, a concept crucial for his idea of the polylogue of civilisations:

> Efforts along these lines should also move us a little closer to what I take to be our shared educational goal of creating a *multi-civilisational universe of discourse* in which problems could be formulated both from Western and from non-Western perspectives and comparisons of Western with Chinese or Indian or Islamic or African modes of thought would come, to an

educated individual, as easily as references to Plato, Shakespeare, Weber, or the great reductionists, Marx and Freud.[13]

The question arises: Whether it is possible to adequately conceive of Western civilisation only within the framework of the modern configuration of values and ideas? This issue might be referred to as the point of departure for Kavolis's notion of the comparative study of civilisations. For him, the comparative study of civilisations was oriented to provide an interpretative and conceptual framework for self-understanding within the idiom of self-and-civilisation. The implication is that comparative studies are interlaced with one's own intellectual and moral biography. That was the way Kavolis arrived at both the civilisation analysis and the history of consciousness. His enthusiasm for, and dedication to, comparative studies had nothing to do with the doctrine of political correctness. Kavolis's civilisationist commitment is much more likely to have been directly related to his intellectual conscience.

This is revealed in one of Kavolis's early Lithuanian essays, "Ir erezija, ir humanizmas" [Both Heresy and Humanism], where Kavolis comes to explicate the concept of humanistic and morally committed individualism:

> The psychological source of humanism—in particular, in the twentieth century—is one's sensitivity to the other human being's pain. An ideological trait of humanism is the recognition of every human being as significant for the rest of humanity. Many of the purposes of their lives may seem to others insignificant, and their values banal and unsophisticated. Yet *every person may be experienced as significant when we come to empathise with his or her pain.* Only when it becomes impossible to pass by the other's pain, can the universality of humanism be conceived of.[14]

And then Kavolis adds an important distinction between Christian and secular humanism regarding the relationship between humanism and conscience, a crucial watershed for a secular liberal thinker: "In its later history, humanism had an autonomous development. In these days, humanism rests not necessarily on the Christian tradition, which was of great importance in maintaining early humanism. Although Christianity often inspires humanity in the sphere of charity, in the realm of conscience humanism is frequently desecrated by barbarians disguised as Christians. Seldom does this occur anywhere else with such naked cynicism and shameless passion as amongst Lithuanians."[15] Kavolis's merciless critique of prejudices and of failures of Lithuanians to match the modern intellectual and moral sensibilities quite often follows and sums up, particularly in his Lithuanian essays, his theoretical insights and analytical emphases.

For Kavolis, modernity was too complex a phenomenon to be reduced to simplistic schemes or over-generalisations. Instead, he took modernity in an all-encompassing variety of its forms and national variants, on the one hand, and thus entailed the analysis of contradictions within modernity, on the other. Tracing some anti-modernist intellectual and moral stances or anti-modernist tendencies of consciousness of a given society (e.g., examining a series of the failed modernisations in Central/East European countries), Kavolis perceived them as an inescapable and unavoidable part of modernisation itself.

Kavolis's attempts at reconciling and bridging those moral cultures and cultural logics that have been separated by modernity were always present behind his scholarly projects and academic activities. The following passage, dealing with the tension between the rational public life and the romantically anarchist intimate culture in the *Santara-Šviesa* movement, shows how deeply permeated by the challenge of modernity Kavolis's individual existence and public life were:

> Perhaps, throughout the history of Lithuanian cultural movements, this tension has nowhere else been so dramatic as in the spiritual universe of the *Santara-Šviesa* where both of these stances—the rational public life and the romantically anarchist intimate culture—are equally intensively emphasised, equally spontaneously accepted.[16]

The theoretical construct, therefore, had to be embodied in cultural practice and mundane reality. On the other side, the theory itself turns out to be quite frequently inspired by a mere human friendship. For Kavolis, *Santara-Šviesa* was not merely a movement; nor was it a mere model of Lithuania as his imagined community. It was instead a community of souls, which almost perfectly embodied the principle of unity in diversity. After all, *Santara-Šviesa* exemplified the Romantic notion of friendship as a joint devotion. Kavolis considered human trust and friendship to be the clue to the puzzle of human connection. Hence, Kavolis's theoretical interest in the history of human friendship and socialisation.

## Criticism, Tolerance, and Openness: Toward a Postmodern Nationalism

One of the most profound and illuminating of Kavolis's insights into the moral origins of the nationalist critique of nationalism, that is, the social and cultural criticism which occurs within the framework of the nationalist moral culture, reveals a hardly identifiable basis for the politically and morally committed criticism of the twentieth century:

> The liberal and romantic moral cultures, after all, are rooted respectively in the individual's rational (ascetic) and emotional (mystical) depth, whereas the nationalist moral culture rests on community, i.e., a historically concrete, "natural" community, which is being, on the voluntary and mystical basis, maintained or revived by the committed individual. The individual finds him/herself as having received a significant part of his/her moral substance from his/her community, and is prepared to hand over this substance, after having it refracted through his/her own experience, to the next generation of the community members. *But inasmuch as his/her community's experience becomes his/her personal substance, part of his/her identity, he/she severely judges this community and its history rejecting those things that are perceived by him/her as the deformation of his/her moral character. At the same time, he/she judges him/herself asking whether his contribution to community coincides with what it needs the most.*[17] (My emphasis.—L.D.)

And then Kavolis ironically sums it up: "What it [community.—L.D.] actually needs, does not necessarily coincide, in the nationalist view, with what its people concretely want. The nationalist follows and conforms to a theory which provides the ready-made answer to what the people do want, not to the polls of population" (ibid.). Therefore, if the social critic, instead of participating in several moral cultures, limits and reduces him/herself to a single nationalist moral culture, it betrays either the symptoms of ambiguity in his/her consciousness and moral stance, accompanied by the striving for intensity and political power, or the shabby individual identity, accompanied by the desperate need for symbolic compensation/dissolution in the mystical collective body.

Along these lines, connected social and cultural criticism might best be defined in the following way: *it implies and rests on one's ability to experience the dynamics and dissemination of one's society and culture as one's own drama, while treating social analysis as the correction of the field of one's own intellectual possibilities and moral choices*. In other words, connected criticism means one's ability to absorb the most symptomatic tendencies of social and cultural change taking place in one's society and culture, and, then, to return them—permeated by one's individual experience and theoretical articulation—to one's community or society, in the form of critical warning or of intellectual and moral trial.

Kavolis's notion of the moral reciprocity between the individual and his or her community, as well as his idea of the mapping of the modern intellectual and modern sensibilities through the individual's imagined community or society or culture, is a logical continuation of his conception of modern individualism. "As an impulse which enables a human individual to differentiate him/herself from the collective and stand for his/her personal faith, individualism has been a potent explosive constantly threatening the rigidity of fossilised dogmas. If the community, before individualism came into existence, was a once-and-for-all *structure* locking up the human being within itself, today it appears as the *process* of the human being's self-examination in history."[18]

While working out a theory of morally committed individualism, Kavolis clearly defines the concept of tolerance, which is a significant part of his liberal social and political philosophy. For Kavolis, tolerance was too important a moral and political phenomenon to be lightly reduced to theoretical curiosity or to what he described in terms of indifference as a symptom of social pathology. Elsewhere he defines indifference as a form of modern barbarity. As the moral and political commitment to stand for everyone's right to freely decide how to express him/herself and how to be a human individual, tolerance has nothing to do with moral relativism and indifference to ethical issues—it was Kavolis's conscious response to the charges of moral relativism and indifference, the constant and unfounded charges against liberals deeply rooted in twentieth-century Lithuania and, in particular, amongst conservative Lithuanian immigrants in the United States. Kavolis's insights into heroism and humanism as moral stances provide an interpretative framework for tolerance, too:

> If the hero is accountable to his consciousness, which represents abstract values, the humanist's conscience assumes the responsibility for flesh-and-blood human beings with whom he or she lives in community. It is not enough to passively tolerate everything around, including dogma, which is always wrong; and blood, even if the blood is of those we do not love; and racist hatred. If tolerance is not a symptom of the pathology of indifference, it should be defined as the commitment to actively stand for everyone's right to have his or her truth and individual existence. It is also the commitment to stand against anybody who wants to control the other's individual existence and penetrate it with the propagandist's fingers, no matter which doctrine the propagandist preaches.[19]

Thus conceived, tolerance may well be translated into the discovery of the Other when studying non-Western societies, cultures, and civilisations. This is exactly what happened in Kavolis's comparative studies. His crucial idea that all theoretically identifiable civilisations, in addition to their cosmologies and ontological conceptions, have the notions of conscience and self rests on the philosophical assumption that self-discovery occurs only through the discovery of the Other. Tolerance is another name for dialogue. Tracing Kavolis's conception of tolerance, we can map its crucial moral and political implications for what he took as the polylogue of civilisations. Such a discursive map would be incomplete without taking into account the discourse about identity, freedom, and nationalism, the latter having been perceived by Kavolis as a symbolic design of modern civilisation and as a pattern of consciousness.

The intense polylogue of moral cultures, modes of self-comprehension, critical intellectual discourses, value orientations, political systems, aesthetic sensibilities, theoretical vocabularies, travelogues, and moral biographies, in order to (re)discover and conceive of oneself in the idiom of self-and-civilisation—this is how Kavolis imagined what he termed a multi-civilisational universe of discourse. Hence, his ideas of local sensibility and intellectual empathy when dealing with non-Western or peripheral-Western—for instance, East European— symbolic designs and structures of sentiments. Having defined the integrating principle of modern Western civilisation as the polymorphous moral-political-aesthetic polylogue, Kavolis asks if Eastern Europe can be expected to come to rely on such a principle.

In doing so, he deeply penetrates the Lithuanian discourse of identity and freedom by recalling the Herderian notion of the nation as the collective individual, still a crucial aspect of the collective identity and political liberty discourse in Central and Eastern Europe. According to Kavolis, in Eastern Europe,

> [t]here is more emphasis than in Western Europe or especially the US on the moral reality of historically durable *"collective* individualities"—nations, religious communities, and so on. (In these respects, as well as in some others, there are similarities with Latin America.) In Eastern Europe, it is not only individuals but also nations that claim "inalienable rights," the latter with more assurance of the justice of the claim (since the individual, not the nation, can be accused, at least by individuals composing it, of selfishness). Desovietisation revives a sense of connectedness within natural-historical collectivities.[20]

Being perfectly aware of how deeply the Herderian discourse is grounded in Lithuanian and Central/East European discourse of identity and freedom, Kavolis found himself quite sceptical about the propensity of the authors of general theories of nationalism to view nationalism either with some hostility, as an unpleasant and temporary aberration of modern Europe, or with anticipation of its inexorable demise within the framework of supranational political and legal systems. Such a myopic standpoint, in Kavolis's opinion, overlooked crucial aspects of nationalism as a civilisational process, let alone the ability of nationalism to shape social reality and consciousness. What is the point in fiercely attacking, demonising, or otherwise discrediting nationalism, which is just another term for the cultural modernisation of Central and Eastern Europe? Kavolis concluded that it would be much wiser to modernise nationalism by opening up its liberal and inclusive traits, instead of conflating the liberal and modernising nationalism with the blood-and-soil, ethnic-cleansing nationalism.

However, the question remains whether the process of political and cultural emancipation of post-Communist Central and Eastern Europe is in tune with the liberal-democratic sensibilities. Having stressed the importance of the process of desovietisation which comes to revive, in Eastern Europe, a sense of connectedness within natural-historical collectivities, Kavolis comes to draw a dividing line between Central Europe and Eastern Europe on the grounds of the presence of what he qualifies as the moral monopolies, a threat to political tolerance and, by and large, to liberal democracy, too:

> This goes along with what are at present peculiarly East European consensual pressures, tendencies to reject on moral grounds those who disagree on political or even strategic matters. This deep cultural tendency is somewhat offset by the more superficial current political reputation (as something "Western" and therefore superior) of tolerance. Political tolerance is perhaps strong enough to have a chance at competing with the moral monopolies only in Central Europe from Hungary to Estonia. It is fragile but of growing strength in Russia. The deep tendency toward moral monopolies undermines the possibility of replacing a rules-oriented by a freedom-oriented moral system. (The sole surviving Western European approximation to a society in which a moral monopoly asserts itself somewhat effectively is Ireland.)[21]

Bearing in mind the historically rooted trajectories of consciousness in Central and Eastern Europe, Kavolis worked out a theory of postmodern nationalism perceived as an attempt to reconcile what has been separated by modernity. At the same time, the idea of postmodern nationalism served, for Kavolis, as an interpretative framework for the split between the modernist and the anti-modernist. He accorded the concept of the postmodern to the process of desovietisation, too:

If desovietisation, in its diversity of forms, continues relatively unhindered and does not become complacent with its own rhetoric, it has the potentiality of becoming a first-rate (that is, "enriching") civilisational movement. If the concept of the "*post*modern" can still be retrieved from the cultists who have made it a monopoly of their own exuberance, desovietisation could even be considered, in some of its cultural emphases, as "postmodern." (I conceive of the "postmodern" not as anti-modernist, but as the building of bridges between the "modernist" and the "anti-modernist.")[22]

Here we have the nexus of Kavolis's intellectual programme. Modernity has come to split up the human world. However, the point is to reconcile those provinces of human existence and distant faculties of the human soul that have been separated by modernity. Kavolis seems to have penetrated the core of modernity and its challenge by offering his inclusive theoretical alternative. How to react to the challenge of modernity? How to accept it? This problematical focus sheds new light on postmodernism as one of the possible responses to the fundamental theoretical alternative and existential dilemma formulated by Kavolis. He considered postmodernism to be the possible way to reconcile those things that have been taken by modernity as incompatible in principle, rather than as a mere theoretical trend in fashion.

How to reconcile and bridge what have been ruthlessly separated by modernity: truth and value; rationality and emotional intimacy; expertise and sensitivity; hierarchy and equality/individualism; tradition and innovation; the classic canon and the released creative experiment; metaphysics and phenomenalistic science; a particular individual and community; a particular community and universal humanity?

One of the possible ways would be to suggest a return to metaphysics and religion (or the traditional concept of transcendence, to use Kavolis's term)—the phenomena that have been, from the point of view of the split between truth and value, neutralised, relativised and, consequently, placed by modernity on the margin of consciousness and existence. Another way, suggested by the sequence and logic of Kavolis's thought and by his ambitious epistemological programme for the social sciences and the humanities, would be an attempt at analytically embracing and, by attaching the dimensions of value and meaning, encompassing the totality of human experience, through the comparative study of civilisations. The latter implies the analysis of the flux of symbolic meaning and of the change of the structures of consciousness over time in Western and non-Western civilisations, by capitalising on the civilisation analysis and the history of consciousness.

Small wonder, then, that Kavolis, in his article "Nationalism, Modernisation, and the Polylogue of Civilisations," defines nationalism in the following way:

> Nationalism is a conception of the cultural identity of a nation which becomes a mobilising political programme even when the nation is (as to some extent it always is) in the process of being invented. National identity is what, unless it is either culturally put into question or politically endangered, does not need to be explicitly declared about one's sense of being more at home in one this-worldly community of participation and historical experience than in any other. The close alignment of culture with politics is perhaps the most general source of the dangers which nationalism has presented not only to the world, but to the members of the nations it sought to represent, to revive, or to "build." This alignment gives to nationalism a deeper, quasi-religious kind of power, an ability to overwhelm, which "normal" political forces generally lack. It leads to the exploitation of culture by politics.[23]

In his short, sharp, and precise formulations regarding the symbolic codes and the structures of meaning within nationalism, Kavolis reveals what other theories of nationalism are missing. Not only does Kavolis show the modernising and liberal potential of nationalism, at the same time clearly pointing out its dubious and dangerous points that largely depend on the political, historical, and cultural context within which a given nation or community builds or revives itself; he also shows the similarity between nationalism and other civilisation-shaping movements, from romanticism to feminism. Kavolis succeeded where other students of nationalism failed. From the point of view of the link between theoretical sophistication and empirical evidence in viewing nationalism as a major civilisation-shaping force, Kavolis far surpasses other theorists of nationalism.

> Democracy in particular benefits from loosening the connections between culture and politics, so that important symbolic quests cannot be monopolised by particular political forces. Like religion, national identity operates optimally in a democratic setting when its distinguishing marks are distributed over a range of political organisations and over a series of cultural programmes, the two distributions far from coinciding with each other, and not divided rigorously along the lines of "majority" and "minority" groups. In what follows we will be mainly concerned with nationalisms as conceptions of collective identity—in their cultural rather than political aspect. In its cultural form, nationalism is similar to other civilisation-shaping movements of the last two centuries—from romanticism to feminism—in that it relates to all levels of modernisation of

culture. In nineteenth-century Germany and Eastern Europe and the present-day Near East, nationalism tends toward the archaic. American nationalism and, to a lesser extent, mainstream French nationalism since the Revolution have been modernising. The crucial issue in distinguishing modernising from archaic nationalism is whether one derives society from individuals having "human rights" or perceives individuals as embodiments of the "collective soul" of the nation.[24]

In his thorough analysis of the four types of nationalism (archaic, modernising, anti-modernistic, and postmodern), Kavolis describes Central and Eastern Europe as a laboratory of the diverse trajectories of the "modernisation of nationalisms." "In Central Europe, Hungarian nationalism has probably changed most since 1939, toward the modernistic model, Yugoslav nationalisms have changed least" (p.135). The incisiveness of Kavolis's analysis is striking—in his analytical study written in 1991, Kavolis predicted the Yugoslav tragedy.

Interestingly enough, the difference between conservative nationalism and liberal nationalism is still overlooked by the current social sciences and critical scholarship in general. As noted, liberal nationalism allows room for cosmopolitan stances and multiculturalism in politics and public discourse, as well as the modernising critique of politics and culture it employs. However insightful, the authors of general theories of nationalism—in particular, Ernest Gellner, Eric Hobsbawm, Anthony Smith, and Benedict Anderson—failed to take into account the importance of national cultures for the political and institutional settings for liberal democracy and the enormous modernising potential of Central/East European nationalism. Finally, they overlooked the ethic of liberal nationalism and its implications for public discourse and social criticism. The merits of liberal nationalism in disclosing totalitarianism are too obvious to need emphasis. It suffices to recall Czesław Miłosz, Václav Havel, Milan Kundera, Tomas Venclova, and other eminent Central European critics of totalitarianism, ideocracy, xenophobia, and manipulative exchanges.

Of Gellner and Hobsbawm Kavolis wrote: "The general theories of nationalism... fail to take into account the importance of national cultures in producing different kinds, or symbolic designs, of nationalism. This has the unjustifiable practical consequence that all nationalisms are treated alike—usually, by most social scientists, either with some hostility or with anticipations of their demise" (p.142).

It makes sense to stress the emergence of what might be described as postmodern nationalism, which, according to Kavolis, "would allow for and recognize the human quality of *openness* and the cultural characteristic of translucence…—a Miłosz-like commitment to one's own nation permeated with a responsiveness to others, a sense of multiple, communicating identities" (p.136). Kavolis identifies a postmodern nationalism in some leading figures of political dissent and emancipation in Central and Eastern Europe. He suggests that anticipations of postmodern nationalism could be found as early as in Giuseppe Mazzini. In bridging the modernist and the anti-modernist/the archaising longings, postmodern nationalism would also serve as a framework for the polylogue of civilisations. Not in vain, Kavolis notes that "postmodern nationalism conceives society as a non-exclusive, open-frontiers, polyphonic, 'multicultural' co-operation integrated by a shared sense of adequacy, an *Angemessenheit* " (p.136).

Defining postmodern nationalism and rethinking civilisation-shaping processes in Central and Eastern Europe, Kavolis was not only describing his future vision of Lithuania. In so doing, he was also finishing his moral autobiography. The concept of postmodern nationalism, as well as the idea of postmodernism as the bridge over the gap between modernistic and anti-modernistic aspects of human existence, sheds new light on why and how Kavolis arrived at the comparative study of civilisations. To stand for every single aspect of human diversity, identity, and freedom; to realise that without you and your community of memory and participation humanity would be incomplete; to bridge your individual existence with societal life of those who, however self-centred and insensitive, need your voice the most; to identify and fight every trace of moral blindness and insensitivity in your community as passionately and uncompromisingly as if it were your own vice; and to be attentive to everything that is happening in the world, for neglect, complacency, and contempt are nothing less than moral provincialism. These moral and political implications of Kavolis's iconoclastic and critical scholarship not only stand as his important lesson for posterity. They refer to the inmost relationship between social criticism and the most inclusive, liberal and humane facet of nationalism.

## The Merits of Fragmentary Writing

Kavolis's articles and books are full of maxims and allusions. His ironic notes and caustic lines, referring to the mainstream of Lithuanian linguistic politics and intellectual culture, are targeted at what he fought passionately and uncompromisingly all of his life—the symptoms of integral and radical nationalism; antisemitism; xenophobia; anti-modernist political and cultural rhetoric; anti-liberal, anti-democratic, and anti-Western attitudes in twentieth-century Lithuania. At the same time, his elegant and insightful critiques touched upon the nerve of Lithuania's political existence and intellectual life: Kavolis made himself clear regarding such peculiar traits of Lithuanian politics and culture as the conflation of political and moral terms, and the resulting propensity to view political problems as moral ones; moral monopolies resulting in the competition over who is the most patriotic; the deep sense of self-righteousness; self-centredness and total indifference to the major intellectual themes and moral issues of the twentieth century.

For instance, Kavolis writes that the never-ending debates about the uniqueness of Lithuanian culture and spirituality sound like a parochial church choir in nineteenth-century Lithuania. Elsewhere, he calls into question the existence of Lithuanian society as such. Kavolis suggests that society, in the deeper sense, signifies the ability of its members to activate and critically question themselves and the object of their joint dedication, not to mention the ability to employ a common moral vocabulary containing keywords for integrity and decency—things that, according to him, are missing in Lithuanian politics, culture, and mundane existence. Kavolis concludes that the inability of a society to make principal ethical distinctions not only undermines its independence and freedom, but also jeopardises its social and moral order. He describes Lithuanian culture congresses in exile as the feasts of exhibitionism. Of racists amongst Lithuanian immigrants in the United States Kavolis wrote that immigrants often adopt the worst traits of their new countries, and that immigrants, in doing so, become caricatures of humankind.

Such sarcastic lines used to appear not in the body of Kavolis's article or book, but in the footnotes and/or endnotes of the text. His footnotes and endnotes were full of metaphors, metonymies, anticlimaxes, antitheses, paradoxes, and other tropes or figures of speech. Analytically accurate, precise, and incisive formulations of Kavolis's thought in the body of the text were accompanied by numerous footnote allusions, elliptic phrases, short comparisons, critical notes, and erudite references to various episodes from the lives and moral choices of theorists, politicians, writers, and artists. Each of them could have been developed into a separate study. The same might be said about Kavolis's working hypotheses and definitions of terms—each of them invited a reconsideration of the theoretical perspectives in which those issues and phenomena were and still are most frequently viewed. Every statement, definition, or hypothesis, in Kavolis's contributions, might have been developed into a monograph. His collage-like insights, maxims, ironic notes, and allusions stand as silent promises of something new to appear in the forthcoming writings. At the same time, they stand as invitation to the universe of dialogue.

A deliberately unfinished work of art has its metaphysics and aesthetics, and so does an unfinished and open-ended thought. Kavolis's maxims and notes may well be compared with the tip of the iceberg beneath which lay the massive foundations of his multidimensional and sophisticated theoretical thought. A major contributor to new methodologies and perspectives in the social sciences and humanities, Kavolis came to provide not only a new theoretical vocabulary, but also an interpretative framework for the most elusive, though dramatic and even tragic, aspects of human experience and existence. In so doing, Kavolis was not only writing his diary and moral autobiography, but also mapping his culture and imagined community of memory and participation.

He greatly contributed to the creating of a new kind of scholarship, the scholarship of the twenty-first century—not bureaucratically "rationalising" and dividing the human world and social reality, not dogmatically rigid and unreflective, not soulless and totally insensitive about its social effects or political and moral implications, but reflective, ironic, critical, attentive to every single detail of human existence, and perfectly aware of the vulnerability and fragility of the human world. It is a scholarship that comes to bridge not only the social science and humanities disciplines, but also the distinct modes of discourse and of self-comprehension. Such a social science with a human face was among the main ambitions of Kavolis. And this is Kavolis's legacy of the polylogue of civilisations.

# Notes

1. Among Kavolis's other books which became his major contribution both to Lithuanian intellectual culture and to international scholarship, the following should be mentioned: (1) *Lietuviškasis liberalizmas* [Lithuanian Liberalism], Editor (Chicago, IL: Santara-Šviesa, 1959); (2) *Žmogaus genezė: psichologinė Vinco Kudirkos studija* [The Genesis of Man: A Psychological Study of Vincas Kudirka] (Chicago, IL: Chicagos Lietuvių literatūros draugija, 1963); (3) *Artistic Expression: A Sociological Analysis* (Ithaca, NY: Cornell University Press, 1968), translated into Swedish and Spanish, Chapter 5 translated into German; (4) *Nužemintųjų generacija: egzilio pasaulėjautos eskizai* [The Generation of the Uprooted: Sketches of the Psychology of Exile] (Chicago, IL: Santara-Šviesa, 1968); (5) *Comparative Perspectives on Social Problems*, Editor (Boston, MA: Little, Brown, 1969); (6) *History on Art's Side: Social Dynamics in Artistic Efflorescences* (Ithaca, NY: Cornell University Press, 1972); (7) *Designs of Selfhood*, Editor (Rutherford, NJ: Fairleigh Dickinson University Press, 1984); (8) *Civilizations East and West: A Memorial Volume for Benjamin Nelson*, Co-Editor, with E. V. Walter, Edmund Leites, and Marie Coleman Nelson (Atlantic Highlands, NJ: Humanities Press, 1985); (9) *Moralizing Cultures* (Lanham, MD: University Press of America, 1993); (10) *Moterys ir vyrai lietuvių kultūroje* [Women and Men in Lithuanian Culture] (Vilnius: Lietuvos kultūros institutas, 1993); (11) *Žmogus istorijoje* [The Human Being in History] (Vilnius: Vaga, 1994); (12) *Civilization Analysis as a Sociology of Culture* (Lewiston, NY: The Edwin Mellen Press, 1995); (13) *Kultūrinė psichologija* [Cultural Psychology] (Vilnius: Baltos lankos, 1995); (14) *Kultūros dirbtuvė* [The Workshop of Culture] (Vilnius: Baltos lankos, 1996); (15) *Civilizacijų analizė* [Civilization analysis] (Vilnius: Baltos lankos, 1998). Thus, Kavolis is the author or editor of 17 books, of around 150 scholarly articles, and of 20 book reviews.
2. For more on this issue, see Vytautas Kavolis, "Structure and Energy: Toward a Civilization-Analytic Perspective," *Comparative Civilizations Review*, 1 (1979), pp. 21–41.
3. For more on the history of consciousness and civilisation analysis, see Vytautas Kavolis, "History of Consciousness and Civilization Analysis," *Comparative Civilizations Review*, 17 (1987), pp.1–19; Vytautas Kavolis, *Civilization Analysis as a Sociology of Culture* (Lewiston, NY: The Edwin Mellen Press, 1995).
4. Kavolis, *Civilization Analysis as a Sociology of Culture*, op. cit., pp.19–20.
5. Vytautas Kavolis, "Šiandieninė pažangumo reikšmė" [The Current Meaning of Being Progressive], in Virginijus Gasiliūnas, ed., *Metmenų laisvieji svarstymai: 1959–1989* [Free Debates of *Metmenys*, 1959–1989] (Vilnius: Lietuvos rašytojų sąjungos leidykla, 1993), p.58.
6. Ibid.
7. Vytautas Kavolis, "Moralinės kultūros: žemėlapiai, trajektorijos, įtampos" [Moral Cultures: Maps, Trajectories, Tensions], in *Metmenų laisvieji svarstymai*, pp.184–185.

8. Ibid., pp.183–184.
9. See Vytautas Kavolis, "Liberalaus galvojimo erdvėje" [In the Space of the Liberal Thinking], *Metmenys*, 63 (1992), p.39.
10. Ibid., p.38.
11. The term "imagined political community," coined by Benedict Anderson for the definition of the nation, seems to express the essence of the nationalist moral culture and of nationalist historical and cultural imaginations. See Benedict Anderson, *Imagined Communities: Reflections on the Origin and Spread of Nationalism* (London: Verso, 1991), pp.5–7.
12. Kavolis, "Moralinės kultūros," op. cit., p.191.
13. Kavolis, "Structure and Energy," op. cit., p.38.
14. Vytautas Kavolis, "Ir erezija, ir humanizmas" [Both Heresy and Humanism], in Virginijus Gasiliūnas, ed., *Metmenų laisvieji svarstymai*, p.47.
15. Ibid., pp.46–47.
16. Kavolis, "Moralinės kultūros," op. cit., p.191.
17. Ibid., p.183.
18. Kavolis, "Ir erezija, ir humanizmas," op. cit., p.44.
19. Ibid., pp.51–52.
20. Kavolis, *Civilization Analysis as a Sociology of Culture*, op. cit., p.161.
21. Ibid.
22. Ibid., p.166.
23. Vytautas Kavolis, "Nationalism, Modernization, and the Polylogue of Civilizations," *Comparative Civilizations Review*, 25 (1991), p.134.
24. Ibid., pp.134–135.

# Chapter Three

## Aleksandras Shtromas: Liberal Nationalism and the Politics of Dissent

> Who can be a critic without a point of view, or a great critic without a profound moral sense?
> Lewis Mumford, *Roots of Contemporary American Architecture*

Aleksandras Shtromas, a British-American political scientist, passed away recently, on June 12, 1999. From 1973 to 1989, Shtromas lived in Great Britain teaching and researching at the Universities of Bradford and Salford. From 1989, he served as Professor of Political Science at Hillsdale College in Michigan, USA. A major figure in the political science world, an erudite writer, and an ambitious thinker, Shtromas had several planes of his identity and moral existence. A human rights activist and political dissident, a dedicated fighter for the cause of Lithuania's independence, Shtromas is reminiscent of the most glorious traditions of the epoch of the springtime of the peoples. Although neglected and even ignored, for a long time, by the mainstream of British and American academics as a maverick and dissenter, he managed to reach the heights of international recognition as a brilliant and talented scholar and as a mesmerising orator. Yet the academic positions Shtromas held reflect merely several episodes from his remarkable biography.

Aleksandras Shtromas (Štromas) was born on April 4, 1931, in Kaunas, Lithuania. A then bilingual boy—Lithuanian and Russian became his native languages—attended a Catholic school, gymnasium of the *Ateitininkai* organisation in Kaunas, where Vytautas Kavolis and Julius Šmulkštys, who would become an émigré political scientist in the United States active in *Santara-Šviesa* (Professor of Political Science at Indiana University, currently—political adviser to President of Lithuania Valdas Adamkus), were among his classmates. After Shtromas's expulsion from the Soviet Union in 1973, life-long friends and classmates would see each other every year, since Shtromas joined *Santara-Šviesa* and started participating in its annual conferences in the United States. Shtromas became a teenager only in 1944, Kavolis in 1943, when the most horrible events of the twentieth century took place in Europe. Shtromas witnessed the clash of the twin totalitarian regimes, which occurred in his country. In 1940, the Red Army invaded Lithuania only to retreat in 1941 when the Nazis came in, the events that meant a double tragedy for Lithuania. First, Lithuania lost its independence for the five decades to come. Executions, mass deportations, and exodus of the most prosperous and educated people—all these calamities were still to come in 1945 when the Soviet Union re-occupied and re-annexed Lithuania, but the destructive military operations and sinister political manipulations of the Soviets in 1940 left Lithuanians in shock and bitterness.

The year 1941 became the most tragic and infamous page in Lithuanian history: the Holocaust commenced, claiming the lives of more than 200,000 Lithuanian Jews. In one of the first slaughters of Lithuanian Jewry, the *Lietūkis* garage massacre orchestrated and operated by Lithuanian collaborators of the Nazis, Shtromas's father, Jurgis Štromas, was killed. One of the most tragic and paradoxical things about his father's fate was that he was a completely assimilated Lithuanian Jew, passionately attached and loyal to Lithuania. Although Jurgis Štromas, particularly after 1933, was increasingly becoming sympathetic to Communism as the supposedly sole alternative to the rising National-Socialist and Fascist regimes in inter-war Europe, he was explicitly pro-Lithuanian. Not in vain, in 1920 Jurgis Štromas served as chargé d'affaires of the newly established Republic of Lithuania in Berlin, Germany. Later he served as a high-ranking official in Kaunas. Deaf and blind to these elusive nuances of the fate of assimilated and modernised European Jews, death found him in Kaunas in the first days of the Second World War, and he died as a Jew.

During 1941–1943, Aleksandras Shtromas, along with his family members, was inmate of the Vilijampolė Ghetto and concentration camp near Kaunas. In 1943, he escaped from the concentration camp in an almost miraculous way. Shtromas and his sister Margaret survived the Holocaust, but their mother perished in the Stutthof concentration camp. Shtromas's mother, Eugenia Kozin-Štromienė, was born and brought up in St Petersburg. She met Jurgis Štromas in Berlin during his diplomatic service. A Russian-speaking lady of Jewish descent, completely assimilated into Russian society and culture of the *ancien régime*, she was not only hostile to the Bolshevik regime, but also contemptuous of the humiliating ghetto existence and Jewish separatism. Symbolically and tragically, she died in the Nazi concentration camp, taking her life three weeks before the liberation of the Stutthof inmates.

Hidden and rescued by Lithuanian Christians, the Macenavičius family, during 1943–1944 Shtromas lived in Kaunas. After the war, he was adopted by Antanas Sniečkus, the First Secretary of the Lithuanian Communist Party (CPL), and his wife Mira Bordonaitė. Yet their paths would diverge soon. Sympathetic to the Red Army and to the "right cause of universal freedom and justice" during the war, an attitude that was quite natural and understandable given the circumstances of political climate in pre-war and wartime Europe, Shtromas radically changed his attitude to the theory and practice of Marxism-Leninism after Stalin's death in 1953. When Khrushchev denounced, in his 1956 speech to the Twentieth Congress of the Soviet Union's Communist Party (CPSU), the "crimes of the Stalin era" and condemned Stalinism as a sinister form of the cult of personality, many young idealists were shocked. Some of them still believed in the possibility of socialism with a human face—a great, though unfulfilled and, therefore, false, promise of Khrushchev's politics of thaw. Shtromas was among those who chose to join the movement of political dissent, thus denouncing the criminal and cynical nature of the regime and demanding to respect freedom of conscience and human rights in general. Later on, his newly formed political views and moral allegiances would greatly disappoint Sniečkus, to whose credit we have to admit that he did his best to understand and tolerate Shtromas's existential choice.

Shtromas's odyssey began in 1948 when, having spent the academic year 1947–1948 at the University of Vilnius, Lithuania, he was admitted to the Law Faculty at the University of Moscow. Having graduated from the University of Moscow in 1952, Shtromas spent some time in Lithuania working as defence lawyer and part-time lecturer in various higher education institutions. During 1955–1959, he pursued postgraduate studies and research at the All-Union Research Institute of Legal Sciences and at the Special Institute of Advanced Legal Studies in Moscow. From 1959 to 1973, Shtromas successively held the positions of Senior Research Fellow, Head of Department, Acting Director, and Reader at various legal research and educational institutions in Vilnius, Ivanovo, and Moscow. It was a decisive period in his life: he actively joined the most prominent Soviet political dissidents. Through their joint devotion, common *raison d'être*, and shared value-and-idea system, Shtromas and Tomas Venclova developed life-long friendship. Leonid Pinsky, a scholar of Renaissance literature and Shakespeare, and Grigory Pomerantz, a philosopher and scholar of Oriental cultures, made a great impact on Shtromas. At the same time, Shtromas knew in person and sometimes co-operated with Andrei Sakharov, Elena Bonner, Andrei Sinyavsky, Yuli Daniel, and Vladimir Bukovsky. Alexander Galich and Alexander Ginzburg were his close friends.

Having experienced political persecution on the grounds of his dissident activities, Shtromas finally had to face the consequences of his political and moral choice. In 1973, he was forced to leave the Soviet Union. Shtromas chose the United Kingdom where he was able to join his sister (later Lady) Margaret Kagan. Here he started his second academic career. From 1974 to 1977, Shtromas was Senior Research Associate in Peace Studies at the School of Peace Studies of the University of Bradford.

Despite his academic credentials and brilliance, he was rejected for a permanent position. No doubt, his outspoken anti-Communism and critical views of the Western peace movement (including much of the new academic discipline of Peace Studies) made him a rather awkward member of a new Department. The Department which was the pride of the then Vice-Chancellor, Ted Edwards, and Pro-Vice-Chancellor, Robert McKinlay, who were responsible for the establishment of what was then an unusual and unique venture in British academia, which received a good deal of media attention. Moreover, the University's valued exchange agreement for Russian language students with academic institutions in the Soviet Union might have been placed in jeopardy by Shtromas's continued employment at the University. It is important to remember that Shtromas was a high-profile dissident, who frequently broadcast on Radio Liberty and Radio Free Europe, and who was vilified in especially the official Lithuanian media.

His merits were quickly realised elsewhere, however. He was welcomed by David Marquand to a more conventional university department, which Marquand created at the University of Salford following his return from Brussels (where he was Roy Jenkins's right-hand man at the European Commission). From 1978 to 1983, Shtromas was Lecturer in Politics at the Departments of Sociological and Political Studies (1978–1981) and of Politics and Contemporary History (1981–1983) of the University of Salford. In 1983, he was appointed Reader. In 1989, Shtromas moved to the United States where he received his tenured appointment as Professor of Political Science at Hillsdale College in Michigan.

A member of many British and international learned societies and associations, Shtromas enjoyed international recognition and co-operated with many prominent British political theorists and social scientists, such as Leszek Kołakowski, Kenneth Minogue, David Marquand, and Bhikhu Parekh. Among leading academics in the United States, whom he could call his friends, were Sidney Hook, Robert Conquest, Morton Kaplan, Robert Faulkner, and David Singer, among many others. Shtromas also held visiting and honorary appointments at the University of Chicago, Stanford University, Boston College, and Assumption College (USA).

Immediately upon his arrival in the UK, Shtromas started lecturing, writing, and broadcasting on the inexorable collapse of the Soviet Union.

Resting his analysis on the assumption that Communism is simply unable to provide any viable social and moral order, he gave numerous examples of the profound intellectual and moral bankruptcy of Marxism-Leninism in the Soviet Union. The British audience must have been astonished to learn that nobody in the Soviet Union takes Marxism-Leninism seriously. The vast majority of the Soviet intelligentsia, as Shtromas pointed out, had become skilled at the ideological cat-and-mouse and hide-and-seek games, constantly wrestling with the Soviet Newspeak and censorship, and employing the Aesopian language and sophisticated literary devices to survive and remain as decent as possible in a world of brainwashing and cynical lies. This was not in tune with a Western image of the Soviet and East European intellectual perceived either as a fool and single-minded fanatic or as a cynical opportunist.

Shtromas was convinced that the break-up of the Soviet Empire would not be long, and was stressing the imperative task for the West to be prepared for such a fundamental change in world history. In this, he was unique in the political science world. Although Dr Rein Taagepera, Professor of Political Science at UCLA, an Estonian émigré scholar in the United States, at this point, also deserves honourable mention (Taagepera was theoretically modelling the decline and fall of the Soviet Union, too), Shtromas was the only political scientist in the world who took an empirically elusive disintegration of the Soviet Union, as early as the late 1970s, as an ongoing process. For Shtromas, the fall of Communism in 1991, a great challenge for the mainstream of sovietologists and political scientists in North America and Western Europe, was nothing more than part of the fundamental change in world order that he anticipated and predicted.

Shtromas's anti-Communism, as well as his uncompromising struggle with Soviet totalitarianism, which he explicitly regarded as a crime against human individuals, historically rooted and culturally formed communities, and humanity, had quite complex implications for his academic career and also for his reputation among his fellow political scientists. Frequently misinterpreted and misrepresented in the political science world dominated by the Left, Shtromas used to be labelled both as a "reactionary" and as a "right-wing hawk." In fact, he was neither. The point was that Shtromas's propensity to mercilessly disclose the blindness and naiveté of his colleagues regarding the alleged humanity and justice of Communism as an important alternative or even as a rival civilisation, as well as his massive attacks on the double standard in assessing National Socialism and

Communism, irritated not a few. Suffice it to recall Shtromas's brilliant eloquence and his delight in being deliberately provocative and challenging.

There was little, if any ground at all to regard Shtromas as a single-mindedly ambitious critic of liberal values. Yes, he was empathising both with rational and moderate right-wing political forces and with conservative political thought, which he perceived as more deeply rooted in history and common sense philosophy. Yet very few are aware of the fact that Shtromas was very liberal and generous in his attitude to nationalism, identity politics, and modes of self-comprehension, not to mention his overall Central and East European intellectual and moral sensibility. Shtromas might best be characterised as a liberal conservative. In his ability to decipher the symbolic codes and interpretative undertones of Central and East European consciousness, politics, and culture, Shtromas was second to none. Being at home in many languages and cultures, he deeply penetrated every single aspect of the characteristically Central and East European fights for freedom and self-determination.

An astonishingly prolific writer, the author of numerous monographs, book chapters, scholarly articles, and essays, Shtromas, perhaps, will best be remembered for his fundamental studies in political change of the Soviet Union, such as *Political Change and Social Development: The Case of the Soviet Union*, and voluminous *The Soviet Union and the Challenge of the Future* (4 volumes, co-edited with Morton Kaplan), as well as for his unsurpassed articles on the Soviet dissidents and on the political dissent in the Baltic countries. At the same time, Shtromas was a major contributor to criminology and forensic sciences, the areas of his expertise and achievement in the Soviet Union.

A Holocaust survivor, dissenter, and iconoclastic intellectual, Shtromas, throughout his lifetime, remained a man of openness and of multiple and communicating identities. Kavolis's words on identity as a dialogue-based framework for self-discovery and for the discovery of the Other perfectly fit Shtromas. Shtromas regarded himself both as a Jew and as a Lithuanian, an identity pattern which is so familiar and understandable to Central and East European Jews, though a rarity in nationalist Europe permeated by the idea of single identity and loyalty. At the same time, he was very much at home in Russian literature and cultural history. While being very attached to his native Lithuania and passionately identifying himself with Central and Eastern Europe, Shtromas appreciated many traits of American politics and intellectual culture, and also had much admiration and affection for Great Britain.

Shtromas's immense erudition and interdisciplinary brilliance made him an untypical political scientist. His capability, from a very young age, to recite by heart the masterpieces of English, French, Russian, and Lithuanian poetry, as well as his overall expertise in world literature, theatre, and arts, struck and fascinated his colleagues and friends. His knowledge of philosophy and sociology was superb. Small wonder, then, that Shtromas's incisive social and political analyses were often complemented by his elegant insights into elusive phenomena of Central and East European consciousness and cultures hidden from the sight of the mainstream of political scientists and analysts.

In twentieth-century Lithuanian intellectual culture, including Lithuanian émigré academics, there was no political thinker of his stature. Aleksandras Shtromas came to join the honourable company of the most eminent critics of totalitarianism, ideocracy, brainwashing, and manipulative exchanges, the company which includes, among others, Hannah Arendt, Karl Jaspers, Karl R. Popper, Raymond Aron, Leszek Kołakowski, and Ernest Gellner, who did academically and theoretically what Yevgeny Zamyatin, George Orwell, Arthur Koestler, Czesław Miłosz, Milan Kundera, and Tomas Venclova did through the means of fiction, literary criticism, and political essays.

Shtromas's *Santara-Šviesa* connection included one more important acquaintance, which sheds new light on his role in the major political processes in Lithuania after 1990. Very much at home and feted in the Lithuanian diaspora around the world, in Chicago Shtromas became a close adviser and friend of Valdas Adamkus, who was elected President of Lithuania in 1998. An internationally recognised environmentalist who spent much of his time in the United States, Adamkus was a life-long friend of Kavolis, and also one of the founders of *Santara-Šviesa*. Shtromas urged Adamkus to run in the presidential campaign in Lithuania, and acted as his adviser all the time. Last but not least, Shtromas was involved in drawing up a new constitution for his native country. A man of ideas and action, Shtromas was able to bridge the world of ideas and the world of public affairs.

## Rethinking Identity, Freedom, and Dissent

Analysing the reasons and sources of the Western misconceptions of the Soviet Union, Shtromas subscribed to the point of view of the French philosopher and political scientist Alain Besançon, who succinctly suggested that "failure to understand the Soviet regime is the principal cause of its successes."[1]

Shtromas starts his harsh criticism of the Western misconceptions of the nature and logic of the Soviet regime from a philosophically and sociologically valuable remark that the Soviet Union by no means represents a continuation of the pre-revolutionary Russian Empire. To think otherwise, according to Shtromas, is nothing more and nothing less than a self-deception, "for the Soviet Union is first and foremost an ideological state whose very substance is Communism and whose rulers have at heart only one single interest, that of Communist domination, not only over Russia and its vicinities, but over the entire world."[2]

Interestingly enough, the distinction that Shtromas makes between the *ancien régime* of pre-revolutionary Russia and the Soviet Union stands in sharp contrast not only to the aforementioned identification of the two widespread in the West, but also to a theory worked out, after 1990, by some politicians in the Baltic countries, according to which the Soviet Union was nothing other than the same old Russian empire masquerading as a Communist state. (For instance, the former Chairman of the Lithuanian Parliament Vytautas Landsbergis, whose name had long been raised as the banner of the independence movement in Lithuania, made himself quite clear several times regarding this issue, namely, that Communism was nothing more than a perfect disguise for Russian imperialism.) Discarding what he perceived as an ill-founded and undifferentiated attitude to Russia, Shtromas points out: "The Soviet rulers are indeed entirely indifferent to Russia and even more so to its genuine national interests. There is little doubt that, if they had to sacrifice Russia to insure the triumph of Communism on a larger scale and on a more secure basis than at present, they would do so without much hesitation. (They are already now conducting their global policy at the expense of the vital interests of the Russian nation.)" (p.21).

Clearly distinguishing between anti-Communist and anti-Russian stances, Shtromas launches his critique of the reluctance of Western politicians and intellectuals to admit that it is Communism, rather than the alleged mysterious traits of Russian consciousness and culture, or the mystique of the Russian soul, that poses a threat to the world.

> The Western refusal to see in the Communist ideology the prime mover of Soviet behaviour, both at home and abroad, is a very dangerous delusion. The substance of that danger was clearly demonstrated to the West in the 1930s when it was dealing under the same "non-ideological" assumptions with Hitler. Alas, the lesson was taught but not properly learned. It seems

that the West simply lacks the imagination and will to take its ideological adversaries for what they really are. Instead, it prefers to project onto them an "isomorphic" image of rationally minded (though somewhat over-rapacious) nation-states and then to treat them in accordance with this false image. The West would not even listen to what its adversaries have themselves to say about their policies and goals, dismissing it all out of hand as mere propaganda, simply because what they say interferes with the West's self-construed, self-comforting, and parochially self-contained image of the world. (Ibid.)

We can understand and even entirely endorse Shtromas's emphasis on the ideocratic nature of the Soviet regime, instead of searching for the beginnings and traces of modern totalitarianism in the depths of Russian consciousness and culture, quite a risky and dubious undertaking. Yet not everything is as clear here as it seems at first sight. It suffices to recall the eminent Russian intellectuals of the *Vekhi* [Landmarks] movement, such as Nikolai Berdyaev, Sergei Bulgakov, Semyon Frank, and Peter Struve, who went so far as to suggest that some trajectories of modern Russian consciousness, as well as some traits of radical Russian intellectual culture, were suicidal for Russian politics and culture. It was they who explicitly held the radical Russian intelligentsia responsible for the fission of the Russian body politic and for the profound crisis that they inflicted on Russian society. However, this does not deny Shtromas's statement that Russia herself fell the first victim to Communism.

In *The Agony of the Russian Idea*, Tim McDaniel gave a plausible example of how culture can shape politics. In a subtle and penetrating analysis of a specifically Russian blueprint both for a social order and for a moral one, which he takes as the "Russian Idea," McDaniel describes why and how Russia's is a culture of binary oppositions and polarities that admit of no compromise—not a solid ground for tolerance, pluralism, and democracy, to say the least. In doing so, McDaniel sheds new light on the legacy of the eminent Russian-Estonian semiotician and literary scholar Yuri Lotman.

> Yuri Lotman, a recently deceased semiotician and cultural historian, developed, together with colleagues, a particularly powerful perspective on the causes of Russian historical breakdowns. In his various books, including his last work, *Kultura i vzryv* [Culture and explosion], he argues that Russian culture, unlike the culture of the West, embodies an underlying binary logic of opposition. Without necessarily being aware of these patterns, individuals and groups conceptualise social life in terms of sets of absolute alternatives that admit of no compromise. There is no neutral ground: either one or the other must be chosen, and in this choice either one or the other must be

absolutely victorious. In terms of human values, Lotman gives the following sets of polar oppositions: charity versus justice; love versus the law; personal morality versus state law; holiness versus politics. As we know from ancient literatures, particularly Greek, the Russians were not the first to perceive the tensions among these qualities. But in Russia, argues Lotman, the tendency is to present the opposition starkly: either one or the other.[3]

At the same time, there is no reason to overestimate the Russian origins of the "Russian Idea," which appears to have been shaped by many trends and tendencies of Western European social and political thought. Another crucial reservation about the kinship of the Russian Idea and Communism is that Communism is a child of the Enlightenment, whilst the Russian Idea seems to have been composed by the most conservative traits of European Romanticism. It is hardly possible to prove the Russian Idea to have been the cradle of the Bolshevik Revolution, which, in its rationalist architecture of the New World and in its endorsement of the Supreme Rationality and Inevitability of Historical Progress, is much more likely to have been a cousin, however distant, of the French Revolution. According to McDaniel,

> [t]he "Russian" idea is not entirely or exclusively Russian. It is not entirely Russian, because many of its elements were in fact borrowed from European social thought. The rejection of egotistic utilitarianism; the desire for community; the suspicion of private property; the hatred of formalism in social relations, especially as concerns law; the desire for a state that will protect the subject against social elites; indeed, the very idea of a distinctive national essence: these key themes of the "Russian" idea can be found in various currents of European thought of the early industrial period, especially romantic conservatism.[4]

Indeed, Shtromas, while quite justifiably separating Communism from the *ancien régime* of pre-revolutionary Russia, might have placed more emphasis on Communism as the failed modernisation of Russia. Although operating as a secular ideocracy—to recall a brilliant term first employed by Aron and then reinterpreted by Gellner—and as a messianic promise of collective salvation, Soviet Communism was always reminiscent of the nearly Byzantine sacrosanct structure of symbolic authority and of the fusion of the sacral and secular elements of power. Modern in intent, yet archaic in symbolic organisation, Soviet Communism is likely to continue puzzling and striking, for a long time, many Western scholars as a false promise of modernity with a human face.

Therefore, Max Weber's comparison of Communism and Protestantism, recalled and reinterpreted by Kavolis, sheds new light on Communism as a failed civilisation-shaping movement. Yet Shtromas's main intention was to show that the Communist ideology, rather than the old-fashioned Russian imperialism and jingoism, was the inner spring of the Soviet regime. In this, he succeeded. He sounds very convincing when pointing out that the West should reconsider the implications of the Communist ideology for world order and world peace, instead of glorifying Communism as an important political and moral alternative to capitalism, and as a rival civilisation.

While assessing, in vigorous terms, "this self-inflicted blindness of the West," Shtromas comes to stress the crucial importance of political dissent in the Soviet Union. "The victory over Communism should and will be decisively won by the determined engagement of the West in the battle of ideas, not of arms. The greatest asset in that battle is that Communism as an ideology is already entirely and irreversibly dead within the hearts and minds of the people ruled by the Communists."[5]

Hence, Shtromas's idea that every Soviet citizen is, at least, a potential dissident. "In spite of the purportedly monolithic structure of Soviet society and the persistent ability of the authorities to orchestrate 'unanimous' support for their every act, it is almost impossible to find any ordinary person in the USSR genuinely committed to the official ideology or truly devoted to the Communist Party and to the Soviet state. Communism and even socialism have become the most discredited words used by the Soviet people."[6]

If so, the question arises: How is the Soviet regime possible at all, once it is so fragile and vulnerable? The answer of Shtromas was that "the Communist regime in the USSR has *no* genuine supporters and exists *only* by oppression and inertia." That is why "its break up is inevitable." Hence, a far-reaching conclusion presented by Shtromas as the working hypothesis: "The slightest instability in the structure of Soviet power could, within a short space of time, cause a complete disintegration of Soviet society... without anyone trying to oppose this flow of events or even regretting it happening. This alone is sufficient ground to regard potential dissent in the USSR as a phenomenon of crucial importance."[7] The incisiveness of this hypothesis is striking. Suffice it to recall the amazing speed, ease, and dynamics of the process of the break-up of the Soviet regime and of the Warsaw Pact alliance to prove Shtromas to have been nearly prophetic in his dynamic premises of, and brilliant insights into, the nature and logic of the Communist regime.

Exactly the same might be said about his concept of dissent. Overt dissent in the USSR, as well as the most visible and eminent figures among the Soviet dissidents, was quite well known in the West. What remained beyond the reach from without and elusive for the conventional academic and political perceptions in the West, was what Shtromas defined as "intra-structural" dissent, i.e., latent dissent well accommodated within the framework of existing political conditions and institutional settings. Whereas "extra-structural," or overt, dissent emerged on the surface of Soviet society, "intra-structural" dissent was deeply rooted in Soviet society, penetrating almost every aspect of societal life.

In fact, what Shtromas described as intra-structural dissent was rather a vague phenomenon ranging from the deeply suppressed, though obvious enough in almost every walk of life, anti-Russian and anti-Soviet feelings among the minor Soviet peoples—more particularly among Ukrainians, Georgians, and Armenians, Lithuanians, Latvians, and Estonians—to the ideas of the "humanisation of socialism" that date back to 1956. Intra-structural dissent may well be characterised as one of the most mysterious phenomena of consciousness and culture ever analysed in the social sciences and political essays. Aleksandras Shtromas and Czesław Miłosz were the major contributors to the analysis of this puzzling trait of societal existence under totalitarianism.

According to Shtromas, intra-structural dissent in the USSR manifested itself in many ways, from the so-called "shadow economy" to attempts of high-ranking Soviet officials to resist Sovietisation and Russification by maintaining the national languages and cultures in their respective republics. Shtromas refers to selfishness, fear, and petty bourgeois aspirations—disguised as a genuine support for the "system"—as the engine of intra-structural dissent. Nobody wanted to sacrifice his or her academic career. Nobody was willing to give up the possibility to go abroad and visit Western countries, whatever the cost. Nobody was willing to abandon his or her safety and security. After all, it was all too human and quite understandable to wish well to one's own family. The system reached the heights of sophistication in manipulating and appealing to such obvious and harmless human needs. The outcome was that, as Kavolis ironically put it, Lithuanians and other peoples under the Soviets "have become skilled at being oppressed." Some people rose to eminence and recognition desperately hiding their "bad" family trees or "dangerous" international liaisons and backgrounds of their parents. In doing so, they elaborated and polished myriad ways of how to praise the system and glorify the wisdom and generosity of the Party, while remaining, deep in their hearts and minds, hostile to the Soviets—alas, this quite often used to take the form of an undifferentiated hostility to, and hatred of, Russians—and patriotic to their country. Yet a more noble cause or reason behind such a conformist stance had to be invented.

Hence, a justificatory and comforting, though obviously deceptive, theory of the necessity to resist the system by joining it and subverting it from within. The theory was worked out to stress the priority of culture over politics: political regimes come and go, so went this logic, but culture and spirituality last forever. Being, by definition, prior and superior to politics, culture and its continuity must be regarded as the priority of the first order, whatever happens in politics which is always a filthy and cynical thing. What is the point in desperately fighting the mighty and cruel regime, thus provoking more meaningless bloodshed and political repression, but weakening the cultural potential of the nation? Small nations must preserve their traditions and values. Survival of the language and culture, whatever cost, is the answer.

In 1992, this theory of cultural resistance, which earlier was severely criticised and explicitly rejected by Tomas Venclova as amoral, would gain new currency. The then President of Lithuania Algirdas Brazauskas, who spent much of his time serving as a high-ranking Communist Party official in Soviet Lithuania and reaching office of the First Secretary of the CPL, went so far as to openly state that nobody of them, i.e., neither he nor his political advisers and former Party friends, ever supported the Soviet regime, and that they were all devoted patriots of Lithuania. This is not to mock Brazauskas who still remains a highly respected statesman in Lithuania. As an issue able to provoke much polemic passion, intra-structural dissent, after 1990, was still on the political agenda in Lithuania. Due to its ambiguity and complex nature, intra-structural dissent turned out to be able to be politically exploited or otherwise misrepresented.

Shtromas adds an important qualification to his analysis of dissent: latent dissenters and overt dissidents are by no means locked up within their once-and-for-all frames of political activity and self-expression. On the contrary, they can freely migrate from intra-structural to extra-structural dissent, save those cases when not a few prominent Russian intellectuals were forced to become overt dissidents. They are "people whom the authorities themselves have pushed into the position of overt dissent." Of one of them, Solzhenitsyn, Shtromas writes:

> Take, for example, Solzhenitsyn. His case is probably typical. He used all the means of his power to maintain his official position as a member of the prestigious Writers' Union. Moreover, efforts were made by him and his friends to acquire for him the Lenin Prize which would have substantially strengthened his official position. Only after he had been expelled from the

Writers' Union in 1969, and after all means of publication in the USSR were completely closed to him, did Solzhenitsyn start to act as a deliberate dissident, publishing books abroad and taking part in some of the overt dissident activities. (p.11)

An overt dissident is thus "created" by the authorities—such is an interesting and provocative Shtromas's conclusion. This reminds us of how Winston Smith, in George Orwell's *1984*, is, in a way, created by O'Brien. (*1984* was among the favourite books of Shtromas.) A latent, or intra-structural, dissenter Winston Smith is identified by O'Brien as a threat to Oceania's Ingsoc only to be consciously transferred to the level of extra-structural dissent. Such a deliberate transfer is the only way to clean up Smith's consciousness, in order to push him to the limit of his dissent and then re-indoctrinate him. The climax of this cynical brainwashing is the fact that the dissident treatise *The Theory and Practice of Oligarchic Collectivism* is written by O'Brien himself disguised as patron saint of Oceanian dissent, rather than by the reputed author and overt dissident Emmanuel Goldstein—a diabolic technique of manipulation invented by the dystopian mental technicians. Thus, Orwell suggests the idea of something like a double conspiracy in a world of the jackboot pressing down upon the human face, the world where even extra-structural political dissent is fabricated by the authorities and, therefore, serves as a mousetrap for potential, or latent, dissenters. Written in 1948, that is, eight years before the actual birth of the Soviet dissidents, Orwell's masterpiece anticipated and depicted, with a stroke of genius, some traits of totalitarian reality. Although far from being fabricated or otherwise manipulated, even the towering figures in Soviet dissent were, in a way, created. As Shtromas points out:

> Sakharov, Sinyavsky, Daniel, Voinovich, Nekrasov, Aykhenvald, mentioning just a few among hundreds of well known and thousands of less known names, also became overt dissidents against their will. Many such overt dissidents were "created" by the authorities after 1956. Official criticism of Stalin aroused in many people an enthusiastic response, but the authorities would not tolerate criticism which exceeded officially established limits, and reacted to it accordingly. (Ibid.)

Shtromas's concept of intra-structural dissent may well be compared to Czesław Miłosz's interpretation of *Ketman*—a time-honoured principle of Islam (although it seems to date back to ancient Persian culture, and the term itself has its roots in the Persian language), according to which, a Muslim is entitled to conceal his or her true faith and temporarily adopt a false one in the face of grave danger to his or her dignity and life. In his thoughtful and subtle analysis of the totalitarian system of brainwashing and manipulative exchanges, Miłosz offers a new version of *Ketman*, translated into a trans-ideological, or even trans-civilisational, idiom equally well operating within religious and secular ideocracies. Miłosz's provocative and thought-stimulating interpretation of *Ketman* enabled him to reveal various literary devices and interpretative techniques concealing one's true political, moral, aesthetic, and religious views—the devices and techniques invented by Central and East European intellectuals who were desperately trying to survive and act decently in a world of cynical lies and severe censorship.

In *The Captive Mind*, Miłosz analyses the following varieties of modern ideological *Ketman*: National *Ketman*; the *Ketman* of Revolutionary Purity; Aesthetic *Ketman*; Professional *Ketman*; Sceptical *Ketman*; Metaphysical *Ketman*; and Ethical *Ketman*. Interestingly enough, the phenomenon of *Ketman* was discovered and described by the notorious founding father of racist anthropology, Comte Joseph-Arthur de Gobineau, a perceptive and interesting, albeit dangerous and sinister, writer, whose *Religions and Philosophies of Central Asia* made it available to a nineteenth-century European readership.[8]

Of the incredible world of *Ketman*, which is beyond the grasp and imagination of Western intellectuals and politicians, Miłosz writes:

> The inhabitants of Western countries little realise that millions of their fellow-men, who seem superficially more or less similar to them, live in a world as fantastic as that of the men from Mars. They are unaware of the perspectives on human nature that Ketman opens. Life in constant internal tension develops talents which are latent in man. He does not even suspect to what heights of cleverness and psychological perspicacity he can rise when he is cornered and must either be skilful or perish. The survival of those best adapted to mental acrobatics creates a human type that has been rare until now. The necessities which drive men to Ketman sharpen the intellect.[9]

Miłosz and Shtromas did not raise the issue of the moral implications of such a technique of survival. The aforementioned theory of cultural resistance and linguistic survival at the expense of political freedom may well be defined as the case of National *Ketman*. However, to judge and dismiss people practising intra-structural dissent or *Ketman* as cowards or cynics or fools was the last thing they would have done. Whereas Miłosz was mapping the existence of the split and paranoid ideological consciousness in the countries of the New Faith, Shtromas was tracing the remains of human dignity and decency in a world of social engineering, political and moral cynicism, and unprecedented manipulations. Here we are in the dark Kafkaesque world of the weak, cornered, and totally confused human being, the world of alienation and anguish. Yet there is ample ground for hope. To the contrary of the Orwellian world of the jackboot trampling the human face, the world where the failure of Winston Smith and Julia's relationship and the triumph of O'Brien over the last individual's striving for freedom, love, memory, and authentic existence signify the end of history, the world of Miłosz and Shtromas comes to witness the triumph of the seemingly little and weak individual over the monster of totalitarian modernity.

Miłosz and Shtromas succeeded where Orwell failed. Whilst Orwell was at his best deeply penetrating the reason and conscience of a separate and isolated individual who was desperately trying to maintain his ability to make logical and ethical distinctions (the heroic attempt at common sense, sound reason, and human connection, indeed, as opposed to the crowd of the true believers and ideological fanatics), Central and East European critics of totalitarianism placed much more emphasis on the collective memory and on the crucial importance of the community of memory and participation. It is hardly accidental that Orwell, who failed to appreciate the merits of liberal nationalism both in exposing totalitarianism and standing for human rights (dying in 1950, he was simply unable to do so), relied only on individual memory, too weak a basis for the sense of history.

For Orwell, nationalism, as well as its derivative phenomena, such as collective identity and collective memory, remained a vague category. Hence, his hostility to nationalism, and also his propensity to accord to the term an exclusively pejorative connotation. Ascribing to nationalism almost every possible manifestation of group stereotyping, political cleavages, social and ideological divisions, and even chauvinism and racism, Orwell is at risk of losing not only the frame of reference, but also the target of his criticism. However insightful and brilliant in his sharp and provocative analysis of what he called "transferred nationalism," i.e., such transposed forms of exclusive ideology as Communism, political catholicism, colour feeling, and class feeling, Orwell failed to understand and appreciate nationalism as a social criticism.[10] The trouble with his concept of nationalism is that nationalism begins to mean everything and, in effect, nothing. Although Orwell, as Timothy Garton Ash suggested, richly deserved to qualify for the honourable title of one of the great Central and East Europeans,[11] an additional remark is needed here. When depicting totalitarianism or deploring the naiveté and myopia of Western intellectuals concerning their attitude to the most "progressive" part of the world,

Orwell reaches the heights of Central and East European intellectual and moral sensibility. Yet on nationalism he writes as a British maverick and dissenter, an *enfant terrible* of British socialism, who deliberately translates the term into a tool of critique targeted at pre- and post-war British and European political realities.

So what was the difference between social or civic dissent—a phenomenon which embraced the whole of Soviet society and which was represented mainly by the Russian nationals themselves—and national dissent represented by the non-Russian nationals? According to Shtromas,

> [t]he non-Russian nationals, those who are aware of their non-Russian identity (about half of the population of the USSR), are dissidents almost by definition. Their deviance has a distinctive cultural background and is based on positive autonomist ideas. There is no doubt that a conscious non-Russian in the USSR dreams about independence for his people or, at least, of some genuine autonomy. This hope can only become a reality when there is a fundamental change in political conditions in the whole of the USSR; it requires, first of all, the abolition of the present Soviet Empire which deserves the title of "a prison of nations" more than Tsarist Russia ever did.[12]

Here we have a new theme in Shtromas's critique of totalitarianism. Social or civic dissent, a phenomenon represented mainly by the Russian intelligentsia, with its emphasis on the universal human rights and political liberty of society as a whole, had little to do with national dissent which was less universalistic, yet more deeply rooted in religion and collective identity. No wonder that Shtromas, in his analysis of the social and political morphology of dissent, links religion to nationalism as one more facet of dissent. "Like nationalism, religion is, in Soviet conditions, a dissident attitude by its very nature" (p.14).

However, nationalism of the non-Russian nationals in the Soviet Union, according to Shtromas, was not limited to intra-structural dissent. It also produced some outbursts in the form of overt extra-structural dissent, as was proved by the Chronicles of the Lithuanian Catholic Church, Ukrainian, Georgian and Armenian Samizdat, "Helsinki groups" in the Ukraine, Lithuania, and Georgia, etc. In spite of the universalistic character of civic dissent in Russia, both forms of dissent were more or less related to each other. Noteworthy is the fact that *The Chronicle of Current Events*, which started circulating in Moscow in 1968, was the obvious model for *The Chronicle of the Catholic Church in Lithuania* which began in 1972. Russian dissent also produced its national movement. Shtromas points out:

> In recent years the non-Russian national movements were joined by a Russian national movement which advocates a Russian national revival in terms incompatible with totalitarian Communist rule (A. Solzhenitsyn, I. Shafarevich, V. Osipov and others are the well-known exponents of this movement). It is remarkable that these Russian national forces, with a few exceptions, favour national freedom for all non-Russian nations of the USSR. Under these circumstances, national dissent being "partial" in essence (i.e. representing the case of one particular nation rather than that of the whole of the USSR), acquires an overall social dimension relevant to political change in the country at large. As one dissident writer stated: "In the Soviet Union the Marxist slogan: 'Proletarians of all countries, unite!' has been strangely replaced by a much more practical slogan: 'Nationalists of all Soviet nations, unite!' In this united shape, national movements are organically joining the democratic movement in its struggle for freedom and human rights." (p.14)

Yet nationalism of the non-Russian movements, by virtue of its ability to enjoy much more popular support and social cohesion than its counterpart in Russia, had an obvious advantage over the noble-spirited, yet disconnected, universalism and secular liberalism of civic dissent in Russia. This is especially true of the marriage of religion and nationalism, so potent in such Catholic countries as Poland and Lithuania, where this alliance came to transform itself into a potent alternative to the regime and its ideology. Although the implications of such an alliance for liberal democracy and pluralism are profoundly problematic, it was operating extremely well as an alternative framework for collective memory and identity and as a mobilising force. Even the greatest of the Russian dissidents may never have achieved such popular recognition and support. The notorious gap between the Russian intelligentsia and common people, the curse of modern Russia, still remained a deep injury on the body politic inflicted not only by Peter the Great and nineteenth-century Russian political and ideological dramas, but also by the recent fission of the body social inflicted by Communism.

Not in vain, comparing dissent in Poland and the Soviet Union (in particular, Russia), H. Stuart Hughes notes:

> Dissent in Poland could count on the backing of a homogenous people— overt support from the working class and tacit sympathy among the peasants. In the Soviet Union it was the reverse: the dissidents formed a beleaguered band drawn largely from the intelligentsia and cut off from the mass of the population by a wall of mutual incomprehension. Polish dissent drew on patriotic traditions reaching back nearly two centuries; Soviet dissent smacked of treason. Such held true for the dominant ethnic

Russians. Among the minor Soviet peoples—more particularly among Ukrainians, Georgians, and Armenians, Lithuanians, Latvians, and Estonians—patriotic resistance here and there united intellectuals and ordinary folk in a common hatred of Russian over-lordship. But movements of this sort languished in obscurity; it was not they that inspired interest and sympathy in the West. Nor was it religious protest, whether Eastern Orthodox or evangelical Protestant; only the pleas of the Jews found support abroad. Yet even Jewish protest fastened almost exclusively on the issue of emigration; such single-mindedness often sounded like indifference to the wider question of arbitrary rule at home. By contrast, the greatest of the Russian dissidents tried to see beyond the plight of their own people to that of the other Soviet nationalities and of humanity as a whole. Their numbers, their eminence, the fact that only they wrote in a major international language, dictate a focus on their struggles and their frustration.[13]

In his attempt to bridge these disunited faculties of dissent, namely, the standing for human rights and the struggle for the national independence cause, Shtromas was among those unique figures in Soviet dissent who combined, on the one hand, the ideals of cosmopolitan tolerance, liberal democracy, pluralism, and ethical universalism, and, on the other hand, local sensibility and fidelity to the cause of the freedom and independence of their native countries. In this, he stands very close to his friends and fellow dissidents, such as Andrei Sakharov, Andrei Sinyavsky, Yuli Daniel, Vladimir Bukovsky, and Tomas Venclova. For them, nationalism, disconnected from the sympathetic understanding of the Other and from an overall dimension of human dignity, decency, and freedom, would degenerate into a tribal sentiment and collective solipsism; whereas a universalistic programme of the struggle for human rights, if lacking in sympathy and sensitivity to the peoples and their cultures under duress of oppression, would turn into a bloodless and soulless political catholicity.

In this political and moral stance, Shtromas and his fellow dissidents are reminiscent of the best moments and the most moving allegiances of the epoch of the springtime of the peoples. The ideals of universal brotherhood and fellowship in a common fight for independence and liberty of the peoples, as the inmost principle and as the starting point in the ethic of liberal nationalism, were still there. "For your and our freedom!" was the war cry, introduced by the Polish fighters for the Italian *Risorgimento* movement and then used as a loan slogan not only by the prominent Russian dissidents, but also by the *Sąjūdis* members in Lithuania as early as 1988. Suffice it to recall Adam Mickiewicz who formed the Polish legion for the *Risorgimento* in 1848, thus keeping his fidelity to Giuseppe Mazzini and Giuseppe Garibaldi, or Tadeusz Kościuszko who fought for independence of America, to conceive of this secular religion of freedom. Only those who are committed to the cause of freedom of other countries may be regarded as patriots of their own country—this legacy of Polish-Lithuanian aristocrats of the nineteenth century stands in sharp contrast to the ferocious and murderous philosophical anthropology of radical and integral nationalism that was yet to come.

A liberally minded cosmopolitan and fighter for human rights in the broadest sense, an extra-structural dissident, in his parlance, Shtromas also was a patriot of Lithuania. A profound moral sense, as well as his tolerant and wise attitude to human virtues and vices, greatly assisted him in grasping the nerve of intra-structural dissent—human fear, selfishness, adaptability, and attachment to mundane stability and predictability, accompanied by the invincible will to live. Shtromas appreciated and analysed every single manifestation of intra-structural dissent, instead of severely judging people for inconsistency, cowardice, lack of principle, and moral compromising. That same moral sense did not deceive him when he described the political and moral impetus of the Soviet regime.

> On a personal level, even high officials are dissidents—including members of the Politburo. (That is one of the reasons why in public they act as automatons—mouthpieces of an abstract ruling body and not like real people; Khrushchev, even when in power, showed something of his personality and, therefore, often sounded like a dissident.) By far the greatest expression of "dissent" is greedy selfishness, a rapacious attitude to the common good which results in cynicism being the dominant attitude towards life. Those in power, although having ceased to believe in Communism and in the infallible virtues of the Soviet regime, are still prepared to defend it by all means in their power but only because they thus protect their enormous personal privileges which they could not maintain in any other socio-political system.[14]

Shtromas dismissed all considerations about the alleged fanaticism and ideological single-mindedness of the Soviet people as vulgar and ill-founded political propaganda, and quite justifiably so. Instead of searching for the special qualities of *homo sovieticus* or depicting the allegedly ever-present fanaticism and ideological zeal of Russians or the "Soviet people," he focused on the analysis of the Communist Party and Communist ideology as the sword and the shield of the Soviet regime. It is the sole political party-based and oligarchic regime, or partocracy, that wages the never-ending war against its own society, while pretending to be constantly surrounded and plotted by external and internal enemies—roughly speaking, such an Orwellian hypothesis regarding the nature of Communism was employed in many of Shtromas's contributions. Although Shtromas made himself quite clear regarding "greedy selfishness" and "rapacious attitude to the common good which results in cynicism being the dominant attitude towards life," he remained a theorist of the alternative possibilities and visions of political existence.

> However, there are millions of people in the USSR who are committed to positive social goals which are incompatible with the totalitarian Soviet regime. In this positive sense the Soviet dissident is everyone who has managed to remain loyal and committed not only to himself as to an isolated individual, but also to the society or simply to the fate of others. These people who are motivated by civic considerations are joined by professionals who cannot help but be critical of mismanagement and other symptoms of decay induced and maintained by the regime, allegedly for ideological reasons, but really to keep in a position of absolute power an ignorant oligarchy. For such professionals the whole rule of that oligarchy (partocracy) seems to be irrational and needs to be replaced by a system based on sound management which they—the professionals themselves—would be able to provide. (p.15)

According to Shtromas, this is more than true of nationalism, which is, almost by definition, hostile to, and incompatible with, the Soviet regime. Being much at home in every aspect of Russian history and culture, let alone his overall expertise in Central and East European politics and societies, Shtromas strongly felt what other political analysts and sovietologists overlooked, namely, that nationalism alone, no matter whether Russian or non-Russian, could destroy the Soviet regime. Tracing nationalism as a political dissent, Shtromas worked out not only a theory of political change focused on the collapse of Communism as a major issue in world history, but also a new identity and freedom discourse which enabled him to theoretically substantiate his statement regarding the liberal nature of nationalism, unless it degenerated into a framework for xenophobic or racist reactions.

At the same time, he explicitly stated that nationalism and national identity, like religion, operates optimally in a democratic setting—in this, Shtromas entirely endorsed Kavolis's conception of identity and freedom. Shtromas also added that nationalism and religion, unless they are distorted by authoritarianism, totalitarianism, or otherwise politically exploited, operate not only as an inescapable right of people to have a collective identity and be rooted in their histories and cultural traditions, but also as a potent alternative to global ideologies that come to deny this right as an obstacle to historical progress or modernisation or the creating of a "new human being" free of history, religion, and tradition. Noteworthy is the fact that Shtromas, an agnostic himself, raised his voice in defence of religion and religious believers in the Soviet Union.

> The Soviet dissident is everyone whose genuine commitment to any social issue is stronger than his egoism and the imposed commitment to the Soviet state. Specifically, it means that all nationalists (including the Russian ones who are already able to distinguish between the Imperial and genuine national interests of Russia and see them as incompatible—Solzhenitsyn is one of them) and all religious believers are unqualified dissidents. (Ibid.)

In order to understand this emphasis on nationalism as a phenomenon radically opposed to global ideologies of the twentieth century, we have to trace Shtromas's conception of ideology and utopia, which was fully developed in his later contributions. Such an analysis is a clue to his ambitious undertaking to map the modern world of political and moral imagination.

### Neither Ideology nor Utopia: Toward a Liberal Nationalism

In his analysis of ideological politics after the collapse of Communism, Shtromas defined ideology as a system of thought and action inimical to, and incompatible with, the principle of reality. Following Karl Mannheim, Shtromas described ideologies and utopias as equally incongruent to socio-political reality. At one point, however, their paths diverged: whereas Mannheim was convinced that utopian ideas, once they have been translated into socio-political reality, become ideological and even make up predominant political ideologies (liberalism and Marxism would perfectly exemplify this statement), Shtromas insisted that ideologies are all global and utopian by nature. For him, non-utopian ideology sounded a contradiction in terms, and so did non-global ideology. Ideology, according to Shtromas, seeks to envision and institutionalise a blueprint for a universalistic and global social order. In doing so, it manifests itself as a promise of collective salvation and as a model of world order. By employing mythological images, utopian ideals of the conflict-free and just society, and quasi-religious priority of the other-worldly ideal or principle over this-worldly reality, ideology operates as a holistic, global, utopian, and, therefore, disconnected alternative to societal existence, the latter being rooted in history, tradition, and collective identity.

As a promise to bridge the world of ideas and socio-political reality, ideology, as Shtromas points out, came into being in the epoch of the Enlightenment. Mapping the increasingly ideological world of modern intellectuals with its pivotal idea of the translation of ideas into reality, Shtromas recalls Antoine Louis Claude, Comte Destutt de Tracy (1754–1836) who coined the term *idéologie* and who defined it as a science of ideas. Shtromas puts it in the following way:

> In his four volume work *Elements d'idéologie*, published between 1801–1813, Destutt de Tracy arrives at a system of such, in his opinion, true ideas (very liberal ones by the way) and then focuses his attention on how to translate these "true" ideas into socio-political reality by conceiving appropriate programmes of political action. Hence, according to Destutt de Tracy, an ideology: (1) is based on a verified cognitive general theory of universal and comprehensive nature explaining human beings and their relationship with the external world, including also other human beings; (2) expresses itself in a programme of social and political organisation of human beings; (3) entails the necessity of struggle for the realisation of this programme; (4) demands proselyting and commitment; (5) addresses the public at large but confers a special role of leadership to properly qualified groups of intellectuals (*les idéologues* or, one would say, the enlightened "vanguard" of society).[15]

Therefore, ideology aims to change the world, instead of interpreting it. The mission of the *idéologues* was to translate ideas into socio-political reality and to change the world around them. In this context, it becomes obvious that the Marxian conviction concerning the real role and place of philosophy in the world—"up till now the philosophers have only interpreted the world in various ways; the point, however, is to change it"[16]—betrays Marx to have been a late and bizarre recurrence of the Enlightenment.

Shtromas suggests that National Socialism and Communism were ideologies *par excellence*—the former favouring the rejection of the present and the restoration of mythological past, the latter passionately denying the past and present of humankind and focusing on the future instead. Their failure means that the world faces the end of ideological politics. However, Shtromas's historical optimism was far from a Fukuyama-like scenario of the end of history. The world may face myriad political dramas and clashes, but they are all about human identity and self-determination, rather than global ideologies or messianic promises of collective salvation. At the same time, Shtromas had much scepticism regarding Samuel Huntington's thesis of the clash of civilisations. According to Shtromas, we live in the world of clashing political programmes and visions of world order, rather than ideologies or civilisations. Therefore, there is no reason to credit some fundamentalist reactions or cynical, ethnic-cleansing, yet highly pragmatic regimes for being religion-sustaining or even civilisation-shaping.

Defining ideologies and distinguishing between them and political programmes, Shtromas goes so far as to state explicitly that feminism, environmentalism, multiculturalism, and welfare-statism must all be understood as political programmes rooted in their respective interest groups, rather than ideologies. The same goes for sinister phenomena of consciousness and politics, such as xenophobia and racism. They, as Shtromas points out, do not make up separate ideologies; nor do they compose political programmes capable of reshaping social reality. Xenophobia and racism are merely negative group sentiments and psychological reactions hostile to what is perceived as a threat to economic and social stability.

The question arises: How about paradigmatic political ideologies of the modern world—liberalism, conservatism, and socialism? The answer of Shtromas is that neither conservatism nor socialism, in the current world, qualifies as a genuinely global system of ideas and values. Conservatism has never been so, and still remains a phenomenon of nostalgia for what Shtromas terms socio-cultural reality's "original or past purity."

> Conservatism is, as a rule, not ideological. It expresses itself mainly in the not necessarily uncritical acceptance of, and accommodation to, the given social-political reality usually accompanied by a certain nostalgia for that reality's original or past purity and a resentment of "bastardising changes" introduced into that reality by recent modernising currents and trends. Traditionalism, the instinctive attachment to familiar rituals and a routine way of life, that is, to what Max Weber so aptly called "the eternal yesterday," is no ideology but a natural result of a successful process of socialisation. It is only when this reality is disintegrating and becomes increasingly unable to secure a successful socialisation into it of substantial numbers of oppressed and/or alienated people that the normally non-ideological conservative orientation may start growing into a set of ideas deserving the name, "conservative ideology." This usually happens when there is an urgent need for the conservatives to present an adequate response to the spread and menacingly increasing impact of revolutionary ideologies.[17]

Yet it did not prevent Shtromas from recognising that Comte Joseph de Maistre's *Considérations sur la France*, one of the key texts of conservatism on its rise, was a call for a revolution against the already established by that time republican regime in France. Therefore, the "conservative revolution" can hardly be seen as an oxymoron. Moreover, Shtromas identified a conservative element in the Fascist and National-Socialist ideologies of the twentieth century. Deeply anti-capitalist and anti-modernist, these ideologies sought to restore what they perceived as the natural and organic communities. But it would be a profound misunderstanding, goes on Shtromas, to treat them as paradigmatically conservative. At the same time, it makes no sense to conflate Fascism and National Socialism, as global, holistic and militant ideologies, with nationalism which has nothing to do with the ambition to establish hierarchy among the nations and rank one above the other or to reshape the entire world on the pattern of a prescriptive *Blut-und-Boden* identity discourse.

Shtromas lists Socialism, Communism, Jacobinism, Fascism, and National Socialism as paradigmatic ideologies. In his view, pre- and non-Marxist varieties of Socialism and Communism also qualify as ideologies. They are: Anarchism, agrarian Socialism (for instance, the Russian *narodniks*), and the modern social-democratic tradition. Yet Socialism, in the second half of the twentieth century, ceased functioning as a global and holistic ideology. If we are not to confound Socialism and welfare-statism, we have to admit that Socialism of Marxist variety has lost its universal appeal. Political programmes, rather than ideologies, which function within the framework of liberal democracy, cannot reject a free-market economy; nor can they deny economic and political realities of a given society. Since no political or ideological programme offers the idea of the radical transformation of social reality, in accordance with a utopian blueprint for a social order, we can safely assume that we live in an ideology-free world. The idea of the end of history is replaced here by that of the end of "isms," that is, ideologies.

However, not everything here is as clear as it seems. By and large, Shtromas makes valuable distinctions, though at the expense of important nuances. It might be suggested, for instance, that not always do ideologies have a separate and autonomous existence. Some of them appear as manifesto ideologies aiming to reshape the world; others are latent or otherwise implicit in philosophical, sociological, religious, mystical, or artistic articulations of the human world. To separate, radically and irreversibly, value and truth in the current social sciences and humanities is the last thing a scholar should do, for ideologies are latent in social and cultural criticism which, for its part, is inseparable from the social sciences and humanities of the end of the twentieth century and of the beginning of the twenty-first. The same is true of utopian consciousness, which is present in the moral imagination and social criticism of our century.

The least convincing part of Shtromas's conception of ideology is his insistence on the mandatory gulf between theory/philosophy and ideology. As if a discovery of a topic were not related to value judgement, which precedes a value-free method as a way to explicate that topic, as Max Weber would have it. In the discursive universe of the social sciences, value always lurks behind fact/truth. The way in which we approach one or another issue, as well as the way in which we make our disciplinary choice and methodological preference, is always determined by our existential and social experience. Our experience inevitably motivates our research and, in particular, a discovery of a topic, for value, within the framework of the social sciences and humanities, precedes and underlines truth. In this sense, the social scientist, in his/her social analysis or interpretation of culture, is constantly correcting or even symbolically constructing social reality and writing his/her moral autobiography. This is more than true with regard to social and cultural criticism, which may well be regarded as a phenomenon deeply characteristic of the current social sciences. The discursive mapping of a social science discipline or of a social theory is unthinkable without including moral choices made by the social scientist. Shtromas's scholarship exemplifies this better than anything else.

Interestingly, Shtromas, following his path of controversy, goes so far as to conclude that Karl Marx was not philosopher but ideologue, and that Marxism should be qualified as ideology, rather than social philosophy.[18] Radically separating theory and ideology as monads being out of touch, Shtromas contradicts himself, for he himself, in his iconoclastic and provocative scholarship, comes to bridge truth and value. Surprisingly enough, it did not prevent him not only from misinterpreting the nature of the social sciences and the social nature of values, but also from falling into a trap of a kind of positivist fiction, which was developed *ad absurdum* in modern analytical philosophy, and according to which, scientific truth and rationality have nothing to do with values, religious and aesthetic experiences, and human subjectivity. In fact, philosophy covers a huge territory of human knowledge and experience, and arbitrary decisions to cut off some of its segments, as well as the amazing ease with which some theorists arrive at the definition of philosophy, thus graciously granting the exclusive rights of existence to some body parts of philosophy, make little sense in our age of inter-subjectivity and interdisciplinary scholarship.

One of the most provocative and challenging parts of Shtromas's theory of the end of ideology is his concept of liberalism. Shtromas qualified

Millian liberalism as militant liberalism and described it as a global, artificialist, and intolerant ideology contemptuous of everything that is rooted in history and tradition—collective identity, communitarian collectivist beliefs and traditions, and nationalism.

> A typical Millian liberal has no patience for or tolerance of communitarian collectivist beliefs and traditions wherever they continue to exist, be it distant India or nearby rural England. They had no understanding of or sympathy for the Irish national struggle and continue to wonder about the passionate attachment of some Welshmen to their "antiquated and useless language," treating the struggle for its preservation as incomprehensible, irrational and thus reprehensible. Millian liberalism is, in fact, militant liberalism. By absolutising individualism and, accordingly, treating every form of collectivism as a reactionary remnant of the "dark ages," a relict of the feudal past and symbol of rural backwardness, it militantly opposes collectivist tendencies and traditions, puts itself into combat for their elimination from the life of contemporary society altogether and does so wherever such tendencies and traditions are to be found (and they are to be found everywhere, indeed). Millian liberalism treats any variety of traditional collectivism, including nationalism, as a phenomenon which, with the further progress of modernity, is bound to vanish into the records of the historic past, anyway, but every true Millian liberal nevertheless sees his task in pushing by all means in his power this process of progressive modernisation (which to him is tantamount to the process of mankind's levelling) forward and thus facilitating and hastening its happy conclusion—the universal predominance of the liberal-individualist uniformity. In this Millian liberalism closes ranks with socialism/communism—they both share the dream about a "new man" who is fully devoid of any national or other traditional collective identity and lives exclusively by the universal values of his respective ideology. (pp.193–194)

Instead, Shtromas favours what he calls Kantian and Herderian-Renanian liberalism. As noted, an arbitrary application of the Kantian notion of self-determination to the ethic of nationalism, widespread among those writers and social analysts who are in favour of nationalism, remains profoundly problematic. However generous and noble-spirited in his attitude to non-German peoples (among them, Lithuanians, whose rights to cultivate their language and culture were advocated by the Königsberg genius), Immanuel Kant can hardly be seen as the founding father of liberal nationalism. Although his contribution to the liberal moral culture is unquestionable, Kant may well be regarded as the Enlightenment philosopher of liberal cosmopolitanism and supra-nationalism, a political philosophy which resulted in his crucial concepts of *phoedus amphyctionum* and *phoedus pacificum*, but not the upholder of the upcoming era of nationalism. This is not to say that there is no such thing as Kantian liberalism. I am only saying that Kantian liberalism by no means automatically implies liberal nationalism. However related in their common history of the eighteenth- and nineteenth-century political dramas and clashes in Europe, liberalism and nationalism cannot be assumed as just two names for the same phenomenon. This is especially true of Kantian social and political philosophy.

At this point, there is much more relevance in Shtromas's admiration and preference for Herder and Renan, whose liberalism he ranks above the Millian version of liberalism. Shtromas's definition of the nation as a collective personality is very much in tune with the Herderian notion of nations as historically unique, self-asserting, and self-sufficient groups of individuals. Not in vain, Shtromas defines the nation as an organic entity shaped by what he refers to as the specific mytho-poetical substance, thus echoing not only liberally minded, though obscure and inconsistent, Herder, but Martin Heidegger as well. Bearing in mind the highly questionable political implications of the Heideggerian notion of *Heimat* and of Heidegger's overall anti-modernism, these two references do not make for a good pair. But it is quite logical that Shtromas recalls the Renanian concept of the nation as an everyday plebiscite, which evidently corresponds with what Shtromas takes as a subjective and liberal definition of the nation. Shtromas might also have added that Joseph-Ernest Renan was engaged in polemic with Heinrich von Treitschke, the historic face-to-face encounter of the leading theorists of liberal and conservative nationalism.

Yet there is no word, in Shtromas's analysis of nationalism and global ideologies, about the capability of nationalism to adjust itself not only to Kantian and Herderian-Renanian Liberalism, but also to Conservatism, Socialism, Fascism, National Socialism, and even Communism, that is, virtually to all major political ideologies. The marriage of nationalism and conservatism is obvious in the case of Heinrich von Treitschke, one of the founding fathers of conservative nationalism and of the prescriptive collective identity discourse. The alliance of nationalism and Fascism, as exemplified with *Action Française* and other sinister ideological movements in inter-war Europe, can hardly be denied, too. And though Shtromas insists on the incompatibility of nationalism and such global ideologies as National Socialism and Communism, arguing that to perceive racism of the Nazis, elevated to the rank of a basis for the new world order, as something related to nationalism would be a profound misunderstanding, it is not difficult to theoretically reconstruct the rhetoric of conservative, radical, and integral nationalism in National Socialism. And whatever Shtromas writes about nationalism and Communism as mutually exclusive and irreconcilable forces, Russian nationalist paraphernalia in wartime Stalin's rhetoric were too obvious to need emphasis.

Regrettably, Shtromas's propensity to pigeonhole nationalism and global ideologies, instead of employing a comparative analysis to trace how these phenomena overlap, did not allow him to substantially explore the morphology of nationalism. His suspicion about universal ideologies and artificially construed modes of collective identity, all of them being regarded as nothing more than the masks of totalitarianism, may easily be found behind his passionate advocacy of nationalism. Hence, his emphasis on the national rights as an important aspect of human rights.

> It is wrong, in my view, to try to counter-oppose, as many scholars do, the rights of nations to individual rights, claiming that the latter take precedence over the former. The rights of nations in principle do not contradict the rights of the individuals, for no nation willingly submits itself to rule by a regime oppressive of the individuals who make up the body of that nation. Repressive authoritarian or totalitarian regimes by violating human rights of their subjects violate at the same time the right of the nation freely to choose the form of rule under which it wishes to live and thus become abusive and oppressive of the nation they falsely claim to rule in that very nation's best interests. It seems to me that the scholars who consider the rights of nations antithetical to the rights of individuals are actually confusing the nation with the nation-state which indeed may submit itself either to an unpopular ideology or to a group pursuing through the state its vested interests at the expense of the interests of the nation and thus becoming oppressive of both the individual and the nation at large. On the other hand, the right of nations to self-determination and sovereignty on a par with other nations can become a real right only if it is rooted in individual human rights and is projected onto the political surface as a natural extension of these rights either exercised or claimed by a multitude of people as individuals in a simultaneous manner. For if the nation is an organic entity with which a great number of people freely identify themselves, no individual belonging to that nation can enjoy any rights accorded to him in an abstract and limited fashion ignoring or even suppressing his collective identity as member of a certain nation. As long as the individual has no right to be what he really is or wants to become—and this, in the first place, means being/becoming a member of what one considers to be one's own nation—he is not free and is thus deprived of his primary right to liberty. This is especially true of individuals who consider

themselves members of one nation but are forced by another nation's state to assume that other nation's identity. (p.202)

Indeed, referring to the national rights as an inseparable aspect of human rights, Shtromas not only shows his Central and East European sensibility, but also comes to oppose those students of nationalism who tend to append to the term an exclusively pejorative connotation. Nationalism has no reason to be apologetic, since it represents the most relevant framework for individual and collective identity. Being a blueprint for a social order, it also provides a moral order—at this point, Shtromas stands in sharp contrast to Ernest Gellner and other generalists of nationalism who were and continue to be rather sceptical about the ability of nationalism to provide a viable moral order. Nationalism, if devoid of such excesses as chauvinism, xenophobia, and racism, is quite a sound phenomenon of politics and culture.

The most important of Shtromas's insights into the nature of nationalism and identity politics is his idea that it makes no sense to counter-oppose the rights of nations to individual rights, since the human identity structure would be incomplete without one of its constituent parts. The individual's sense of belonging, as well as his/her right to be a member of the community of memory and participation with which he/she wishes to identify him/herself, is one of the essential human rights which must be defended against the ideologies of human facelessness, denationalisation, anonymity, and uniformity. Inclusive and sound nationalism, operating in a liberal-democratic setting, should be neither demonised nor otherwise misrepresented as a deviation from what is supposed to be "normal." This is a crucial lesson that we can draw from a human rights activist and critic of ideologies.

Interestingly, Shtromas refers to Aristotelian ethical theory as "the best available guide for determining the moral quality of every variety and aspect of nationalism and also for defining which elements in any nationalism are evil and reprehensible and which ones are benign and commendable" (p.203).

> According to Aristotle, good and evil are quantitative rather than qualitative categories. This is to say that excess or defect of a certain orientation or attitude are what makes it evil, but if this orientation or attitude expresses itself as the mean between these two extremes, then it is good. In this sense courage is the good and virtuous mean between the two bad extremes of rushness and cowardice, the virtue of generosity is the mean between the two blameable extremes of extravagance and stinginess, etc. Nationalism *per se* should be then also understood as the virtuous mean between the two

immoral extremes of chauvinism and abstract (a-national or even anti-national) catholicity, the former being the excessive and the latter the defective expression of an individual's or a group's sense of collective national identity. Xenophobia, though less excessive than chauvinism, will find its place in the quantitative continuum between good and evil in a space closer to the excessive extreme than to the virtuous mean. Hence, chauvinism and xenophobia, as excessive expressions of nationalism, are reprehensible and should be ethically evaluated as evil, but not less so is catholicity which fully ignores or even actively negates national identity and usually tries to substitute for it a universal ideology based and artificially construed collective identity, such as, for example, a certain world religion, a certain world wide social class or, ultimately, the mankind as a whole. (Ibid.)

In his scepticism about artificially construed and pseudo-universalistic systems of ideas and values—for which cosmopolitanism, however, is not the most accurate word—Shtromas stands close to Kavolis. The problem of incomplete humanity in modern consciousness was at the core of the works by two of the most ambitious and eminent of Lithuanian social and political thinkers in the twentieth century. However distinct in the frame of reference and theoretical idiom, Shtromas and Kavolis were very close in their local sensibility and in their intellectual courage to raise the most painful and controversial issues concerning human awareness, morality, and sensitivity. Of the danger of the simulations of openness and of the travesties of the polylogue of civilisations, which occur in a world of "political correctness" and of the faceless and anonymous ideological bodies disguised as the bearers of sensitivity and politeness, Kavolis wrote:

> The polylogue of civilisations and cultures can occur wherever minds open up beyond the taken-for-granted systems of categories and balancing styles of one civilisation. This could be the universal purpose of post-high school humanistic education. Its primary social supports will be the universities, world media, international scholarly associations, and culture-critical movements—to the extent that they are all set up in such a way as not to consist of "official representatives" of collectivities or ideological bodies; and, on the other hand, are not committed to some blandly programmatic "citizenship of the world" (the incomplete humanity of which becomes evident when it comes to raising one's children).[19]

However, what Shtromas's critique of ideologies is missing is the analysis of prejudice and irrationality, which is a strong point in Kavolis's critical scholarship (suffice it to recall Kavolis's contribution to the study in comparative social pathology), and which reaches its culmination in Tomas Venclova's political essays. A rationalist political thinker and a rational-action theorist, Shtromas underestimated the irrational and lunacy, the crucial importance of which for the moral and political imaginations of the modern world was so elegantly articulated in the works of the most brilliant critics of Western consciousness and modern civilisation, such as Zygmunt Bauman, Jean Baudrillard, and Umberto Eco.

To further compare Shtromas and Kavolis, Shtromas lacks Kavolis's attentiveness to meaningful details of human experience and existence, since he is preoccupied with big issues and global scenarios of political change. Another dividing line between them would be their attitudes to history and tradition: Shtromas speaks out in favour of what Kavolis criticises as archaising longings. However accurate from the point of view of political history, such remarks of Shtromas as, for instance, that that "Britain and other colonial masters claimed to exercise, with regard to their colonies, a civilisatory mission which, after having been successfully accomplished, would allow them to release their colonies into, first, autonomous and, later, independent existence" (and this, according to Shtromas, had indeed become the case) are reminiscent of the "white man's burden" mentality.[20]

For his part, Shtromas surpassed Kavolis in his first-hand knowledge of the primary Central and East European sources and in the scope of his political analysis. A classical type of scholar, Kavolis was technophobic and relied only on books and professional journals. He refused a computer and hated travel. Although his remarks and insights into the dynamics of Lithuanian politics and culture are astonishingly sharp and precise, Kavolis had little interest in empirical observations of societal life. A lonely generalist of genius, Kavolis's participation in social reality was conceptual and symbolic. Shtromas, instead, had much to say about the hottest political processes, flesh-and-blood political actors, and newly found political heroes of many countries all over the globe. A curious social scientist, a political adviser of Russian democrats and liberally minded politicians, an expert on Lithuanian domestic and foreign policies, and a travelling scholar, Shtromas had never lost touch with the reality of the major social and political processes. For him, knowledge occurred *only* through direct participation in socio-political reality.

There is no reason, however, to exaggerate their ideological and political differences. No doubt, Kavolis, patron saint of Lithuanian liberalism, was a consistent and dedicated liberal, a man of moderation, whereas Shtromas's relationship with liberalism is marked by inconsistency and ambivalence. A conservative in intent, Shtromas was a liberal in dissent. Such a combination of conservatism in theory and liberalism in practice shows

Shtromas to have been a man of passion and iconoclasm. Their principal similarity lies in the vigorous criticism of the moral provincialism and naiveté of those Western scholars and politicians who were and still are contemptuous of Central and Eastern Europe, particularly those who are still inclined to treat the rest of Central and Eastern Europe as fundamentally misinterpreting and misrepresenting the Soviet Union and Russia, or "progressive" political forces in general.

They were both passionate, though sceptical and ironic, intellectuals. Both combined liberal cosmopolitanism and liberal nationalism, the happy complementarity that equally justifies and gives sense to these forms of identity and freedom. Both were very attached to their native Lithuania, though Shtromas was far less critical to Lithuanian consciousness and culture than Kavolis. This is why Shtromas may well be described as a critic of the contamination of consciousness, brainwashing, totalitarian and ideocratic regimes, and global ideologies, whereas Kavolis was a critic of society and culture in at once the most inclusive and exclusive sense.

Their differences might best be defined in terms of stylistic preference. Kavolis favoured the ellipse, and Shtromas preferred the straight line.

## Thinking Unthinkable: The Discourse about the Holocaust

The most controversial and moving part of Shtromas's legacy is his reflections on the metaphysics and ethics of the Holocaust. The Rabbi Joseph Klein Lecture, "The Jewish and Gentile Experience of the Holocaust: A Personal Perspective," which Shtromas gave on April 10, 1989, at Assumption College in Worcester, Massachusetts, USA, sheds new light on him as a political and moral philosopher whose inquiry cannot stop from entering at the gates of the metaphysics of human existence. The questions Shtromas raises here drive him to core questions in ethics. Far from being merely a passing reference, his idea of the overcoming of the division of humankind into "us" and "them" provides an interpretative framework for the new identity and freedom discourse.

Shtromas starts by mentioning the French philosopher Henri Bergson whose *Two Sources of Morality and Religion*, a book published in 1931, not only becomes a source of the discourse about the open society and the closed society, the fact acknowledged by Karl R. Popper, but also addresses the issue of an instinctive division, by each individual, of the rest of humanity into two basic categories, those of "us" and "them." The division has sinister implications for politics and morality. Shtromas provides here a discursive map of the Holocaust and of the two totalitarian regimes of the twentieth century. In doing so, he recalls Nietzsche's famous dictum that mediocrity is death. "For it is the mediocrities, people unable to produce any innovative and constructive ideas, who, in a desperate attempt at realising their frustrated will to power, conceive and propel ideologies the only goal of which is to incite the alienated masses of modern urban societies to engage in a resolute struggle against their alleged exploiters and oppressors, a struggle which, without solving any of the authentic and, no doubt, grave problems of these masses, is ultimately only able to bring about total destruction and death."[21]

The mapping of the Holocaust would be unthinkable without mentioning the conspiracy theory of society. Although Shtromas was not concerned with in-depth exploration of the conspiratorial view of the world present in major ideologies, or prejudice-stricken sets of ideas responsible for group stereotyping, he explains why and how the seeds of collective hatred fell in quite a fertile soil. Tracing prejudice, superstition, and antisemitism, in the countries occupied by and incorporated into the Soviet Union, back to the eve of the Second World War, Shtromas makes a valuable contribution to the study of the historical and political context within which the Holocaust and the final solution became possible.

> It seems to me, and here I may be at odds with some historians of the holocaust, that the idea of the final solution of the Jewish problem by means of total physical extermination of the Jewish population of Europe struck the Nazis only after they had attacked the Soviet Union in June 1941 and witnessed there mass killings of Jews initiated and perpetrated by local inhabitants themselves. Used to Stalin's ways of dealing with real or alleged enemies, and knowing that the Nazis considered Jews and Communists their avowed foes, some Soviet citizens in the territories abandoned by the retreating Red Army did not waste time in waiting for instructions from the new authorities, but started exterminating Jews and Communists on their own. It must be said that, at the time, a great many gentile Ukrainians, Belorussians, and Great Russians themselves perceived the hated Communist Soviet regime as a Jewish conspiracy against their nations, attributing, in an undifferentiated manner (and thus entirely falsely), the responsibility for the enormous atrocities of Communist rule to the Jews. For them, as well as for many Lithuanians, Latvians, and Estonians, Communism was a Jewish cause, and a gentile Communist was, though their own compatriot, no more than a mere Jewish groveler. (p.10)

Indeed, the spread of the conspiracy theory in the twentieth century might be exemplified by recalling such ideological recurrences, or prejudice-stricken sets of ideas in group stereotyping, as the theory of the historic guilt of the Jews for the occupation of the Baltic countries by the Soviet Union. This theory, which is still alive and well in Lithuania and Latvia, though to a much lesser extent in Estonia, deals with a Jewish segment of the Soviet regime as the most influential and even decisive. At the same time, this theory includes some considerations on the allegedly subversive and treacherous activities, on the eve of the Second World War, of local Jewry, the latter being perceived as lacking in civic loyalty, patriotism, and civic-mindedness in general. This kind of embarrassingly inadequate and sinister reasoning is also deeply characteristic of its derivative theory of two genocides, which provides an assessment of the Holocaust and of local collaborators of the Nazis in terms of the revenge for the Soviet genocide of local population conducted by Jews.

Many explanations might be offered to answer the enigmatic question: How is it possible that people still take such "troglodytic theories"—this is the term coined by Tomas Venclova for the theory of two genocides—seriously? One of those explanations might be focused on the aggressively defensive stance of the Balts in the face of never-ending accusations of the extermination of the Baltic Jews during the Second World War. However, there are many reasons to believe that such an attitude has always been deeply grounded in the perception of the Jews as an alien and subversive element, which, if accepted or otherwise "tamed," could jeopardise or even destroy the organic unity of the nation. This attitude seems to have been the case in inter-war Lithuania, too.

Discarding these pearls of the conspiratorial view of the world as pure nonsense, Shtromas, however, employs the term "conspiracy," reserving it for the Holocaust itself. According to him, no particular nation as a whole can be held responsible for the Holocaust.

> The holocaust was indeed a conspiracy secretly planned and executed by an ideologically zealous ruling clique behind the back not only of the German nation, but also of the directly uninvolved membership of the Nazi party itself. No particular nation can be held responsible for such a conspiracy, but the members of all nations, Germans and non-Germans alike, who participated in it should be pronounced guilty of the parts they personally played in the execution of that mass-murderous conspiracy. (p.15)

Shtromas worked out a theory of responsibility, his major contribution to the Holocaust ethics, within which he came to examine great moral and political events of humankind in the light of the Holocaust. With heroic objectivity and remarkable power to make fundamental ethical distinctions,

Shtromas dismissed the idea of collective guilt of the entire nation as politically dangerous and morally barbarous. He described the increased tendency on all sides to ascribe collective guilt to entire nations as one of the worst traumas of the Holocaust.

A nominalist and rationalist thinker, Shtromas leaves aside the relationship between the symbolic codes of culture and violence in politics. This is more than true with regard to Central and Eastern Europe that, as Charles Péguy put it, everything begins in mystique and ends in politics. Although Shtromas was perfectly aware that ferocious and murderous ideological or political rhetoric, politically irresponsible and sinister modes of discourse, and the atmosphere of hatred also count. For who can measure the damage that a culture, permeated by the demonisation of the Other, group stereotyping, and hatred, may inflict on society, its consciousness and politics? Tomas Venclova would point out that it is a moral choice, as well as an ethical act, not to distance oneself from one's nation in the worst moments of its history. Such a stance is about moral, rather than legal, responsibility, for nobody can safely and lightly assume that a crime against humanity does not concern me, inasmuch as a small group of people was involved in it. Vytautas Kavolis, for his part, would suggest that we, in a way, are all responsible for the Holocaust insofar as we share the responsibility for perpetuating the mode of thinking and speaking that turned out to be employed in initiating or justifying the Holocaust.

Of the Holocaust and its crucial political and moral implications Shtromas thought and wrote as a man of multiple and communicating identities. Shtromas's thorough analysis of the Holocaust in Lithuania, marked by his ethical universalism and attempts at thinking unthinkable and comprehending incomprehensible, must have been a culmination of the intense dialogue of a Jew and a Lithuanian, the dialogue that occurred within his soul. Neither side has the right to demonise the Other, and there is no point in stigmatising one another—roughly, this is the message of Shtromas. Echoing Talmud and subscribing to the point of view of Martin Buber, Shtromas implies that there is no ethical scale to measure the virtues and vices of the nations. No nation can be ranked above or below the rest of the nations. Hence, his idea that responsibility can only be individual as far as a legal assessment is concerned.

> The holocaust affected very deeply indeed both the Jews and the gentiles who lived through it. Its traumatic experiences and subsequent complexes are very difficult for all sides to overcome. Perhaps the worst legacy of the holocaust is the increased tendency on all sides to ascribe collective guilt to entire nations and groups, and the enhanced unwillingness, also on all sides,

to differentiate between the guilty, innocent and virtuous individuals who were present in all the nations involved, including the Germans and the Jews themselves, not to mention the Poles, Lithuanians, and other lesser protagonists of that awful bloody drama of European history. (p.23)

Shtromas does not consider the indifference, as Kavolis would have it, as social pathology. Having admitted that there was a tiny group of those Lithuanians who were active in the slaughter of Jews, and a tiny group of those Lithuanians who risked their lives and the lives of their families to rescue and hide Jews, he states explicitly that those who remained indifferent and assumed that it was "none of their business" were in a majority. The indifferent majority might indeed be considered as a dangerous symptom of moral insensitivity and lack of compassion. Yet Shtromas's objectivity and impartiality, once again, find a way to avoid projecting such symptoms of amorality onto other nations. In so doing, he even engages in a risky mental experiment, thus practising in a kind of counter-history of human morality and moral imagination:

> I sometimes wonder how the Jews would have behaved if they had changed places with the Lithuanians after the holocaust. Would there have been fewer Jewish Lithuanian-killers than there were Lithuanian Jew-killers? Would there have been as many Jews ready to risk their lives and the lives of their families in order to save Lithuanians as there were Lithuanians who did so for the Jews? I doubt it. What I am, however, sure about is that the majority of the Jews, as was the case with the majority of Lithuanians, would try to stay out of the whole bloody business of the holocaust. Not a very moral position but much better than involvement in vengeance and death. (pp. 22–23)

Shtromas seems to set aside a time-honoured tradition of what Czesław Miłosz called petty antisemitism, a phenomenon deeply entrenched in Central and East European consciousness, politics, and cultures: "And if the hatred of the Jews towards the Poles, in view of their extraordinary forgiveness of the Germans and Russians, deeply disturbs and hurts me, I must admit that petty anti-Semitism gets under the skin just as much as crime because it is an everyday occurrence."[22] Yet the Jews have to find strength to resist temptation to indict entire nations and cultures. Deriving his liberal ethic of nationalism from Herder's idea that there cannot in principle be such a thing as *Favoritkulturen*, Shtromas explicitly states that all nations—particularly when their heroic histories, established identities, cultures, and values are put into question or otherwise jeopardised—are equally tinged with the sense of self-righteousness and self-centredness.

Recalling Lewis Coser's words that we are likely to be especially critical of the things we love, we can identify Shtromas as perpetuating a characteristically Central and East European ethic of liberal nationalism and applying it to the Holocaust ethics.

In the context of this identity formula, the individual's self is not only part of the moral substance of the community of memory and participation whose collective sentiment he/she shares, but also part of the moral substance of the community whose history and culture he/she can judge as his/her own universe of symbolic participation and correction. Speaking out as a Holocaust survivor and as an East European Jew, Shtromas rejects the indiscriminate accusations of entire nations as an inversion of antisemitism. By accusing entire nations and demonising their cultures, Jews fail to diminish prejudice and hate in the world. Instead, they fall into a trap of what they have been suffering from themselves, throughout their history, namely, the barbarous idea of collective responsibility and the sinister metaphysics of blood. Unable to resist and overcome the collective hatred, they come to revive it and even let it triumph over their minds and hearts. Anti-Germanism, anti-Polishness, or anti-Lithuanianism, must all be understood as a profoundly amoral search for collective enemies and as a kind of inverted antisemitism. The Holocaust is not over insofar as the idea of collective responsibility and the accusations of entire nations are alive. One of the crucial moral implications of Shtromas's discourse about the Holocaust is that if we are incapable of empathising with sufferings and pain of other individuals and peoples, we fail to draw the most important lessons from the Holocaust as the axial event in human history.

> The same indiscriminate accusations of entire nations of the murderous acts perpetrated by some members of those nations, either because of their ideological blindness or for the attainment of personal gain, are not alien to the Jews either. Don't we hear from some Jews that the entire German nation should be held responsible for the holocaust, although, as I pointed out above, most Germans, in contrast with the Lithuanians, Poles, Ukrainians, Russians, and other East Europeans in whose territories the holocaust was executed, did not even know much about the final solution, let alone the massive, industrial scale of its implementation? Are there not enough Jews convinced that the Poles, Lithuanians, Ukrainians and other peoples in whose territories the mass exterminations of Jews took place are in their entirety the nations of Jew-killers and Jew-haters, despite the indisputable facts that so many Jews were saved by the members of these nations and that the majorities of these nations were uninvolved in the Jewish holocaust at all?[23]

The most challenging and provocative part of Shtromas's analysis of the Holocaust and of its moral lessons for humanity is his idea that only the mutual forgiveness and reciprocal reconciliation of the Jews and European nations, in whose lands the Holocaust took place, can overcome the legacy of the Holocaust and avert new holocausts. Having mentioned the eminent Polish writers and literary critics Jan Błoński and Pawel Spiwak, and also Tomas Venclova as the first Polish and Lithuanian intellectuals who fully admitted the crimes of their respective nations against the Jews and humanity, Shtromas points out that the mutual wall of misunderstanding, that erected, in the twentieth century, between the Jews and their Central/East European compatriots, thus causing much animosity, prejudice, misrepresentation, and demonisation on both sides, Jewish and gentile, was a consequence of their lack of intellectual and moral sensibility. Not only did Poles, Lithuanians, and other Central/East European nations remain deaf and blind to Jewish anguish, isolation, alienation, and traumas; according to Shtromas, all too many Jews, for their part, were astonishingly indifferent and totally insensitive to the major political and social concerns of their gentile compatriots, to their losses, fears, and tragedies. The gap between "us" and "them," lack of human exchanges, and unwillingness, on both sides, to introduce a dialogue prepared the seeds of hatred that fell into a fertile soil of mutual indifference, intolerance, suspicion, and stereotyping.

Shtromas crossed the boundaries of what was supposed to be politically correct by stating explicitly that such forms of modernisation as quasi-messianic ideologies of universal equality and collective salvation, which resulted in Communism, subversive political activities, and the denial of Western civilisation, were a tragically inadequate response of many Jewish intellectuals and young dissenters, who came only to increase the fatal gap between "us" and "them," instead of abolishing or minimising it. The trouble with such a turn of Shtromas's historical narrative and socio-cultural analysis is that he does not critically question a completely false proposition that major historical and socio-political processes can be impersonated and represented by interest groups or alienated intellectuals or clandestine organisations. Although it might have been that Shtromas, a provocative and emphatically open-minded writer, deliberately adopted some propositions and working hypotheses completely alien to him, and then pushed them to their limits, in order to show their logical conclusions and moral implications.

However, Shtromas briefly mentions the clichés, prejudices, and other pearls of conspiracy theories that regard modernity as a characteristically

Jewish invention. Antisemitism had existed and flourished in Central and Eastern Europe long before the Bolshevik internationalism and other paraphernalia of the soulless and faceless modernity crossed nationalism. On the other side, to paint a picture of the twentieth-century world as a struggle of impersonated agencies of power means to endorse the conspiracy theory of society or otherwise please the conspiratorial view of the universe deeply inherent in anti-modernist reactions to modernity.

To portray the waves of completely anonymous and uniform processes of the global "rationalisation" and modernisation of the world, as well as anti-modernist reactions to them, as a series of betrayals of national interests or as the broken nationalist allegiances is to grossly misinterpret the clash of the modern and the anti-modern in the twentieth-century world. Shtromas was perfectly aware that the troubled anti-modernist and conspiratorial imagination sooner or later finds and singles out a group target, which comes to signify and personify history. Why should Jews be held responsible for the marriage of antisemitism and non-acceptance of Western liberal democracy, capitalism, and bourgeois cosmopolitanism, the marriage whose offspring were the modernity of antisemitism and the modernity of the conspiratorial view of the world?

Yet Shtromas deplored what he perceived as a lack, on the Jewish side, of local sensibility, fidelity to their native countries in Europe, and civic-mindedness in general. Lithuanian Jews reacted to the loss of Lithuania's independence as if it were something beyond their lives and concerns. Why did, Shtromas asks, so many Lithuanian Jews remain indifferent to the occupation and annexation of Lithuania by the Soviet Union, which meant a tragedy for the Lithuanians? It was not only the end of the uniquely self-contained and sophisticated culture of Lithuanian Jews, a world within the world, but also the grand failure, on both sides, to reach the sympathetic openness and conceive of a common tragedy. Shtromas admits that such forms of self-righteousness and self-centredness were unpardonable in the light of the destruction of what was a common home of the Lithuanians and Lithuanian Jews. To sum it up, both sides, according to him, greatly contributed to the gulf of alienation, mutual exclusion, and stigmatisation.

However provocative and challenging from the point of view of socio-cultural analysis, the following passage from Shtromas's work reveals his heroic objectivity and great sensitivity towards his native country and gentile compatriots:

> Not knowing of any such words [as those of Błoński, Spiwak, and Venclova.—L.D.] coming from a Jewish writer's pen, I feel it to be my duty to start filling this gap. Yes, we Jews lived together with our gentile hosts—

Germans, Poles, Lithuanians, and others—for many centuries. We speak their languages, we are a part of their history and culture. There were some mutual grievances between us, but they cannot overshadow our commonalty or change the fact that we are continuing to move together along the same path. Anti-Semitism is horrible, as anti-Germanism, anti-Polishness, anti-Lithuanianism, and all other "antis" are horrible. But it would be wrong on our part to pretend that all anti-Semitism is born merely in pure fantasy and prejudice of the gentiles, and does not at all, even in part, represent an exaggerated reaction to the real wrongs which some of us really did. As a Jew, I must reject the assumption that we Jews forever were just the faultless and powerless victims of other peoples' abuse and injustices, and must admit our own true faults, such as, for example: our certain insensitivity to some of the grave problems facing our gentile landsmen; our self-centredness that only too often urged some of us to seek our particular goals without giving much consideration to how the achievement of these goals would affect the interests of others; the frivolousness which more than once led quite a number of us to assume that what is good for Jews must be even better for the gentiles. Too many of us, led by such considerations, were more than ready thoughtlessly to engage ourselves in all kinds of subversive and revolutionary activities threatening the integrity and even survival of our host countries. For this we have to confess our guilt. We must understand forever that the losses and defeats of our host nations are our own losses and defeats, and that their gains are also ours; that by the will of history we form with them, for better or worse, one people, and have to think and behave accordingly. (pp.25–26)

What is unique about this passage is that Shtromas adopts, for the first time in the history of European Jews, a specifically East Central European discourse of identity and freedom to explain the fate of European Jewry. In his discourse, Jews appear as an inseparable part of Central and Eastern Europe in terms of their national loyalties and patriotic allegiances. Whereas the mainstream of Lithuanian writers would tend to describe Lithuanian Jews as a monadic entity which was out of touch with political and cultural reality of Lithuania, a significant part of the glorious story of multi-ethnic, multi-religious, and multi-cultural Lithuania, Shtromas harshly criticises a separate and self-contained world of Lithuanian Jewry in inter-war Lithuania, as well as Jewish separatism in general, as a self-imposed ghetto existence. This, as Shtromas implies, sheds new light on why the modernisation of Jewish consciousness and culture, in Lithuania and other Central and East European countries, took so radical a shape and acquired such disconnected forms.

It might be suggested that those subversive and revolutionary activities mentioned by Shtromas, in which not a few of Central and East European Jews were engaged, were quite a logical and unavoidable consequence of the character of modernisation in Central and Eastern Europe. The peripheral variants of European modernity were simply unable to provide such liberal-democratic institutional, political, and cultural settings for the emancipation of all segments of society that were more or less developed in North America and in Western Europe.

Noteworthy is the fact that even Jewish self-hatred, that is, Jewish antisemitism, so aptly described by the German-Jewish writer Theodor Lessing and then plausibly reinterpreted by Isaiah Berlin, appears to have been a Central European phenomenon, which stressed the failure of many talented Jews to liberate themselves from antisemitic stereotyping deeply embedded in gentile societies. Jewish self-hatred also sprang from their acceptance of the modes of discourse and the images of societal life full of modern antisemitic references, innuendoes, and clichés. Thus, the modernity of antisemitism has acquired its plane in the philosophy of history. It is especially true of a sinister tendency of nineteenth-century consciousness imposed by gentile societies on some emancipated European Jews, namely, the propensity to personify socio-political reality and its major processes—such as scientific, technological, and religious "rationalisations" of the modern world—and then project them onto the most familiar and recognisable idiom of otherness, that is, the Jews. Exactly the same might be said about the propensity to refer to the Jews as "rootless," "immoral," "profit-calculating," "insensitive," "incapable of patriotism," "alien and hostile to the modern intellectual and moral sensibilities," "devoid of aesthetic sense," and the like. At this point, suffice it to recall Karl Marx, Walther Rathenau, Arthur Trebitsch, Otto Weininger, and, in a way, even Ludwig Wittgenstein.[24] We could also recall this strange phenomenon—the very triumph of antisemitism and of the most inhumane and ugly facet of modernity—as widespread in inter-war Poland, as depicted in Isaac Bashevis Singer's short stories.

It might also be noted that an apology of a Lithuanian Jew for the aforementioned subversive and revolutionary activities and for a lack of sensitivity and concern on the Jewish side cannot affect the dominant attitude of genuine antisemites. The modern ideological antisemite is unable to employ any other mode of discourse or explanatory framework than that which rests on the assumption that the Jews are a necessary reference point when dealing with suspect and alien values of modernity, cosmopolitanism, and liberal democracy. It is a matter of the frame of reference, ideological idiom, and vocabulary, rather than conscience and common sense. Modern ideological antisemitism comes into being as a way to categorise the world by reducing it to the clash of village and city, tradition and modernity, community and individual, community and humanity, and by personifying these forces.

Therefore, nobody should assume that the number of antisemites in Lithuania and elsewhere had decreased because of Shtromas's discourse about the Holocaust, the divide of humanity into "us" and "them," and the impossibility of such things as collective guilt and collective responsibility. Antisemitism may flourish even where there are no Jews left. As a kind of modern demonology and as a form of technocratic consciousness, which allows room for the ideas of infinite manipulation and omnipotence of clandestine political and intellectual elites, antisemitism may have nothing to do with flesh-and-blood human beings. Shtromas had done what so many Lithuanian nationalists demanded and expected to be done, namely, he admitted that some Lithuanian Jews were active in the Communist Party and in the repression against citizens of occupied and annexed Lithuania. However, it would be more than naïve to believe that an outspoken and provocative Rabbi Klein lecture delivered by Shtromas pacified or otherwise affected antisemitism in Lithuania and elsewhere.

Yet Shtromas's discourse far transcended the frame of reference of the mainstream of Lithuanian nationalism. By admitting that Lithuanian Jews were also not without sin and by asserting that it makes no sense to divide the world into the ever-lasting righteous and sinners, Shtromas rediscovered a symbolic code, so plausible and easily recognisable in Central and Eastern Europe, to theoretically establish an inclusive discourse about the equality of nations as moral entities. In the context of Lithuanian social criticism and intellectual culture, Shtromas and Venclova pioneered in raising the idea that it is a duty of intellectuals to criticise their own society and culture, instead of negatively fixing on the neighbouring countries or searching for internal and external enemies. The critical assessment of the virtues and vices of Russian and Polish societies is the responsibility of Russian and Polish intellectuals, according to this moral logic. I am an inseparable part of the object of my critique, and I critically question my society and culture if they become a threat to my moral character or if they deviate from what I take as my moral substance—this moral logic, which is absolutely alien to conservative and radical nationalism, was perpetuated and developed by Kavolis, Shtromas, and Venclova, the three greatest critics of society and culture in twentieth-century Lithuania.

There are many more polemical points in Shtromas's iconoclastic and provocative scholarship. Some of his philosophical and sociological ideas, in virtue of being derived or loaned from rather conflicting sources, sound less plausible than his dynamic premises regarding political change in Europe or his brilliant insights into the origins and nature of political dissent. Even so, his concept of legal and moral responsibility invites a reconsideration of the nation as a collective moral actor in history and as an agency of consciousness. Most importantly, Shtromas's incisive and critical scholarship reveals key aspects of Central and East European sensibility, such as:

(1) The priority of historically and culturally rooted modes of identity over artificial ideological constructs;

(2) The primacy of natural community over abstract and logically derived humanity;

(3) The ability and willingness of the social scientist—though this is not exclusively the case, since the same might be said about literary scholars, poets, and other intellectuals or "mundane" social actors of Central and Eastern Europe—to participate in several cultures and moral logics;

(4) A comparative perspective when viewing the modes of moral imagination and political existence;

(5) Liberal cosmopolitanism whose essence lies in a clear realisation that without me and my community of memory and participation the humanity would be incomplete, and, *vice versa*, that my individual and collective self exists insofar as it is engaged in a dialogue with other actors of history;

(6) The idea that collective individuals—i.e., historically and ontologically unique, self-asserting, and self-sufficient cultures—can claim the same rights of independent existence and self-determination as political individuals;

(7) A firm conviction that politics should be moral;

(8) The assessment of totalitarianism as a political and moral criterion to evaluate politicians and intellectuals;

(9) The ethic of liberal nationalism which stresses freedom of choice and individual conscience as the routes to authentic moral existence of the nation; and

(10) The crucial role of poetry and literary scholarship for politics and public discourse.

The ethical message of Shtromas is also of great importance. His humanity and sensitivity were instrumental in constituting his scholarship. Like Kavolis, Shtromas regarded his research and lecturing as a significant part of his moral autobiography. A maverick and dissenter by moral choice, he was incompatible with hypocritical and cynical power games, demagoguery and manipulative exchanges, contempt for humanity, or ideological zeal and fanaticism of all shades. For sinister things originate in obscure thought and ambiguous soul. Shtromas powerfully stood against all forms of modern barbarity, not only as a humanist thinker, but also by virtue of the clarity of his thought. An East Central European thinker and writer capable of participating in several cultures and modes of discourse, Shtromas—by virtue of his intellectual breadth, clarity of thought and expression, and humanist concerns—was never confined to the specifically Jewish causes. In this, he reminds us of the best traditions of Central and East European Jewry, who not only pioneered in modernity, but also stood for all possible forms of human sensibility and fulfilment.

As far as the clarity and availability of truth are concerned, the straight line has its advantages over the ellipse.

# Notes

1. Quoted from Alexander Shtromas, "To Fight Communism: Why and How?" *International Journal on World Peace*, Vol. 1, No. 1 (1984), p.20. Shtromas is the author or editor of 12 scholarly books, of 9 short books (pamphlets and monographs), of around 30 book chapters, of around 70 scholarly articles, and of around 60 articles in general interest and cultural periodicals in English, Japanese, Russian, Polish, Hungarian, and Lithuanian.
2. Ibid., p.21.
3. Tim McDaniel, *The Agony of the Russian Idea* (Princeton, NJ: Princeton University Press, 1996), p.17.
4. Ibid., p.24.
5. Shtromas, "To Fight Communism," op. cit., p.27.
6. Alexander Shtromas, *Who Are the Soviet Dissidents?* (Bradford: University of Bradford, 1977), p.2.
7. Ibid., p.4.
8. For more on this issue, see Czesław Miłosz, *The Captive Mind*, trans. Jane Zielonko (New York: Vintage, 1990), pp.54–81.
9. Ibid., p.78.
10. For more on this issue, see George Orwell, "Notes on Nationalism," in George Orwell, *Decline of the English Murder and Other Essays* (Harmondsworth, Middlesex: Penguin, 1970), pp.155–179.
11. See Timothy Garton Ash, *The Uses of Adversity: Essays on the Fate of Central Europe* (London: Penguin, 1999), p.154; p.157; p.191.
12. Shtromas, *Who Are the Soviet Dissidents?* op. cit., p.13.
13. H. Stuart Hughes, *Sophisticated Rebels: The Political Culture of European Dissent, 1968–1987* (London & Cambridge, MA: Harvard University Press, 1988), pp.94–95.
14. Shtromas, *Who Are the Soviet Dissidents?* op. cit., p.15.
15. Aleksandras Shtromas, "Ideological Politics and the Contemporary World: Have We Seen the Last of 'Isms'?", in Aleksandras Shtromas, ed., *The End of 'Isms'? Reflections on the Fate of Ideological Politics after Communism's Collapse* (Oxford & Cambridge, MA: Blackwell, 1994), p.184.
16. Karl Marx, "Theses on Feuerbach," in Robert C. Tucker, ed., *The Marx-Engels Reader* (New York: Norton, 2nd ed., 1978), p.145.
17. Shtromas, "Ideological Politics and the Contemporary World," op. cit., p.194.
18. Ibid., p.188.
19. Vytautas Kavolis, "Nationalism, Modernization, and the Polylogue of Civilizations," *Comparative Civilizations Review*, 25 (1991), p.132.
20. See Shtromas, "Ideological Politics and the Contemporary World," op. cit., p.193.
21. Aleksandras Shtromas, *The Jewish and Gentile Experience of the Holocaust: A Personal Perspective* (Worcester, MA: Assumption College, 1989), p.4.

22. Quoted from Tomas Venclova, *Forms of Hope: Essays* (Riverdale-on-Hudson, NY: The Sheep Meadow Press, 1999), p.17.
23. Shtromas, *The Jewish and Gentile Experience of the Holocaust*, op. cit., p.22.
24. For more on Wittgenstein's idea that Jews can only interpret the world, never producing anything original and creative, and on his comparisons of Mendelssohn and Brahms at this point, see Ludwig Wittgenstein, *Culture and Value*, ed. G. H. von Wright in collaboration with Heikki Nyman, trans. Peter Winch (Chicago, IL: University of Chicago Press, 1984). For more on the phenomenon of Jewish self-hatred, see Sander L. Gilman, *Jewish Self-Hatred: Anti-Semitism and the Hidden Language of the Jews* (Baltimore, MD, & London: The Johns Hopkins University Press, 1986).

# Chapter Four

## Tomas Venclova: Ethical Universalism and the Discovery of the Other

> Every man of talent or genius is political who makes his heart a battleground for conflicting tendencies of culture.
>
> Lionel Trilling, *Beyond Culture*

Tomas Venclova may well be regarded as the most influential social and cultural critic in twentieth-century Lithuania. Having passed from intra-structural to extra-structural dissent, he repeated the sequence of the phases of political dissent so aptly described by Shtromas. A national poet of Lithuania, a liberal critic of conservative nationalism, and a brilliant essayist, Venclova may be said to have quite legitimately joined the honourable company of the most prominent critics of society and culture in Central and Eastern Europe, such as Czesław Miłosz, Adam Michnik, Václav Havel, Milan Kundera, and Joseph Brodsky.[1] As a critic of Communism, and as a human rights activist, he was a major figure in the human rights movement in the Soviet Union and beyond. Yet Venclova's critiques and humane concerns far transcended the limits of the conventional political dissent and entered the discursive universe of the critical questioning of his society and culture. Prejudice, superstition, irrational fear of modernity, antisemitism, xenophobia, self-centredness, and self-righteousness are key words to define the object of his criticism targeted at Lithuanian society and culture.

Tomas Venclova was born on September 11, 1937, in Klaipėda, Lithuania. His father, Antanas Venclova, was a famous Soviet Lithuanian poet and writer, and even a high-ranking official within the Soviet power structure. From 1940 to 1943, Antanas Venclova held the post of Soviet People's Commissar of Enlightenment, that is, the Minister of Education of the Lithuanian Soviet Socialist Republic (LSSR). In 1943, he worked in the Communist International (the Comintern) Radio in Moscow. In 1944, he returned to Lithuania and was employed, until 1946, at the Faculty of History and Philology of the University of Kaunas. In 1949, he became a Member-Correspondent of the Academy of Sciences of LSSR. From 1952 to 1964—a member of the Central Committee of the Lithuanian Communist Party. In 1954, Antanas Venclova was elected Chairman of the LSSR Writers' Union.

Of his father Tomas Venclova wrote: "My father, Antanas Venclova, was a convinced communist. I have respected him and I continue respecting him as a human being. It was from him, among others, that I learned to be loyal to my principles. But as I observed life and took part in it, I early formed a world-view different from that of my father. My later experience merely served to confirm it. This was not a secret to my father or to anybody else."[2] Venclova wrote these words in his famous letter to the Central Committee of the Lithuanian Communist Party dated May 9, 1975. They clearly indicated his political and moral stance. Unwilling to continue his life and work in the Soviet Union where he felt "barred from any more extensive and public literary, scholarly and cultural activity,"[3] Venclova asked to allow him to go abroad with his family.

The similarity of Shtromas's and Venclova's biographies lies in the fact that both, in a way, broke away from ideological and political allegiances that were more or less rooted in their families. Both grew up in a safe and secure world of privileges and stability; yet both rejected that world. Shtromas's mother was very proud of her family tree and celebrated her aristocratic descent. Venclova's maternal grandfather was the renowned professor of classical philology, Merkelis Račkauskas, whose brother Karolis Vairas-Račkauskas was an émigré intellectual, diplomat, and literary translator. Venclova grew up surrounded by books, manuscripts, and literary debates. His milieu was deeply permeated by world literature and intellectual culture. Whereas Shtromas, who was six years older and with whom he would develop a life-long friendship, survived the Holocaust and early experienced the clash of the most cynical, criminal and murderous political regimes of the twentieth century, Venclova remained, for a long time, disconnected from the brutality of political reality.

Small wonder that he entered this-worldly reality as a total stranger, judging it by the intellectual and moral standard of the other-worldly reality, a world of literature and humanistic studies, the realm of *Bildung* and *das rein Geistige* where he was much more at home than in a barbarous world outside his library. As Shtromas incisively noted, in Venclova's world of self-cultivation and self-dedication, Lithuanian ethnocentrism was unthinkable.[4] The same might be said about Lithuanian nationalism which was regarded, by Venclova's father and other people of his circle and ideological background, as a sign of Lithuanian provincialism and of those allegedly reactionary attitudes that were deeply rooted in inter-war Lithuania. What Venclova formed very early by himself was his ethical universalism, a profound sense of universally valid moral values that later would turn out to be irreconcilable and incompatible with Communist ideology.

Having graduated from the University of Vilnius in 1960, Venclova later was appointed a lecturer in literature, linguistics, and semiotics at his *alma mater*. This appointment lasted from 1966 to 1973. At the same time, he began translating American, English, Welsh, Irish, French, Greek, Russian, Polish, and other continental European literature into Lithuanian, quite early establishing his reputation as a master of the translation of modern literature. In the area of the translation of twentieth-century literature, Venclova has always been and still is regarded as second to none in Lithuania. His interest in semiotics and literary theory led him, in the late 1960s, to the University of Tartu, Estonia, where he attended Yuri Lotman's seminar of semiotics and structural poetics. In 1966–1971, Venclova pursued his graduate studies in semiotics and Russian literature at the University of Tartu. Yuri Lotman, who was a semiotician and literary scholar of world stature and who was offered full professorship in Estonia after the antisemitic purge in Leningrad (now St Petersburg), attracted not a few writers and literary scholars from the circles of political dissent. A strong opposition to Marxist-Leninist ideology was therefore paralleled by the quest for an alternative to dialectical and historical materialism as a mandatory methodology in the humanities and social sciences. In those days, such methodological preferences and disciplinary choices as semiotics and structural poetics were an obvious and significant part of dissent.

A clue to Venclova's political and moral choices is the fact that he has never been a typical representative of Lithuanian Catholic and nationalistic dissent. However respectful of *The Chronicle of the Catholic Church in Lithuania*, Lithuanian Samizdat and other forms of political dissent, Venclova may never have fallen into the category of the mainstream of Lithuanian patriotic and nationalistic dissent. Venclova describes his double dissent in the following way:

> I could regard myself neither as professional writer nor as professional scholar; I was rather professional translator. In the eyes of society and government, I was an obvious non-conformist. I would say, I was even a double non-conformist. I was at odds not only with official values, but also with those values that usually signify, in the Baltic countries and in the Soviet Union, non-acceptance of the regime. For instance, I did not have a strong interest in the new music of the West; nor was I interested in its technology and fashion. And seriously speaking, I never was a nationalist and xenophobe. The Soviet regime does not regard mundane non-conformity with great suspicion. Moreover, it has even learned how to "co-

opt" and integrate such a form of non-conformity. Yet they must have been puzzled with my case. The Lithuanian intelligentsia was not sympathetic to me either.[5]

In 1960, Venclova met Alexander Ginzburg, who at that time edited an underground literary journal, *Sintaksis* [Syntax], and who was willing to publish a special issue of the journal in Lithuanian. Venclova gave him some of his poetry to publish in this issue. Much around the same time, he participated in establishing a Samizdat publishing group, *Eglutė* [Christmas tree], and a literary scholarship and culture studies group. As Venclova remembers it himself, all these initiatives ended up with interrogations. Happily, it was a post-Stalinist epoch, and nobody was jailed. Although Venclova's name was put on the KGB blacklist at that time, he was left to his own devices for some time. In 1968, Venclova, along with many Russian dissidents, signed a letter of protest regarding the case of Alexander Ginzburg and Yuri Galanskov (224 persons signed the letter). This time he was neither interrogated nor otherwise punished, although the real consequences of his dissent were still to come. Venclova's application for membership of the LSSR Writers' Union was denied. He was also not allowed to visit Hungary where his book of poetry was about to appear.

According to Venclova, the fact that he was the son of Antanas Venclova protected him from big trouble at the beginning of his dissident activities. Although Antanas Venclova did nothing to promote his son or to secure his position as a poet and translator, the authorities were reluctant to do harm to the son of a prominent Soviet poet and statesman. However, things have changed after Antanas Venclova's death in 1971, which coincided with the beginning of an increasing Brezhnevist reaction. In 1973, Venclova lost his position at the University of Vilnius, and a number of his texts did not get through political censorship, and, subsequently, were refused by editors of literary magazines. (During the period of 1974–1976, he served as a Junior Fellow at the Institute of History of the Academy of Sciences of LSSR.) Being deeply convinced that much of his creative and intellectual endeavour was simply being ignored, Venclova decided to write the aforementioned letter to the Central Committee of the Lithuanian Communist Party, a decisive action and a dangerous undertaking in those days.

Having written this letter on May 9, 1975, he was certain that a severe reaction of the authorities, including the possibility of being put in jail or psychiatric hospital, would not be long. Surprisingly enough, instead of punishment, the new job offers came up, such as the translation of

Shakespeare's *Tempest*. An émigré historian in the United States, Vincas Trumpa, wrote a public letter to Venclova, which was published in a liberal American-Lithuanian monthly *Akiračiai* [Horizons]. In this letter, Trumpa warned Venclova about the possible hardships and difficulties of living in the West if he, a Lithuanian poet and an East European intellectual, should leave for the West instead of staying with his people. Trumpa implied that a foreign country would fail to appreciate Venclova's talents and that he would therefore be unable to fulfil himself, outside Lithuania, as a poet and translator. Moreover, Trumpa's letter acquired a moral plane suggesting that the real responsibility of a national poet and eminent intellectual is to do his or her best to improve things in his or her country, instead of emigrating. Having mentioned Socrates and Ovid, one of whom preferred death to exile from Athens, and another, to Dacia, who was banished from Rome to Tomi without being able to choose, Trumpa wonders at the modern poet's, that is, Tomas Venclova's, willingness to leave his country without being brutally forced to do so.

Venclova's response to Trumpa, published in *Akiračiai* (surprisingly enough, the text has reached the United States), contains some crucial points of his moral philosophy, the philosophy of ethical universalism and cultural dialogue. Here Venclova passionately and explicitly denies the idea that we can allow moral compromise for the sake of our national culture and its survival. Venclova also reminds of the importance of émigré culture and émigré existential experiences, a phenomenon which he describes as the second voice of culture and which acquires crucial significance when the first voice either remains silent or sings the wrong and imposed melody. The following passage sheds new light on Venclova as representing a new type of Lithuanian émigré, who, in the admirable words of Kavolis, comes to choose exile only to be able to speak the truth and keep faith with his ethical principles and moral integrity.

> You say that our writers are corrupt and enjoy many benefits of the regime. The writers, who really deserve this title, have, in our country, such existential experiences that I would not wish you to have. You are talking about Socrates and Ovid. Unfortunately, these analogies are misleading. The country in which I live has little to do with Rome, and definitely nothing with Athens. It is an absolutely new phenomenon in world history. I could discuss it in detail, but writers, who are better than I and with whose works you can easily familiarise yourself, have already done it. I also wonder that you, historian, did not recall such exiles as Adam Mickiewicz, Herzen, and many Lithuanians. Their way to exile much differs from that of Socrates and Ovid. I am very happy that I managed to write without lies for many

years (not always, though). It is equally true that I, in doing so, was not alone—in fact, there are a number of people of this sort in our country. Yet, in recent years (roughly, since 1968), non-Marxist and non-dogmatic intellectuals are bound to choose between compromising with their conscience and being marginalised. There is an opinion that compromises are justifiable and even indispensable for the sake of national culture. In my view, no demoralisation—bearing in mind that compromise is the beginning of demoralisation, and sooner or later has very sad consequences—has ever been, is, and will be of value for culture.[6]

At that time, Czesław Miłosz extended an invitation to Venclova to lecture at the University of California-Berkeley, USA. Venclova fought one and half years for his right to go to Berkeley. He remembers that period of his life as intense, unpredictable, even pleasant. According to Venclova, the Soviet authorities would have been happy to get rid of him; yet they did not know how to achieve this. The cat-and-mouse game cornered the authorities; therefore, something had to be done. In 1976, Venclova joined the Lithuanian Helsinki group where he acted along with Viktoras Petkus, a human rights activist in Lithuania. The first conference of the Moscow Helsinki group, which took place on December 1, 1976, in Yuri Orlov's flat, Moscow, and where Venclova participated together with many other prominent dissidents, such as his old acquaintance Alexander Ginzburg, was the last thing the Soviet authorities would have tolerated. Suffice it to recall that Natan (Anatoly) Sharansky served, in this Helsinki group initiation conference, as an interpreter from Russian into English. The reaction would not be long. Some of the Helsinki group members were jailed, others—Venclova among them—thrown out of the Soviet Union.

On January 25, 1977, Tomas Venclova left for Paris, France. Having spent three weeks in Paris, he went to the United States. On June 14, 1977, in accordance with a special decree of the Supreme Soviet, Venclova's Soviet citizenship was terminated "on the grounds of his actions incompatible with the title of the Soviet citizen." Shortly afterwards, Venclova was granted political asylum in the United States. Such a legal procedure—termination of Soviet citizenship—was applied not only to Venclova, but also to such celebrity writers and artists as Aleksandr Solzhenitsyn, Vassily Aksyonov, and Mstislav Rostropovich.

As Venclova later would point out himself, he could only speculate about the reasons behind the decision to allow him to emigrate. According to him, one of such reasons might have been his family name, quite inconvenient for the Soviet authorities. After all, Venclova's case was too well known in the West for them to ignore Western political and moral opinion. Most importantly, the KGB files provided Venclova's psychological portrait where he must have been depicted as an indulgent boy of the Soviet privileged class—wishy-washy, vulnerable, and, in a way, unstable. It might have been expected that Venclova, having failed to adjust to highly competitive and insensitive Western society, would certainly ask for permission to return to the Soviet Union, which would be his grand failure, yet the very triumph of the Soviet authorities. Instead, such a naïve and unrealistic portrayal of Venclova proved to have been the grand failure of the authorities, KGB and Soviet press alike.

Having spent one semester as Regents Professor of Slavic Literatures at the Department of Slavic Languages and Literatures of the University of California-Berkeley in 1977, Venclova received a lectureship at the Department of Slavic Languages and Literatures of UCLA (1977–1980). Whereas Czesław Miłosz invited him to Berkeley, Marija Gimbutas, the prominent American archaeologist of Lithuanian descent, stood behind his appointment at UCLA. In 1978, he was appointed Morton Professor at the Department of Philosophy of Ohio University. In the United States, Venclova started his second and actual academic career, simultaneously acting as PhD candidate, and serving as Lecturer and Acting Instructor of Slavic Literatures at the Department of Slavic Languages and Literatures of Yale University (1980–1985). Having earned his PhD from Yale, he was appointed Assistant Professor in that same Department (1985–1990). In 1990–1993, he was Associate Professor. In 1993, Venclova was promoted to the title of Professor of Slavic Literatures at Yale. His honorary appointments and titles include lecturing at Harvard University and honorary doctorates from the Maria Curie-Skłodowska University in Lublin in 1991, and from the Jagiellonian University of Kraków in 2000.

When Lithuania and Poland, after the break-up of the Soviet Union, became independent and achieved a historic breakthrough in their relations, Venclova's political voice and humanist message were recalled in both countries. Venclova received the supreme Lithuanian and Polish honours. In Lithuania, he was awarded, in 1995, the Third Degree Order of Gediminas for his major contribution to the improvement of the relations between Lithuanians and Poles, and also between Lithuanians and Jews. In 1999, Venclova received the Fourth Degree Order of the Vytis Cross for his dissident activities. In Poland, Venclova was awarded, in 1996, the *Krzyż Komandorski* [the Order of the Commander Cross] for the enhancement of mutual trust and respect between the two nations. In 2000, Venclova received Lithuania's National Prize for Culture and Art for his poetry and essays of the period of 1995–2000.

In the United States, Venclova joined *Santara-Šviesa*. A close friend of Czesław Miłosz and Joseph Brodsky (who dedicated his poetic masterpiece, "Lithuanian Divertissement," to Venclova, cherishing the remembrances of their discussions and evenings in the Vilnius café Neringa, a favourite place of Russian and Lithuanian dissidents and non-conformist intellectuals), Venclova was much at home in this liberal intellectual and cultural movement of Lithuanian émigrés. It was quite logical that he established close relationship with *Santara-Šviesa*. It would be difficult to imagine him somewhere else in American-Lithuanian circles. Being at odds with the mainstream of Lithuanian immigrants in the United States regarding many points of Lithuanian identity and freedom issues, the liberal and cosmopolitan Venclova was frequently referred to by the conservative part of Lithuanian community in the United States as a Russophile, Polonophile, and, *horribile dictu*, a Judophile.

Although nobody in Lithuania and beyond has ever critically questioned or otherwise doubted his major contribution to the human rights movement and to the Soviet political dissent, it is difficult to get rid of a feeling that Venclova has met more sympathy, respect, and understanding in Russia and Poland than in his native Lithuania. However cherished and respected by his friends and fellow dissidents in Lithuania, Venclova has always been alienated from the mainstream of Lithuanian culture and from the Lithuanian intelligentsia. Not in vain, his close friend Vladimir Bukovsky, one of the towering figures in Moscow circles of overt political dissent, once made a joke: "The Lithuanian people—after two thousand years of working so hard on it—gave birth to its first Jew. The name of the Jew is Tomas Venclova."[7]

Quite early establishing his reputation as a citizen of the world, Venclova moved the centre of his Lithuanian political and cultural concerns towards core issues in ethics, political philosophy, and metaphysics of human existence. He might well be regarded as the founder of modern Lithuanian ethical universalism. At the same time, he, along with Kavolis and Shtromas, laid the foundations for the ethic of Lithuanian liberal nationalism. There are many reasons to treat Venclova as a major figure in the philosophy of history and moral philosophy, too. His concept of nations as moral actors of history is much in tune with the humanistic pathos of Shtromas's ethical theory of nationalism, and also is reminiscent of the best traditions of German and Russian philosophies of history and culture, and of the dialogue-based ethical personalism as well, the latter ranging from Nikolai Berdyaev to Martin Buber. Venclova's symbolic citizenship of the world, complemented by his Central and East European intellectual and moral sensibilities, makes him stand close to such great émigré poets and thinkers as Adam Mickiewicz, Giuseppe Mazzini, Alexander Herzen, Joseph Brodsky, and Czesław Miłosz. Actually, Venclova is inseparable from this gallery of intellectual and cultural heroes of Central and Eastern Europe. He would certainly qualify for the honourable company of people whom Kavolis described as post-modernist nationalists. Having said that, I have to explain Venclova's quite complex attitude to nationalism. This is only possible to achieve within the universe of his philosophy of ethical universalism.

## The Dialogue-Based Personalism and Ethical Universalism: Nations as Moral Actors of History

Kavolis and Shtromas, though operating within distinct theoretical idioms and disciplinary contexts, attempted a symbolic reconciliation of nationalism and ethical universalism, both within themselves and Lithuanian culture. Their efforts to achieve this may be said to have culminated in Venclova's philosophy of history and moral philosophy. Shtromas's article on universalism and nationalism in the discursive universe of Tomas Venclova provides an interpretative framework within which we can map these intellectual tendencies and trajectories of consciousness. Shtromas here goes so far as to explicitly refer to Venclova as a nationalist, a reference point which can hardly be expected to be enthusiastically endorsed by Venclova himself, bearing in mind his overall scepticism regarding the ups and downs of nationalism in Central and East European politics. Yet Shtromas attempts an incisive discursive map of Venclova's ethical universalism and liberal nationalism, the map which has yet to be surpassed in Lithuanian philosophical and sociological literature. Shtromas notes:

> Yet Tomas Venclova differs from other Lithuanian nationalists, inasmuch as Lithuanian-ness and its concerns have never been the substance of his political life. He was approaching nationalism carefully, slowly, closely viewing and combining every small step towards it with those universally valid ethical dimensions that have always constituted the foundations of his worldview. I think, the idea that nationalism can be absolutely in tune with the norms of universal humanistic morality came to Tomas's articles under the influence of the personalist philosophy of R. T. Flewelling, E. Mounier, J. Maritain, and, in particular, N. Berdyaev. This philosophy pronounces the nation a sort of collective personality and applies to it the same general

ethical and teleological criteria that are applied to a human individual, including inescapable human rights that should be respected in every single case. It undoubtedly served as an orientation point that enabled Tomas Venclova to firmly identify himself with nationalism, not rejecting any single principle of his earlier formed worldview.[8]

Defining the dialogue-based personalist ethics as the starting point of Venclova's moral philosophy, Shtromas gives a clue to Venclova's concept of nation. Distinguishing between nationalism and patriotism, Shtromas defines Venclova as a nationalist in the paradigmatic sense, that is, as an intellectual perpetuating the ethics of compassion and the politics of collective identity and freedom. That individual freedom, reason, and conscience are prior to collective liberty and other collective sensibilities, according to Shtromas, is an indisputable fact. All liberal nationalists agree upon this: the human individual ontologically and ethically precedes the nation as collective individual or collective personality. Only conservative and backward-looking nationalists tend to derive the human individual from the ever-present metaphysical substance of the mystical cohesion of the nation. The same goes for the blood-and-soil nationalists.

Whereas nationalism perpetuates its ethics of the sympathetic openness to, and understanding of, otherness, patriotism manifests itself in an uncritical acceptance of socio-political reality: its essence lies in the assumption "My country, right or wrong." Many Lithuanian and Russian nationalists were fundamentally opposed to Communism and wished for its demise, without having any feeling for the fate of the Soviet Union as their country. A patriot is unable or unwilling to draw a dividing line between his/her country and its political regime. A nationalist, on the contrary, harshly criticises the authoritarian or totalitarian regime inasmuch as he/she takes it as incompatible with the vision of his/her nation as a free political and moral actor of history discovering and disseminating itself in concert with other nations. To identify his/her country with an undemocratic political regime or authorities is the last thing a genuine nationalist would do. In this sense, concludes Shtromas, all Russian nationalists among political dissidents were unpatriotic. Shtromas's valuable insights into the nature of, and differences between, such empirically elusive phenomena of consciousness as nationalism and patriotism allow us to critically reconsider the assumption of not a few of the contemporary Lithuanian writers and politicians that Communism was nothing more and nothing less than a mask on the face of Russian imperialism.

On the other side, it makes no sense to strictly separate nationalism and ethical universalism. According to Shtromas, to be an internationalist without being a nationalist is a contradiction in terms. Genuine internationalism—if not confounded with transnationalism, which denies nationalism and speaks out in favour of abstract globalisation and various kinds of supra-national systems of world order—is a logical continuation and consequence of nationalism. Chauvinism, imperialist jingoism, blood-and-soil integral and radical nationalism must all be understood as deviations from the ethic of inclusive and liberal nationalism, which not only allows room for cosmopolitan stances in politics and culture, but logically and ethically should be derived from universalism. Moreover, they are complementary phenomena, for universalism without nationalism turns into a sort of totally disconnected, bloodless and soulless catholicity, while nationalism free of ethical universalism quickly degenerates into xenophobia, demonological chauvinism, jingoism, and other forms of social pathology. Shtromas's attempts to reconcile nationalism and ethical universalism in Venclova's worldview culminate in this passage:

> Reflecting on Lithuania and raising the crucial points of the existence of the Lithuanian people, Tomas Venclova, on the one hand, views Lithuania as a cosmopolitan ethicist and humanist, and, on the other hand, he approaches the universal ethical values of humanism from a Lithuanian perspective. His methodology and position uncover the new page in the history of Lithuanian thought. Earlier having defined Tomas Venclova as a nationalist, I included him in a general tradition of Lithuanian thought. Now I will call him the Lithuanian universalist, thus trying to define a new current in this tradition, the current whose founder and representative he undoubtedly is. I am convinced that future historians will describe this book [Tomas Venclova's book *Lietuva pasaulyje* [Lithuania in the World] published in Chicago, IL, 1981.—L.D.] as nothing other but the primary source of Lithuanian universalism. We, contemporary people, who co-operate, engage in polemic with him, or simply follow his current activities, can be proud of having stood, together with him, close to this source. Lithuanian universalism, in my view, is not opposed to Lithuanian nationalism. Moreover, Lithuanian universalism should be regarded as a perfectly consistent and pure expression of Lithuanian nationalism. (pp.113–114)

In this context, we could recall Venclova as saying that after Communism, nationalism is the second doctrine unacceptable to him. He had long been reluctant to endorse nationalism as a blueprint for a viable moral order. As Shtromas correctly points out, Venclova, along with other members of overt dissent, clearly realised that nationalism represents an explosive force and a great threat to the Soviet regime. The incompatibility and mutual exclusiveness of the two enabled many liberal-democratic dissenters to reconsider their sceptical and critical attitude to nationalism. Yet Venclova's idea that universal human rights should be given priority over independence at any cost was at odds with a feeling shared by the vast majority of the Lithuanian intelligentsia, namely, that the respect to human rights, political pluralism, openness, and tolerance would automatically result from the independence of Lithuania. In his essay, "On the Choice between Democracy and Nationalism," Venclova remembers:

> I have often encountered a curious delusion. Some Lithuanian intellectuals have said to me, "Yes, we understand your tactic: you cannot openly defend Lithuania under Soviet conditions and that is why you defend human rights." (It seems that was precisely the way of things in some other national Helsinki groups.) It always cost me a lot of effort to explain that for us human rights are not a question of tactics but one of principle. No matter how much we loved Lithuania, this principle was more important to us. If in the independent Lithuania of the future human rights were violated, it would be rather difficult to love it. There usually followed a response like, "But this is impossible. An independent Lithuania means a free and democratic Lithuania." The only thing left to say was "I, too, am hoping for this. I am not, however, confident that one is the automatic result of the other." [9]

When Lithuania regained its independence in 1990, Venclova wrote that national euphoria is not the answer to many challenges Lithuania is about to meet. The national mystique, which came to occupy the former place of Marxism-Leninism, is a psychologically and sociologically understandable phenomenon. Yet it would be more than naïve to assume that the nation is the paramount value or the end-in-itself. In the situation of moral vacuum and anomie, many people are tempted to write the word "nation" with a capital letter. Venclova made it clear that there are values, which are more important than the nation. "Shouldn't we reserve capital letters for them? Let a Christian reserve the capital letter only for God, and a liberal for Conscience."[10]

Venclova's discourse about priority of human rights over an abstract independence did not prevent his remarkable emphasis on the relationship between individual and collective rights. Here we have an example of liberal nationalism, which Venclova approaches from a cosmopolitan perspective. His arrival at the ethic of liberal nationalism is not accidental and has something of the epoch of the springtime of the peoples. That is why it is difficult to resist an idea that Venclova, being much at home in every aspect of aristocratic and Romantic nationalism of the nineteenth century, rejects its transformation into a doctrinaire, mass-oriented, and defensive phenomenon which departs from the intellectual and moral sensibilities of the epoch of the springtime of the peoples. Recalling Kavolis's idea of the nationalism's cycle of virtues and vices, that is, its transformation from the Romantic ethics of compassion and the discovery of the Other into a kind of zoological defence of its own nation, accompanied by total insensitivity towards the rest of humanity and by the cult of the dead, we can easily understand where Venclova's distaste for integral, radical, and doctrinaire nationalism comes from. Hence, his distinction between moral and amoral nationalism implicit in his vigorous assessments of the theory and practice of Lithuanian nationalism.

> The rights of man are the rights of the individual. But there are also collective rights, including the right of an ethnic group to preserve (if that is what it wants) its culture and language, as well as to create its own state. An independent national state is perhaps not the only guarantee, but it is undoubtedly the best guarantee that the language and culture will be preserved. There can be doubts here with regard to very small groups, or groups that live in diaspora, but the Lithuanians, as well as the other Baltic peoples, do not belong to this category. What is more, Lithuania has already been an independent state twice in the course of its history. The first independence was forcibly suppressed by czarist Russia, the second by the Stalinist Soviet Union. Sometimes people affirm that Lithuania is striving for independence only because it wants "to jump from a sinking ship," meaning that Lithuania would stay within the Soviet Union if it were flourishing economically and were democratic to boot. This is ridiculous. Besides the economic considerations, there are such things as national consciousness, national ambitions, the aspiration to play an independent role in history, and, finally, the ancient and not so ancient injuries. They should all be taken into account, and they can be stronger than the purely pragmatic points.[11]

Having said that, Venclova sums up his considerations by suggesting: "These rights of the nation cannot be questioned. In this sense, nationalism is not a negative phenomenon. It is something inalienable and has often brought forth wonderful fruit in the course of history" (p.88). Yet it does not mean that nationalism is just another term for human rights. However interrelated and complementary, these phenomena are not just the same.

> One should not forget, however, that individual rights have logical precedence over collective rights, that is, human rights have logical precedence over national rights (which is the same as saying that the rights of the nation are the result of the rights of man, but not vice versa). To the extent that conflicts tend to spring up here, one should grant precedence to

the rights of man. Forgetting to do this has led to grave consequences. People in our part of the world tend to affirm—directly and even more often between the lines—that there can be no contradictions at all between democracy and nationalism. This, of course, is incorrect. Democracy tolerates nationalism and gives free range to the development of the national idea, but the opposite is not always true. Nationalism tends to limit democracy, and constant efforts are needed, especially on the part of intellectuals, to oppose this tendency. (pp.88–89)

Venclova's definition of the logical and metaphysical precedence of individual rights over collective rights serves here as a watershed between liberal and conservative nationalism, since the latter assumes that human rights, individual reason, and individual conscience are all logically and theoretically derived phenomena, and must therefore be ontologically and even ethically held secondary to the mytho-poetic substance of the organic people. Another crucial implication of his incisive description of the tension between democracy and nationalism is that nationalism can only be democratic and inclusive if it operates in a democratic setting and, subsequently, is complemented by a culture of discussion and opposition, and by social and cultural criticism. As Kavolis would have it, nationalism is modernising and progressive insofar as political modernity meets cultural modernity. Nationalism, if it happens to be devoid of liberal-democratic sensibilities and of intellectual and ethical pluralism, turns into a mere cult of homogeneity, and, consequently, degenerates into a set of tribal subordination imperatives. On the other side, nationalism remains a key word for the morphology of human diversity, ranging from historical memory and symbolic codes of history to collective sentiment and mundane—linguistic, social, and cultural—solidarity. Demonising or otherwise misrepresenting nationalism as evil, neglecting or even ignoring nationalism as a social and moral philosophy and as a call for the critical questioning of one's society and culture, we are at risk of denying and, finally, losing an important aspect of modern human experience.

What really matters in evaluating nationalism, its political and cultural quality, and also its potential for sensitivity and humanity regarding otherness, is a dominant nation's attitude to its minorities. Venclova was the first among Lithuanian intellectuals to single out this as one of the principal criteria to assess nationalism. A nation which fails to respect its minorities and which identifies its dignity and pride solely with the territory it possesses or claims is incapable of discovering and embracing otherness— this is an ethical message of Venclova regarding the high and low points of nationalism. The worst thing that can occur to a nation is an unshakeable belief in its self-righteousness. As he points out,

> [a] dominant nation which suppresses and tramples upon minorities for the sake of its own "sacred rights" turns out to be a pathetic slave itself. If somebody emphasises the "nation's sacred rights" to territory, to the spread or preservation of its influence, this can lead and has led to wars more than once, including world wars. Unfortunately, the dignity of a nation is often seen only in the possession of territories and in the expansion of those territories (while it can also lie in self-limitation). People often say that a small nation is always on the defensive, while a large one is always on the offensive, and that is why the small ones are always right. This is true in many cases. But the line between defence and offence is, alas, shaky enough and it is a dubious thing to insist on one's eternal and absolute rightness. Moreover, it is inappropriate to see the relations between states, nations and ethnic groups through the Darwinian model, according to which the strong ones "naturally" strive to devour the weak ones because they cannot do otherwise. This model was very widespread in the nineteenth and in the first half of the twentieth century. Even nowadays, it has preserved its influence over many minds, including some in Lithuania. But this model is simplified—primitive, to be more precise—and can be harmful. (p.89)

And then Venclova sums it up by stressing: "It would be useful for the Westerners to treat nationalism with slightly less caution, to admit that under certain circumstances it is legitimate and sound. But we, people in the former Soviet Union—and not only Russians—have to admit that nationalism can be illiterate, uncritical, and extremely harmful to democracy when it assumes this shape" (ibid.). Venclova's harsh criticism of illiberal, insensitive, and morally provincial nationalism may well be perceived as a political and moral encounter of two conflicting and even mutually exclusive facets of nationalism, namely, the aristocratic and noble-spirited ethic of liberal nationalism, permeated by the ideals of tolerance and universal brotherhood/sisterhood, and rigid, militant, doctrinaire, mass-oriented, victimised, aggressively defensive, and exclusionary nationalism. In brief, Venclova's social criticism obviously represents the encounter of two incompatible patterns of nationalistic ethics and of two contrasting modes of being of nationalism in general.

The dialogue-based personalist ethics of Venclova comes into being along with his concept of moral responsibility. Having accepted Shtromas's idea that legal responsibility concerns only those individuals who have been directly involved in crimes against humanity, he extends the validity of moral responsibility to the nation as a whole. In this, Venclova stands very close to Karl Jaspers, who, in his post-war essay on the question of guilt, described legal, moral, and metaphysical aspects of guilt. Venclova is also reminiscent of Emmanuel Lévinas, according to whom the miracle of morality disappears as soon as the question "Why should I be moral?" is asked. An evident intellectual and moral kinship relates Venclova to Martin Buber, too; namely, the idea that I can be free in this world insofar as the Thou recognises my freedom, and that being-in-the-world is a dialogue. At this point, Venclova not only joins the gallery of the most eminent existentialist and personalist thinkers of the twentieth century, but also comes to enrich the dialogue-based ethics of personalism by expressing his Lithuanian and overall human sensibility, the sensibility of a human rights activist and political dissident, who, even in his society and culture, has always been and remains a maverick and dissenter.

The following passage from Venclova's famous essay, "Jews and Lithuanians," is perhaps the most moving and authentic of all attempts to symbolically restore the Jewish-Lithuanian dialogue and co-existence after the Holocaust. Of the Holocaust in Lithuania and of the moral sense of belonging to one's nation Venclova writes:

> What can I say, having heard all the testimony? Yes, totalitarianism distorts human nature and motives; yes, violence bears violence; but evil always remains evil, murder murder, and guilt guilt. Nothing on earth will change the fact that at the end of June 1941 some Lithuanians, in front of the very eyes of a crowd of Lithuanians, annihilated defenceless people, even the fact that in the twentieth century many—almost all—peoples have done something similar. And I, a Lithuanian, am obliged to speak of Lithuanian guilt. Sadism and looting, hatred and shameful indifference to people cannot be justified—worse, they cannot be explained; they live in such dark corners of personal and national consciousness that to search for their rational origins is a fruitless labour. Some will say: "Well, the Jews were killed not by Lithuanians, but by riffraff (or, even better, by 'bourgeois nationalists'), utterly unrelated to the Lithuanian people." I, myself, have said similar things from time to time. But this is not true. If one can consider the nation a greater self—and direct experience says that this point of view is the valid and fair one in the moral world—then all members of the nation, both righteous people and criminals, are included in this self. Every sin committed is a burden on the conscience of the entire nation and the conscience of each member of the nation. One must not dump one's own guilt on other nations. They will figure out their own guilt. We must figure out our guilt and repent for ourselves. Properly speaking, this is the very essence of what it means to belong to one nation or another. (pp.49–50)

Venclova therefore describes the sense of a common universe of moral discourse as the ontological and ethical grounds to regard oneself as a member of one nation or another. A human individual searches in his/her community and culture for a moral code. In doing so, he/she severely judges those traits of his/her community and culture that he/she finds the deformation of the moral character of the community of his/her memory and participation, let alone his/her individual moral character—Kavolis's incisive characteristics of the nationalist moral culture serves here as a clue to Venclova's ethic of liberal nationalism. One would think that it is of Venclova that Kavolis wrote about the committed individual, who, "inasmuch as his/her community's experience becomes his/her personal substance, part of his/her identity... severely judges this community and its history rejecting those things that are perceived by him/her as the deformation of his/her moral character," and who "judges him/herself asking whether his/her contribution to community coincides with what it needs the most."[12]

To Shtromas's note concerning a major influence that such personalist moral philosophers as Flewelling, Mounier, Maritain, and Berdyaev made on Venclova—and references can also be made to Jaspers, Lévinas, and Buber—I would add that Venclova's emphasis on the nation as a moral actor of history dates back to the Russian philosopher Peter Chaadayev, one of the first eminent critics of Russian society and culture, and also one of the most dramatic and tragic figures in nineteenth-century Russia (his predecessor and soul-mate Alexander Radishchev may well be said to have been the most dramatic and tragic figure in eighteenth-century Russia). In his famous *Philosophical Letters*, the first literary and philosophical manifesto of the kind of intellectual called by the great Russian poet Alexander Pushkin "the superfluous man," Chaadayev wrote that "peoples are moral beings in the same way as individuals are."[13] It is not accidental that Alexander Herzen described Peter Chaadayev himself as "the first superfluous man" of Russian society and culture.

Implicit in Venclova's philosophy of history and moral philosophy is also a concept of history as the process of the education of humankind/nations, the concept put forward by Herder and then reinterpreted by Chaadayev. Deeply influenced by German social philosophy of his time—Herder's philosophy of history and culture, and, in particular, Schelling's idea of organic peoples—Chaadayev provides an interpretative framework for a kind of social and cultural criticism based on the notion of history as universal educational process, the process that can only be viewed in a comparative and critical perspective. At the same time, this process can only be joined by critically reflecting on one's own nation's political practice and cultural accomplishments. To achieve this, the nation has to act in concert with other nations. Chaadayev sounds astonishingly similar and close to modern Central and East European critics of society and culture. At this point, he may be said to have anticipated the crucial intellectual and moral sensibilities of Central and Eastern Europe: "If we want to have an outlook similar to that of other civilised nations, we have somehow to repeat the whole education of mankind. In this we can be assisted by the history of other nations, and we have before us the products of the ages."[14]

The essence of Chaadayev's notion of history as the universal process of the education of nations, is, perhaps, best expressed in the following passage:

> Every nation has its period of stormy agitation, of passionate unease, of hasty activities. In such a period men become wanderers over the world, both in body and spirit. This is an epoch of strong emotions, great undertakings, great national passions. At such times nations toss about violently, without any apparent object, but not without benefit for future generations. All communities have gone through such a phase. Such a period provides them with their most vivid memories, their legends, their poetry, their greatest and most productive ideas; such a period represents the necessary basis of every society. Otherwise, they would have nothing valuable or cherished in memories; they would cherish only the dust of the earth they inhabit. This fascinating phase of the history of nations represents their adolescence, the age when their faculties develop most vigorously, and whose remembrance brings both joy and wisdom to their maturity. (p.110)

Venclova definitely has something of the spirit and of the frame of mind of the nineteenth-century Russian Westerners, or *Zapadniks*, who were the first liberal critics of Russian society and culture and among whom were such émigré philosophers and writers as Chaadayev and Herzen. People who were deeply attached and morally committed to their country, yet unable to fully express themselves and, consequently, not at home in crucial aspects of their country's intellectual development and political existence—such is the model of Russian political émigrés' existential situation whose undertones and nuances might easily be found in Venclova's life and works. To emigrate in order to be able to speak the truth and keep faith with one's principles and moral integrity—Kavolis's definition of the political motives and ethical programme behind Venclova's emigration perfectly fits nineteenth-century Russian Westernising liberals as well.

I would even risk a comparison of Venclova and early Russian political émigrés in the light of the concept of "the superfluous person." In a way, Venclova was also "the superfluous man" of Lithuanian society and culture. We would deceive ourselves or pronounce half-truth by depicting Venclova as "the superfluous man" only to the Soviet regime. And the truth is that he was equally unacceptable for genuine communists and radical nationalists. Hence, a lonely moralist vigorously and courageously opposing himself to a crowd of the indifferent and to an ideologically zealous—or cynically pretending to be so and therefore playing a complex game with the regime—elite. Such a lonely moralist, a sort of the personification of conscience, appears as nearly an archetype of the East European intellectual.

The way in which Chaadayev describes the frame of mind of "the superfluous man" might be seen as almost prophetic vision and anticipation of the fate not only of the Russian intelligentsia, but of Central and East European intellectuals as well.

> Look about you. Don't you think that we are very restless? We all resemble travellers. Nobody has a definite sphere of existence; we have no proper habits; there are no rules, there is no home life, there is nothing to which we could be attached, nothing that would awaken our sympathy or affection—nothing durable, nothing lasting; everything flows, everything passes, leaving no traces either outside or within us. In our own houses we seem to be guests, in our families we look like strangers, in our cities we look like nomads, even more than the nomads who drive their herds in our steppes, for they are more attached to their deserts than we to our cities. And don't think that this is not important. Poor souls that we are, let us not add to our other afflictions that of not understanding ourselves, let us not aspire to the existence of pure intelligences; let us learn to live sensibly within our given reality. (pp.109–110)

A significant part of Venclova's ethical universalism comes from Russian literature and philosophy. Along with it comes a sceptical attitude to nationalism, a phenomenon that has never been rooted in Russia, if we are not to conflate nationalism with other forms of collective identity, collective memory, and collective sentiment. Instead, such phenomena of consciousness as *Landespatriotismus* and territorial identity have been developed in Russian history, politics, and culture. Deeply grounded in modern secular consciousness and moral egalitarianism, nationalism may have always remained something foreign and artificial to Russian religious and ideological consciousness. Hence, a juxtaposition of nationalism and universalism, which is very widespread in Russia, though to a lesser extent in Western and Central Europe. Hence, too, an idea that any kind of nationalism threatens the universality of human nature, and, thus, represents incomplete humanity. As we have seen in the cases of Kavolis and Shtromas, liberal nationalists would state exactly the opposite: disconnected and abstract universalism is perceived by them as representing incomplete humanity, and, consequently, fundamentally misrepresenting the need for the sense of history and collective identity.

Although the distinction between particularity and universality is very intense in Russian thought, modern Russian philosophy, as well as mainstream Russian intellectual culture, provides little grounds for a balanced and multidimensional analysis of nationalism. Nationalism, in its paradigmatic shape, seems to have been suppressed in mainstream Russian culture and relegated to the margins of Russian consciousness. The elements of liberal nationalism might be found in Russian social and cultural criticism, and also in Russian/Soviet political dissent. For instance, as a social and moral philosophy, nationalism is implicit in Chaadayev's critique of Russian politics and culture. Small wonder, then, that the Russian *Zapadniks* of the nineteenth century, such as Chaadayev and Herzen, have much in common with their contemporaries Jules Michelet, Edgar Quinet, and Giuseppe Mazzini.

My hypothesis would be that there is something characteristically Russian in Venclova's ethical universalism, although he always finds, in an extremely erudite and precise manner, Lithuanian idioms and reference points when translating his universalism into the Central European frames of political/cultural meaning and, more specifically, into the Lithuanian frame of reference. Venclova's remarkable ability to transpose nationalism into universalism and *vice versa* might be regarded as a phenomenon of his mobile, multiple, and communicating identities. He easily and naturally migrates between Lithuanian, Russian, Polish, and even Jewish sensibilities, thus bridging these cultures and modes of discourse. In this, Venclova remains unique among Lithuanian writers and thinkers. Through his political and moral stance, Venclova reinterprets the ideal of Renaissance and Baroque Lithuania—multi-ethnic, multi-religious, and multi-cultural. Born in Klaipėda and raised in Kaunas, Venclova, in his essays and poetry, comes to project his worldview onto Vilnius, a characteristically Central European city—inclusive, tolerant, multidimensional, and cosmopolitan—around whose poetic vision revolves the entire map of his thought. This is revealed in "A Dialogue about a City," a masterpiece of the epistolary genre written by Venclova and Czesław Miłosz.

Venclova's notion of Europe as a value-emanating symbolic entity also comes from Central and East European—particularly, Russian—sensibilities. Suffice it to refer to Chaadayev's vision of Europe as a unifying principle of being and creation, reminiscent of the Schellingian philosophy of history: "At the time, in Europe everything was animated by the vivifying principle of unity. All emanated from it and all converged into it. The whole intellectual movement of those times tended to build up the unity of human thought, and all incentive had its source in this powerful need to arrive at a universal idea which is the genius of modern times" (p.117). The image of Europe as a blueprint for a universally valid moral order and as the configuration of values and ideas had its sources in not a few Central and East European essayists. The image may become a source of symbolic, or even actual, exclusion, too. Venclova, however, does not fall into the category of writers who tend to create a myth of Europe, uncritically praising and describing it exclusively in superlatives. In sharp contrast to Milan Kundera who, astonishingly enough, excluded Russia from the symbolic universe of Europe—an intellectual move unpardonable for the writer and thinker of his stature, the move not endorsed by Václav Havel or György Konrád, and effectively criticised by Joseph Brodsky—Venclova holds Russia an inseparable part of this universe of symbolic participation, construction, and correction.[15]

Objecting to the outlook, which is quite popular in Lithuania and elsewhere in post-Communist Central Europe, and which betrays a xenophobic anti-Russian sentiment, namely, that "the Russians are not Europeans but an assimilated Russian-Tartar-Mongol composite for whom the manifestations of European culture are incomprehensible, foreign, and by the Soviet standard even hostile and dangerous," Venclova, in his essay, "Russians and Lithuanians," writes:

> For me, as no doubt for every rational person, this statement is unacceptable. I would never agree that Chaadayev or Nabokov "are not Europeans" or that for them "the manifestations of European culture are incomprehensible, foreign." Regrettably, the Lithuanians have so far produced no Europeans of their stature. I am also convinced that by their efforts both Solzhenitsyn and Sakharov are realising the very same ideals that evolved over the ages in Europe. Besides, the very opposition of "European" against "Asiatic" is a dubious and slippery affair. Russians are being aligned with Tartars and Mongols, but there is nothing simple in this. First of all, it still has not been proven, and most likely never will be, that an "assimilated composite" is worse than the "racially pure." Second, the Tartars and Mongols deserve no more derision than any other group. The

Crimean Tartars, who experienced Stalinist genocide, earned universal respect by their heroic (and very European) struggle for human and national rights. And the Mongols gave us not only Genghis Khan but also a refined Buddhist culture, just as the Germans bequeathed not only Hitler but also Goethe and Hegel. Whether the European cultural manifestations are "hostile and dangerous by the Soviet standard" is an issue still open to debate, because Marxism, to which the Soviet leaders pledge their allegiance to this day, was hatched in the universities and libraries of Europe and nowhere else. Incidentally, it is worth remembering an old Muscovite joke. The main street in Moscow, the Marx Prospect, starts with a library and university and ends with the Lubyanka edifice (headquarters of the KGB): yet it does start, after all, with a set of purely European establishments. Many who know their Marx will admit that the layout of the Prospect has an intrinsic logic.[16]

Yet Venclova's ethical universalism can barely be reduced to his close relationship with Russian literature and intellectual culture. However important, Russian universalism constitutes only one of many aspects and perspectives within Venclova's world of intellectual and moral awareness. His universalism also springs from the dialogue-based personalist ethics and from the concept of otherness inherent in this kind of moral reflection. Venclova's concept of otherness has very little, if anything at all to do with the Hegelian notion of otherness; nor is it related to Heidegger and Sartre's concepts of otherness. Instead, it stands very close to that of Lévinas. Algis Mickunas describes the relationship with the Other in Lévinas's philosophy of dialogue, responsibility, and freedom in the following way:

> The relationship with the other, presupposed by representation, is identified by Lévinas as the domain of ethics. This relationship does not emerge from representation of objectivities but is attained as a response recognising an appeal, an interrogation, an imperative making demands on me, requiring of me justification, conscience and apology. The movement of critique, contestation, appeal and justification in a dialogue wherein a world is objectified, constitutes the ethical dimension of cognition. It is this dialogical process, this fundamental relationship with the other as ethical that, according to Lévinas, might have compelled Plato to elevate the Good above Being. The ethical dimension has very little to do with rules of behaviour or principles of duty; rather it is a dialogical encounter wherein first one-sided and truncated understanding is contested, interrogated, justified and appealed, wherein the ethical dimension of cognition is in gestation.[17]

Establishing the dialogical relationship with the Other—an other nation, an other culture, an other mode of discourse, an other mode of sensibility, or, simply, another human individual—Venclova rejects the monologue-based speaking and thinking. The monologue, no matter whether individual and collective, is just another word for intolerance. The monologue is a reference to ideological discourse, a mode of discourse within which the thoughts, actions, exchanges, dreams, imaginations, and creative endeavours of other human beings all become instrumental in manipulating and technologically/ideologically reshaping the world around us. The metaphysics of the monologue rests on the assumption that truth can never be established in a dialogue, since truth represents something that can only be described in terms of the ever-presence. Finally, the monologue serves as a perfect basis for political demagogy, brainwashing, indoctrination, and manipulative exchanges. In so doing, the monologue comes to distort the reality of human individuals and inter-subjectivity. The inability to engage in a dialogue means the denial of responsibility. Therefore, where is no dialogue, there is no responsibility; and where is no responsibility, there is no freedom. As Mickunas notes,

> [w]hat passes for speaking and thinking is quite frequently a mere playing with words and concepts constituting a succession of egocentric monologues. We may subsume objectivities, events and things under our egocentric categories, but speaking becomes serious when the other contests our views, our categories and even our truths. It is while responding to the other that the self experiences an altereity and an awareness of the arbitrary, limited and egocentric views attained by an uncriticised freedom. In responding to the challenge of the other, the self becomes responsible.[18]

Such is the philosophical substance of Venclova's ethical universalism. Only individuals can act in history as moral agents. Unanimous forces and faceless processes of social change can never be regarded as politically aware of, and morally responsible for, the vulnerability and fragility of the human world. But if the nation may be assumed as a greater self and as an extension of the human individuality, it should be regarded as a moral actor of history. If so, it is morally aware and responsible. Whereas the monologue can only lead to clichés, stereotyping, xenophobic prejudice, and demonisation of the Other, the dialogue results in responsibility, tolerance, and discovery of the Other. Tomas Venclova's political essays remind us of this truth better than anything else.

## Representations and Misrepresentations

The Herderian concept of the nation as collective individual, refracted through Venclova's Central/East European intellectual and moral sensibilities and through the dialogue-based personalist ethics, allowed the eminent Lithuanian poet and literary scholar to join the glorious gallery of East Central European internationalists and cosmopolitans, such as Tomáš Masaryk, György Konrád, Václav Havel, and Adam Michnik. (It is not without reason that Herder may well be perceived to have been the first Central European thinker in this sense.) All of them represent the most liberal and humane facet of nationalism. This sort of generous, inclusive, and sophisticated nationalism paved the way to genuine internationalism—the term spoiled and compromised by the Soviet propaganda, yet politically and morally still valid and significant in the context of East Central European intellectual culture.

Their political and moral stance, however, is tinged with splendid isolation, solitude, and aristocratic detachment from popular consciousness and mainstream culture. This makes the possibility to reach a wider audience profoundly problematic. And the question that arises here is this: Is it possible to transform such a liberal and sophisticated nationalism from the political and moral stance of a tiny minority of Westward-looking, cosmopolitan, secular-humanist, and rationalist intellectuals into a blueprint for a viable moral order? Of this East Central European political and moral dilemma Timothy Garton Ash writes:

> Another line of general criticism would be this (and I exaggerate deliberately): Konrád, Havel and Michnik are merely the latest scions of a tradition that has been present in Central and Eastern Europe since the Enlightenment: the Westward-looking, cosmopolitan, secular-humanist and rationalist element, what Thomas Mann contemptuously called the *Zivilisationsliteraten* (before becoming one himself). True, the *Zivilisationsliteraten* are now saying different things from what they were saying half a century ago: indeed, in crucial respects they are saying the opposite. But one thing has not changed: they have always been a tiny minority. They were a tiny minority before the First World War, impotent against the nationalism that tore that Central Europe apart. They were a tiny minority before the Second World War, impotent against the imperialism which tore *that* Central Europe apart.[19]

Tomas Venclova is undoubtedly one of the *Zivilisationsliteraten* of Central and Eastern Europe. Quite sceptical of the mystique of the collective soul and of the glorification of the village green—things that constitute an indispensable element of every single case of nationalism as a mass-oriented political and cultural movement—Venclova distanced himself from a parochial and defensive nationalism deeply grounded in twentieth-century Lithuania. He states explicitly that if we wish well to our country, we cannot isolate it from the challenges of the contemporary world. Lithuanian culture can only experience and try out itself acting in concert with other cultures. The attachment to and respect for one's nation cannot minimise or, worse, eliminate, the moral requirements to it, let alone the critical questioning of what departs, in one's society and culture, from the universally assumed human rights and ethical norms.

The size of a country is not an excuse to justify one's prejudice and superstition. There cannot in principle be any double standard in assessing what is supposed to be our own and what is perceived as alien. Kavolis held that we tend to be critical of the things we respect, since what is unworthy of respect deserves no critique at all and should be ignored. Venclova identifies the reluctance to critically question one's society and culture as intellectual and moral provincialism that can be harmful in many ways. According to him, there are two kinds of provincialism: the province is what claims to be the centre of the universe, a sort of global provincialism that Venclova accords to the former Soviet Union; and the province, not to a lesser extent, is what regards itself as a province, a sort of parochial provincialism whose elements he finds in Lithuanian culture. A critical approach is the only cure from this sort of collective inferiority complex. Most importantly, a critical approach to oneself serves as a self-discovery, since an exclusive emphasis on the real or imagined vices of other countries and their cultures betrays the reluctance or inability to face up one's own past and present.

> A fully integrated personality esteems all others equally; the same principle should apply in regard to collective personalities. And if we declare ourselves enemies of totalitarianism, we must be careful to erase traces of it within ourselves. There is no doubt that David rouses more sympathy than Goliath; a nationalism of the smaller countries draws more justification than the nationalism of a great hegemony. But one should not consider a nation to be the highest value. There are values which are more important than the nation: for a Christian, that is God; for a non-professing liberal, it is humanity and truth. To save the nation by forfeiting our humanity would be worse than to experience the reverse. *Totalitarianism provokes absolutising of the nation, which in itself is the form of totalitarian consciousness.* Quite often we turn a foreigner into a projection of all kinds of evils, first and foremost the evils that are our own. A mature nation that is determined to survive and to grow

has to remain critical of itself, not just of its occupier or neighbour. And it is better to overdo the criticism than to diminish it.[20]

The problem of the representation and misrepresentation of the Other, therefore, becomes central in the most internationally acclaimed of Venclova's thoughtful and penetrating political essays, such as "Jews and Lithuanians," "Russians and Lithuanians," and "Poles and Lithuanians." A brilliant writer, an erudite scholar, and an elegant thinker, Venclova, in the aforementioned political essays, formulates his thought in an exceptionally clear and understandable way, as if deliberately trying to make himself heard and read by a larger audience of his compatriots. He is by no means an elitist writer. Doing his best to increase the readership of his essays and to enhance his political and moral appeal to as many people as possible, Venclova radically differs from Kavolis who was foremost a sophisticated academic writer. Venclova differs from Kavolis from the point of view of the linguistic expression and composition of the text, too: Venclova places in the body of the text and even italicises what Kavolis used to relegate to the endnotes of his articles, namely, reference points and allusions concerning Lithuanian antisemitism, xenophobic sentiments, prejudices, and conspiracy theories. This is not to say that things that are central to Venclova were of the second order or even marginal for Kavolis. The point is that Kavolis's political and moral concerns are contextualised within the framework of his broader social analyses and interpretations of culture, whereas Venclova derives all major themes from his direct experience not only as a writer, but also as a human rights activist and political dissident who spent much of his time in Lithuania and Russia.

In more than one way Venclova differs from Shtromas, too, since Shtromas, in his political analyses and passionate essays, placed more analytical and critical emphasis on Communism and the Soviet regime than on Lithuanian misrepresentations of other nations and cultures, thus showing more forgiveness of Lithuanian prejudices and superstitions than Venclova and Kavolis. And although we can only speculate about the short- and long-term effects of Venclova's social criticism on Lithuanian society and culture, the charge of being too disconnected from the ordinary readership or of being inaccessible to a wider audience in terms of his exaggerated linguistic and stylistic sophistication, in Venclova's case, would be totally unfounded. If Venclova remains a maverick and dissenter even in present-day Lithuania, the reasons lie elsewhere.

One of the reasons, most probably, is Venclova's cosmopolitanism and internationalism, the attitudes that are much misinterpreted and misrepresented in present Lithuania. For most Lithuanians—not excluding writers, artists, journalists, academics, public officials, and politicians—internationalism still remains a pejorative term reminiscent of the worst nightmares of the Soviet propaganda and political demagogy, and quite justifiably so if the term is placed exclusively in the context of Soviet reality. Alas, an alternative to the Soviet interpretative vocabulary has yet to be worked out in Lithuania. This is also more than true with regard to cosmopolitanism, which is increasingly being depicted as a threat to Lithuanian identity and national culture, thus using the term as a mere euphemism for the supposedly "Jewish insensitivity and indifference" to the utmost Lithuanian patriotic concerns and providing quite a rich soil for the similar pearls of group stereotyping and antisemitic wisdom. For the vast majority of present-day Lithuania's intellectuals, the internationalism and liberal cosmopolitanism of Venclova and his fellow dissidents sound more than odd and are simply inconceivable. To blame them for this is the same as to blame people for being unable to speak a foreign language. It is little wonder that Venclova openly challenges a sort of reverse Soviet demonology, or even a bizarre combination of Soviet mentality and demonological nationalism, by writing the following on Moscow and Russia:

> Many Lithuanians, on hearing the word "Moscow," feel nothing but a sense of enmity; and that is natural. I am definitely an exception to this. Moscow is for me a sombre, miserable yet oddly splendid city; the city of Pasternak, Solzhenitsyn, and Sakharov. Moscow also is where Vladimir Bukovsky lived, in the infrequent periods when he was not in prison. In January 1977, when he was already in the West, Bukovsky said: "By oppressing other nations, the Russian nation can only lose its freedom, not gain it. It's fortunate that the Russians are growing more and more aware of this. In this sense, we have been working a long time together with the movements in the Ukraine, in Armenia, in the Baltics and in other nations." And in 1975, while still in prison, he declared: "I am a nationalist. A Ukrainian, Armenian, Jewish, Czech, Polish, Maori, Peruvian nationalist." I will confess that when I see such people, and at the same time observe the symptoms of a totalitarian thinking among my own compatriots, I too become a nationalist. A Maori, Peruvian, German, Jewish, Polish nationalist. Sometimes, even a Russian nationalist.[21]

This little manifesto of internationalism and liberal cosmopolitanism sheds new light on why and how Venclova, in the eyes of conservative or radical nationalists, is still open to the charge of treason. Crossing the boundaries of cultures and raising the pivotal political and moral issues of modern human experience and existence, he quite naturally transcends the limits of a single loyalty. This constitutes an identity formula that is simply beyond the reach and understanding of a doctrinaire and mass-oriented nationalism. The defence of his nation at any cost and at the expense of the universally valid moral criteria, suggested and even explicitly preached by Lithuanian mainstream nationalism, is as alien to Venclova as the idea of irresponsible determinism was to Kavolis. Equally unacceptable to him is the idea that criticism of inconvenient facts of the nation's history must come "in time," since, otherwise, it may be harmful to the image of the country. For instance, Venclova has always been opposed to the idea that the time has not come yet to fully assess the Holocaust in Lithuania because it would be useful only for those who do not wish well to Lithuania.

It is not difficult to imagine that Venclova's internationalism and liberal cosmopolitanism, combined with his expertise in other Central and East European cultures and in world literature in general, in the eyes of Lithuanian traditionalists and conservative nationalists (or, worse, antisemites and xenophobes), passes for a recurrence of the Soviet ideology or, *horribile dictu*, for his far-reaching intentions to please the omnipotent and clandestine international/Jewish organisations. Since these two discourses of identity and freedom are simply out of touch, Venclova is condemned to remain, in his own country and amongst the majority of émigrés, a dissenter almost to the same extent he was in the former Soviet Union.

> As for me personally, for some ten years in Lithuania I was, and in emigration still am, of course, accused of something like betrayal of my nation. The reason is that I'm a cosmopolitan, Judophile, Polonophile—a Russophile even, and the Lithuanians often irritate me simply because they are my people. The Lithuanian Helsinki group has been blamed because we are not Lithuanian dissidents but "general Soviet" dissidents. And how can it be any other way? The effort is hopeless unless it is joint, and we feel emotionally tied to everything that happens there. When I say there, I don't mean in the Soviet Union only, but in the whole of Eastern Europe. We are East European dissidents or simply East Europeans—which means the same thing. (pp.39–40)

Like Shtromas, Venclova drew a sharp dividing line between Russia and the Soviet Union. One of the worst misrepresentations of another society and culture in Lithuanian consciousness is that which depicts Russia as evil by definition. People who have zero expertise in Russian history and culture tend to describe Russia as a threat to Europe and Western civilisation, and as an embodiment of merciless and cynical imperialism. Challenging this stereotype of barbarous Russia, supposedly irreconcilable to Europe and to its European neighbours, Venclova discarded the unfounded and false identification of Russia with the Soviet Empire. Viewing the Soviet Union as a logical extension of tsarist Russia, we fail to take into account the global ideological, ideocratic and logocratic nature of the Soviet regime incompatible and irreconcilable with deeply religious Russian consciousness and classical Russian culture. According to him, however problematic and tinged with imperialism and imperialist jingoism, tsarist Russia represented a sort of classical and old-fashioned empire, not dissimilar to those of Britain and France. If so, it cannot be equated with the regime which represents a *sui generis* phenomenon in world history and which has neither reverence nor pity for Russian intellectual traditions and culture.

> And Russian dissidents are well aware of the Russian predicament. Not only those who support Sakharov, but also quite a few Russian nationalists, will attest that only a firm rejection of imperialism would save their nation morally, economically and culturally. The parting of the ways is not between nations but between the democratically minded people (which includes even some moderate nationalists) and a totalitarian system. (p.63)

Another representation of the Other, that turns out to be one of the most vicious misrepresentations deeply rooted in Lithuanian consciousness, is that of the Poles. Here I rush to admit that it has been a relatively long time since publication of "A Dialogue about a City"—this masterpiece of epistolary literature written by Venclova and Czesław Miłosz in 1979—and that Polish-Lithuanian relations, spoiled by immense mutual hostility and unfavourable political memories that resulted from a complex historical legacy of the Polish-Lithuanian Commonwealth and, in particular, from the occupation of Vilnius by Poland in 1920, have ever since improved beyond recognition. A major contribution to the new politics of reconciliation, mutual understanding, respect, and tolerance, made by Venclova and Miłosz, is too obvious to need emphasis. They anticipated and shaped the politics of reconciliation, which was later endorsed and implemented by politicians. Literature preceded politics. They, too, came to bridge the modern literatures and intellectual cultures of both nations. (Although the role of Adam Michnik and of his generation of Polish intellectuals, particularly those from the Solidarity movement, also deserves honourable mention.)

What Venclova referred to in his political essays was the Polonophobic attitude, which was and still is rather strong among not a few Lithuanian academics and politicians, and which deeply disturbed him. As he wrote to Miłosz:

> For me personally, the antagonisms between our nations seem colossally stupid and I would like to regard them as conquered. I think that a significant part of the younger generation in Lithuania does not feel any hostility towards the Poles. I suspect that it is the same the other way around; perhaps somewhere the feeling of Polish superiority and haughtiness still lingers, but perhaps not. We have passed out of that era and the old squabbles seem meaningless. (p.34)

Poland and Lithuania may best exemplify one of the greatest paradoxes of nationalism, namely, the struggle of historical memories and collective sentiments of the actors of history who have long had a common state and even a common culture. Nationalism as a radical reinterpretation of history definitely is one of the principal reasons behind the parting of, and numerous political tensions—throughout the twentieth century—between, Poland and Lithuania. The worst consequence of such a reinterpretation of political and cultural histories of the two nations, on both sides, was a fatal weakening of the sense of common history, of common intellectual and cultural legacy, and of a common, i.e., Central European, identity, let alone the propensity to see a historically formed and ever-lasting enemy in one another. As Venclova, along with many Lithuanian historians of the younger generation, noted, the only side that benefited from this clash of Poland and Lithuania was the former Soviet Union, particularly in the inter-war period. A pointless process of the demonisation of the Poles could lead nowhere but to a loss, on the Lithuanian side, of a significant part of Polish-Lithuanian culture. Sadly enough, the divorce of the two cultures not only tragically narrowed the Lithuanian frame of reference and Lithuanian historical horizon, but robbed Lithuania of its multi-ethnic and multi-cultural past, thus jeopardising and putting into question its status of a Central European country.

Suffice it to say that one of the consequences of the marriage of culture and state, that is, nationalism, and of the divorce of the two nations, whose cultures had long shared a common universe, is that Czesław Miłosz, who was born in Lithuania and without whose intellectual and poetical voice the modern Lithuanian discourse of identity and freedom would be unthinkable, can no longer be regarded as the great Polish-Lithuanian poet. The disrupted tradition of intellectual polyvocality and multiculturalism—disrupted not only as a result of a nationalist reinterpretation of history and of a reinvention of national traditions, but also as a tragic consequence of the Holocaust—is the most dramatic thing that occurred to modern Lithuania, and this fact still remains insufficiently understood in Lithuania.

Commenting on the feelings of Polish superiority and Lithuanian inferiority, Venclova writes:

> Personally I do not have any feelings of national inferiority; the young Lithuanian generation is freeing itself from this because Lithuania is no worse than any other East European country. But certain stereotypes remain and can be revived, especially because the experience of totalitarianism in general does not foster wise and tolerant attitudes. There is a tradition of demonising the Poles. According to this mentality (which still has influence, albeit vestigial), Poles throughout the centuries have had one goal: to annex Lithuania to Poland, denationalise it, and oppress it. The Poles are thought to be more dangerous than the Russians because they are Catholics as well as Europeans. The stereotype of the Machiavellian Pole, who always gets his own way, if not by force then by treachery, lingers on. Here, in emigration, I often come in contact with this mentality and I always feel a terrible shame because it is an immaturity straight out of Gombrowicz. A mature nation, which Lithuania undoubtedly is now, cannot be denationalised even if someone wanted it. This stereotype is one of inertia and regression and can only be convenient to the regime. So, we and the Poles must remember this, and we must avoid activities which incite and rekindle these feelings. (p.35)

Yet Venclova's criticism of the misrepresentations of the Other culminates in his interpretation of the Holocaust in Lithuania. The interpretation that constitutes the most challenging part of his ethical message.

## Rethinking the Holocaust in Lithuania: Toward a Jewish-Lithuanian Dialogue

Fully subscribing to Shtromas's point of view, Venclova notes that: "First, one cannot be silent about any crime. Second, there were and are collaborators in fewer and greater numbers, depending on the historical circumstances, but there is no such thing as a collaborating nation" (p.38). He differs from those inter-war Lithuanian intellectuals—such as the writers Vincas Krėvė-Mickevičius and Juozas Tumas-Vaižgantas, or the philosopher Stasys Šalkauskis—who were sympathetic to the Jews and who empathised with Lithuanian Jews from a genuinely Christian standpoint. In a way, Venclova also differs from the post-war liberal-humanist element in

Lithanian émigré culture in the United States, such as the poet Algimantas Mackus, a member of *Santara-Šviesa*, who, in one of his poems, depicted the tragic fate of a Jewish boy. For Venclova, the Holocaust and the martyrdom of Lithuanian Jewry are not only a matter of sympathetic understanding and compassion, but also the crucial question of Lithuania's present and future. Venclova conceives of the destruction of the Jewish community in Lithuania as the destruction of the civic and moral foundations of Lithuania. A sense of metaphysical guilt here clearly means a realisation that I am part of a tragic history, since I belong to the country where a catastrophe occurred; I share the language, historical memory, and culture of the country where there occurred a crime against humanity.

> The Jews were killed by Lithuanians and I am Lithuanian. Jews were killed in Kaunas and Kaunas is my city: I know its every building, every tree on its Liberty Avenue; I know its dusty gardens, its crowded cinemas. I cannot exist without the Lithuanian language—it is my natural space; I write verse only in Lithuanian. There are cultures much more powerful than Lithuanian culture, but for me it cannot be compared with any other. I know that a lot of good things may be said about it. For centuries we Lithuanians were proud of our own integrity, honesty, stubbornness, and kindness. We have a sense of history which, I believe, is characteristic of few peoples: we remember our past and are usually able to check our present against the past. I am also proud of the fact that in the overwhelming majority of cases Lithuanians behaved themselves with dignity in the concentration camps; the greatest contemporary Russian writer wrote about this and he knows of what he speaks.[22] I love the Jewish people as well. Their cultural role and their very fate are so enormous that they are for me the primary proof of the transcendental design which determines our historical existence. What occurred in the first days of the war was a catastrophe for the Jews, but it was an even worse catastrophe for the Lithuanians. (p.44)

Venclova's humanism manifests itself not only in his great sensitivity, but also in his rejection of rational and deterministic explanations of the Holocaust. Elsewhere he reminds us that every crime, like every act of heroism, contains a kind of "transcendental remainder," which powerfully resists all rational-action or rational-choice explanations. Ultimately, such explanations are worthless.[23] Having stressed that the Kaunas pogroms contradict the entire Lithuanian historical tradition marked by religious and political tolerance toward Jews and by peaceful coexistence of both peoples, Venclova breaks all Lithuanian political and cultural taboos by touching upon the nerve of the story.

One of such taboos in Lithuanian history and historical memory still is the role and place of the Lithuanian Activist Front (LAF) in the 1941 uprising to restore Lithuania's independence and in the spread of antisemitic propaganda in Lithuania. In 1941, the provisional government of Lithuania started playing a complicated game with the Nazis, sincerely hoping to restore Lithuania's independence. The game, as Venclova notes, was inexorably doomed to failure. It is difficult to imagine something more dubious than choosing between Stalin and Hitler. Nobody can deny the fact that the provisional government was inspired by the LAF. And the point is that it was members of the LAF who launched antisemitic propaganda employing such pearls of the Nazi rhetoric as "the Judeo-Bolshevik conspiracy," "a plot of the Jewish bankers and communists," "the Jewish yoke and exploitation," and the like. This is not to say that the entire 1941 uprising should be regarded as an overture to the Holocaust. But its fallacies and grave mistakes have to be admitted. Venclova was the first to do this. In his articles, he openly challenged the romanticised and patriotic version of the Second World War history, which tends to glamorise both the LAF and the 1941 uprising, thus calling for a transvaluation of those values. Quoting from editorials in wartime Lithuanian papers, Venclova showed black on white that some Lithuanian politicians, intellectuals, and ordinary Lithuanians, on the eve of World War II, were influenced by Nazism.[24] Needless to say, the conservative and ultrapatriotic circles, particularly amongst émigrés, reacted noisily, thus adding insult to injury.

Even so, it seems there is a long way from propaganda, however ferocious and sinister, to mass murder. Yet Venclova places his interpretative emphasis and moral evaluation on the empirically elusive world of human connection and inter-subjectivity, rather than political history written in a conventional academic manner. In a world of moral choices and ethical self-fulfilment, nothing is unimportant, and every single detail of human experience or attitude acquires its meaning. Being much in tune with Shtromas's idea that many tragic events of the twentieth century have resulted from the division of people into "us" and "them," Venclova comes to stress the spiritual isolation which manifests itself in the division of people into categories. By distancing ourselves from a group of other human beings or our fellow citizens, we create a kind of political and moral vacuum, which sooner or later will be filled with theories and practices of exclusion and hatred—one more political and ethical message of Venclova's theory of otherness, dialogue, and inter-subjectivity. Venclova points out:

> It seems there is a long way from a particular pronunciation of the word to a pogrom. But in the spiritual world—if we are at all capable of making judgements about this world—this distance, apparently, approaches zero. Whoever sets apart a particular group of people—a nation, religion, class, or any other group—and considers himself spiritually in no way related to this group, in essence, is preparing a pogrom, concentration camp or totalitarian system. This is as basic and true as a-b-c. Like any basic truth, it is quite frequently forgotten.[25]

Here we are, again, in the sphere of the ethics of dialogue, inter-subjectivity, and of the discovery of the Other as opposed to the ethics of monologue. A world of self-centredness, insensitivity, and neglect of the Other, where a particular group is set apart as a dangerous alien, or, worse, as an enemy, ultimately, is dominated by the ethics of monologue, a kind of collective solipsism. Such an ethics is only able to forge consciousness where there is no room allowed for tolerance as the discovery of the Other. Why do we need the Other? Because the Other is what comes to establish dialogue and inter-subjectivity. Because the Other is a pivotal dimension of human awareness without which I am incomplete as a human being. Because without otherness I am unable to conceive of myself. Because the Other is just another word for being-in-the-world. Finally, because the discovery of the Other, if properly understood, is a self-discovery. If a nation is a greater self, within which human individuals search for the symbolic designs of human existence, modes of discourse, images, and memories to experience themselves in all dimensions of history and collective identity, it is also unthinkable without otherness.

> This is not a rending of one's shirt; this is a spiritual repentance. But we must speak about everything which took place, without trying to protect ourselves, without any internal censor, without propagandistic distortions, without national complexes, without fear. We must understand forever that the destruction of the Jews is the destruction of ourselves, that the offence to the Jews is an offence to ourselves, that the liquidation of Jewish culture is an attempt on our own. (p.50)

The parallel existence of Lithuanian and Jewish cultures in inter-war Lithuania throws some light on the gulf, if not abyss, between Lithuanians and Jews before World War II. Exactly the same might be said about the existence of gentile hosts and Jews elsewhere in East Central Europe, with a relative exception of Russia where Jews not only had access to the mainstream of Russian modern culture, but also played an important part in Russian literature, theatre, and arts. The alienation of cultures, as Venclova suggests, may have dangerous political implications. First and foremost, it results in spiritual isolation, which is the cause of many misfortunes. Although there were attempts, on both sides, to overcome this wall of mutual indifference and isolation, the most remarkable achievements and cultural accomplishments of one side went almost unnoticed by the other. In inter-war Lithuania, even well-educated ethnic Lithuanians knew little about the Jewish Enlightenment, the Haskalah, and other phenomena of Jewish emancipation, and next to nothing about such things as the Yiddishist movement and Yiddishist modernism in general. For their part, Lithuanian Jews, with minor exceptions, had little interest in the intellectual dramas and cultural stirrings of their gentile compatriots. As Venclova observes,

> [n]evertheless, despite their centuries-long experience of intercourse, Lithuanians and Jews, in practice, lived in completely separate worlds. We, Lithuanians, knew not a little about Polish culture and something about German and Russian cultures, but we hadn't the slightest idea about Jewish culture which was unfolding in our own country in front of our very eyes. The religion, language, alphabet, and customs turned out to be too great a barrier. The Jewish community was understood as an exotic enclave spiritually unrelated to us. It is clear that this was a grave mistake. The Jews, also, knew little about Lithuanian traditions and culture. Those who assimilated usually adopted Russian, or sometimes German. Two national renaissances—Lithuanian and Jewish—blossomed simultaneously and contiguously, but in different dimensions. This recalls a Bradbury story about Earthlings and Martians who live on the same planet but can meet only in a rare, lucky coincidence. The first cautious attempts to overcome this impenetrable barrier, to become acquainted with one another's cultural potential, occurred in the inter-war years. The Jews took the initiative. In the later years of the inter-war period there also appeared Jews who wrote in Lithuanian about their problems. The best known among them is I. Meras. He left Lithuania for Israel and his name is no longer mentioned in the Lithuanian press. (pp.46–47)

Venclova considers this spiritual isolation, indifference, and alienation to have been instrumental in erecting, on the eve of the Second World War, the fatal wall of mutual misunderstanding between Lithuanians and Jews. Of course, it might be suggested that much of Lithuanian antisemitism was and still is rather indifference to, or defensiveness about, certain aspects of the past. It might also be pointed out that those things sprang from the fear of modernity—and, in particular, of such unavoidable aspects of modernity as internationalism, secularisation, and "godlessness," all of them, supposedly, militating against the preservation of Lithuanian identity and national culture—largely represented and even embodied by European Jews. Yet to justify and defend his nation is the last thing Venclova would do. Instead, he penetrates the substance of the problem, reaching the gates of core questions in ethics.

Venclova's discourse about the Holocaust is unique in the context of Lithuanian scholarship, literature, and social criticism. He was the first to state explicitly that the destruction of the Jews signified the destruction of Lithuania, and that the Jewish pogroms in Lithuania were not only a catastrophe for the Jews, but an even worse catastrophe for the Lithuanians. He stressed the Holocaust as a fundamental examination of Lithuanian nationalism and of its maturity. He, too, defined the attitude to the Holocaust as a watershed between the Westward-looking, liberal-democratic, universalistic, and cosmopolitan Lithuanian-ness and the aggressively defensive, exclusionary stance of ethnic homogeneity and tribal subordination. Finally, he proclaimed the Holocaust a great challenge to, and transvaluation of, a time-honoured Lithuanian tradition of the fear of modernity. Rethinking the Holocaust and creating a new ethical discourse about it, Venclova put forward a framework for a new identity and freedom discourse, too.

Most importantly, Venclova's discourse about the Holocaust serves as a landmark in restoring the symbolic Jewish-Lithuanian dialogue. Symbolic, because there is no such thing in mundane reality as the Jewish-Lithuanian dialogue. Lithuanian Jews who actively engaged in Lithuanian politics and culture did so not because they were preoccupied with a certain dialogue of imagined collective bodies, but because they were Lithuanians, not only Jews. Symbolic, because such a dialogue would be impossible in a country where a tiny Jewish minority is diminishing all the time, and is no longer capable of a dialogue, or intellectual and creative exchanges, with mainstream culture. The Jewish-Lithuanian dialogue is therefore a symbolic reference to Lithuania's political and ethical self-discovery, and to Lithuania's dialogue with its own historical past and present. It refers to Lithuania's dialogue with its modern history as it actually happened. The Jewish-Lithuanian dialogue also serves as a symbolic code for the rediscovery of Lithuania's obsessions, phobias, fears, longings, expectations, disappointments, and traumas. In fact, there is nothing else behind such a dialogue with oneself, or self-discovery, that the Jewish-Lithuanian dialogue might signify. Venclova provides an ethical framework within which this dialogue comes into being.

Along with Kavolis and Shtromas, Venclova may be said to have initiated an entire current in Lithuanian intellectual culture recently endorsed and joined by a number of young Lithuanian historians and literary scholars, namely, a comparative and critical study of Lithuanian society and culture accompanied by an ethical reflection on the identity and freedom discourse, the latter manifesting itself throughout the history of modern Lithuania.

## Towards a New Identity and Freedom Discourse

Stressing every nation's historical memory and a distinctive project for the future, Venclova envisions Lithuania as cherishing its diversity. In doing so, he describes a nation as an open system that has a dimension in time.

> A nation may be understood as a certain unity, the parts of which complement and sustain, regulate and sometimes replace each other. They can even contend among themselves with no loss of their essential unity. Such an outlook is equally acceptable, I think, to the scholar who has a rationalist orientation (for instance, in cybernetics) as to the thinker who has a religious orientation: they view the same phenomenon from different perspectives, though without negating each other. Furthermore, a nation (just as an individual) is a system that has a dimension in time. It lives up to its name only when it has acquired historical memory and a distinctive project for the future. The attempts of contemporary totalitarian states at denationalisation are aimed primarily at this temporal dimension: the historical memory of nations is damaged in every way. Trends in "mass culture" within the democracies of the West work in a similar manner, yet it is after all another—and complex—problem. The obliteration of national differences would no doubt spell the end of world culture, at least of the culture we know and cherish, one that really is worth cherishing. Luckily, it appears that such obliteration remains a utopia. (pp.56–57)

In his emphasis on historical memory and a distinctive project for the future, rather than ethnic origin or the blood-and-soil cultural logic, Venclova explicitly challenges ethnic nationalism, speaking out in favour of civic nationalism—civic-minded, tolerant and inclusive. Being perfectly aware of the historic struggles to preserve and revive the Lithuanian language, Venclova, though, moves the centre of his considerations toward a free existential choice as the routes to the nation as the community of memory and participation. Indeed, by the beginning of the twentieth century, Lithuanian was rather a peasant language, and the Lithuanian intelligentsia, themselves trained at Polish and Russian universities, formed a very tiny layer of the fluent speakers of Lithuanian. For Lithuanians, the Lithuanian language is nothing less than their natural space, to recall Venclova's admirable formulation. Even so, to describe the national language and culture as something that should be in the fighting trim all the time is the last thing he would do. Instead, Venclova emphasises what he terms the "gravitational field" of a culture, a quality that attracts and invites to participate people from other cultures. Such a "gravitational field," rather than a purity of blood or an uncritical acceptance of one's linguistic and cultural milieu, shows the real potential of a culture.

> It should be added that every nation is an open system. Its worth and potential are not by any means gauged by a purity of blood; more likely, it's the reverse. A large number of people of different background always enters the "gravitational field" of a stronger culture. There are well-known instances in Russian history: Gogol was Ukrainian; Dostoevsky, if not as Lithuanian as has at times been claimed, then certainly Belorussian; Mandelstam a Jew. It is interesting that the Lithuanians have a similar "gravitational field" as well. More than one German has chosen Lithuanian culture as his own (from those who prepared the seventeenth-century hymnals, all the way to, let's say, the twentieth-century scholar and journalist Joseph Ehret), more than one Russian (Lev Karsavin), more than one Jew (Icchokas Meras), more than one Pole (though in the last case the reverse of this process has been more pronounced). The open systems that nations are can interrelate normally, in order to enhance and enrich each other, only under conditions of unforced sovereignty and democracy. (pp.57–58)

In Venclova's discourse about identity and freedom, identity becomes a matter of free choice and of self-determination, rather than ever-presence. Endorsing the view, according to which established identities tend to be, in effect, empty, he describes identity as activity, an intense process of the choosing among many possibilities of human self-fulfilment and self-discovery. For example, what is behind one's being Lithuanian is an important aspect of freedom, not historic destiny or ethnic inheritance. Of a number of possibilities to be a history-conscious human individual and a member of the community of memory and participation, I choose one. Although this is not exclusively the case: I can choose several modes of existence as an actor of history and culture. I can confine myself to one symbolic design of human awareness and experience, or one community of memory and participation, on condition that it does not contradict or exclude my participation—at least theoretically—in others. Nobody can determine my moral substance but myself; this is equally true of the right to decide how to be a human individual. Identity and freedom complement and sustain one another: my identity, both individual and collective, is an extension of my freedom as a social and cultural actor, whereas freedom, disconnected from human identity, turns into a logically derived and abstract principle. Moreover, identity and freedom are virtually impossible without each other, for how can I be free without awareness of who I am and where I belong?

The most important of the philosophical and political implications of Venclova's social criticism is that he reconciles Lithuanian nationalism with ethical universalism. It was not accidental that Shtromas analysed Venclova as the founder of modern Lithuanian universalism. In addition, Venclova may well be regarded as one of the founders of Lithuanian internationalism and liberal cosmopolitanism. If liberal nationalism can be defined as a social criticism, this is more than true of Venclova's essays and critical scholarship. In the context of Venclova's works, Lithuanian mainstream nationalism appears as a deviation from the values and ideas recognised and fully endorsed by the ethic of liberal nationalism, that is, the initial stage of Lithuanian nationalism. Most importantly, Venclova succeeds in reconciling, in the discursive universe of his philosophical and political essays, truth with value, which is a great yet unfulfilled ambition of very many of the contemporary humanists and social scientists. Having started as a lonely moralist and representative of the conscience in Lithuania, he joined the company of the cosmopolitan exiles of East Central Europe whose works, lives, and personalities contain significant alternatives to their native countries and cultures.

Venclova's criticism gives us a clue to the conflicting tendencies of modern Lithuanian consciousness and culture. The intellectual and political dramas of his culture have been refracted through his social and existential experience, and internalised as his own. The boldness of Venclova's statement, as well as the public appeal of his essays, owes much to the brilliance of his style and even his linguistic virtuosity. Venclova is a master of political essay *par excellence*. As an essayist and critic, he is second to none in Lithuania—given the very high degree of linguistic and overall philological sophistication of Lithuanian writers and critics, this is quite a serious achievement. Venclova's attentiveness to the language is clearly seen in his works on the logocratic nature of the Soviet regime, and also on the Soviet Newspeak. Simplicity, clarity, and decisiveness, the three graces of academic writing, have become the distinctive features of his humanist message, and have made his essays and critiques a landmark in twentieth-century Lithuanian and European social and cultural criticism.

If Vytautas Kavolis is the writer of the ellipse, and Aleksandras Shtromas of the straight line, Tomas Venclova achieves their synthesis.

# Notes

1. Tomas Venclova is the author of 13 books of poetry in Lithuanian, English, German, Swedish, Polish, Hungarian, and Slovenian; of 6 books of essays in Lithuanian, English, Russian, and Polish; of 4 books of literary scholarship in English, Russian, and Polish; and of around 100 scholarly publications. His poems are translated into more than 20 languages.
2. Tomas Venclova, *Forms of Hope: Essays* (Riverdale-on-Hudson, NY: The Sheep Meadow Press, 1999), p.3.
3. Ibid.
4. For more on this issue, see Aleksandras Štromas, "Universalizmas ir nacionalizmas: prieštaraujančios ar suderinamos koncepcijos? (Tomo Venclovos atvejis)" [Universalism and Nationalism: Conflicting or Compatible Conceptions? (The Case of Tomas Venclova)], *Politologija*, Vol. 2 (1991), pp.109–118. N.B.: in Aleksandras Shtromas's Lithuanian contributions, his last name is spelled Štromas.
5. Tomas Venclova, *Vilties formos: eseistika ir publicistika* [Forms of Hope: Essays and Reviews] (Vilnius: Lietuvos rašytojų sąjungos leidykla, 1991), p.10. This book has also been translated into Russian as Tomas Venclova, *Svoboda i pravda* [Freedom and Truth] (Moscow: Progress, 1999).
6. Ibid., p.23.
7. Quoted from Tomas Venclova, *Kad išliktų bent vienas...* [To Have at Least One...] (Vilnius: Algimantas, 1995), p.3.
8. Štromas, "Universalizmas ir nacionalizmas," op. cit., p.113.
9. Venclova, *Forms of Hope*, op. cit., p.86.
10. Venclova, *Vilties formos*, op. cit., pp.250–251.
11. Venclova, *Forms of Hope*, op. cit., p.88.
12. Vytautas Kavolis, "Moralinės kultūros: žemėlapiai, trajektorijos, įtampos" [Moral Cultures: Maps, Trajectories, Tensions], in Virginijus Gasiliūnas, ed., *Metmenų laisvieji svarstymai: 1959–1989* [Free Debates of *Metmenys*: 1959–1989] (Vilnius: Lietuvos rašytojų sąjungos leidykla, 1993), p.183.
13. Peter Chaadayev, "Philosophical Letters: Letter I," in James M. Edie, James P. Scanlan, Mary-Barbara Zeldin, eds., with the collaboration of George L. Kline, *Russian Philosophy*, Vol. 1 (Knoxville, TN: University of Tennessee Press, 1994), p.112.
14. Ibid., p.111.
15. For more on Kundera's attitude to Russia, see Timothy Garton Ash, *The Uses of Adversity: Essays on the Fate of Central Europe* (London: Penguin, 1999), p.166; Milan Kundera, "The Tragedy of Central Europe," *The New York Review of Books*, Vol. XXXI, No. 7 (April 26, 1984): pp.33–38.
16. Venclova, *Forms of Hope*, op. cit., pp.53–54.

17. Algis Mickunas, "Two Philosophers of Lithuanian Origins: Emmanuel Lévinas and Alphonso Lingis," *Lituanus: The Lithuanian Quarterly*, Vol. 24, No. 1 (1978), p.50.
18. Ibid., p.51.
19. Ash, *The Uses of Adversity*, op. cit., p.186.
20. Venclova, *Forms of Hope*, op. cit., p.58.
21. Ibid., p.63.
22. Venclova refers here to Aleksandr Solzhenitsyn.
23. For more on this issue, see Venclova, *Vilties formos*, op. cit., p.147.
24. For instance, Venclova quotes from an editorial in *Naujoji Lietuva* [The New Lithuania] (July 4, 1941): "The greatest enemy of Lithuania and other nations was and in some places remains a Jew... Today, as a result of the genius of Adolf Hitler... we are free from the Jewish yoke... A New Lithuania, after joining a New Europe of Adolf Hitler, must be clean from Jews... To exterminate the Jewry and Communism along with it is a primary task of the New Lithuania." See Tomas Venclova, "A Fifth Year of Independence: Lithuania, 1922 and 1994," *East European Politics and Societies*, Vol. 9, No. 2 (1995), p.365.
25. Venclova, *Forms of Hope*, op. cit., p.47.

# Bibliography

Amalrik, Andrei. *Will the Soviet Union Survive until 1984?* New York: Harper & Row, 1970.

Anderson, Benedict. *Imagined Communities: Reflections on the Origin and Spread of Nationalism.* London & New York: Verso, 1991.

Arendt, Hannah. *The Origins of Totalitarianism.* London, New York & San Diego, CA: Harcourt Brace Jovanovich, 1979.

Ash, Timothy Garton. *The Uses of Adversity: Essays on the Fate of Central Europe.* London: Penguin Books, 1999.

Baudrillard, Jean. *Cool Memories III, 1990–1995.* London & New York: Verso, 1997.

Bauman, Zygmunt. *Community: Seeking Safety in an Insecure World.* Cambridge: Polity Press, 2001.

———. "Intellectuals in East-Central Europe: Continuity and Change." *East European Politics and Societies*, Vol. 1, No. 2 (1987): 162–186.

———. *Intimations of Postmodernity.* London & New York: Routledge, 1992.

———. *Legislators and Interpreters: On Modernity, Post-Modernity, and Intellectuals.* Ithaca, NY: Cornell University Press, 1987.

———. *Life in Fragments: Essays in Postmodern Morality.* Oxford & Cambridge, MA: Blackwell, 1995.

———. "Making and Unmaking of Strangers" in Sandro Fridlizius and Abby Peterson, eds. *Stranger or Guest? Racism and Nationalism in Contemporary Europe.* Stockholm: Almqvist & Wiksell International, 1996: 59–79.

———. *Modernity and Ambivalence.* Cambridge: Polity Press, 1991.

———. *Modernity and the Holocaust.* Ithaca, NY: Cornell University Press, 1991.

———. *Postmodern Ethics.* Oxford & Cambridge, MA: Blackwell, 1993.

———. *Postmodernity and Its Discontents.* New York: New York University Press, 1997.

Baumer, Franklin L. *Modern European Thought: Continuity and Change in Ideas, 1600–1950.* New York: Macmillan, 1977.

Ben-Israel, Hedva. "From Ethnicity to Nationalism." *Contention*, Vol. 5, No. 3 (1996): 51–68.

Berdyaev, Nikolai. *The Russian Idea.* Hudson, NY: Lindisfarne Press, 1992.

Berlin, Sir Isaiah. *Russian Thinkers.* Harmondsworth, Middlesex: Penguin Books, 1979.

———. *Vico and Herder.* London: Hogarth Press, 1976.

Bertens, Hans. *The Idea of the Postmodern: A History.* London & New York: Routledge, 1996.
Billington, James H. *The Icon and the Axe: An Interpretive History of Russian Culture.* New York: Vintage Books, 1970.
Bottomore, T. B. *Elites and Society.* Harmondsworth, Middlesex: Penguin Books, 1966.
Brubaker, Rogers. *Citizenship and Nationhood in France and Germany.* London & Cambridge, MA: Harvard University Press, 1992.
———. "Citizenship Struggles in Soviet Successor States." *International Migration Review*, Vol. XXVI, No. 2 (1992): 269–291.
———. *Nationalism Reframed: Nationhood and the National Question in the New Europe.* Cambridge: Cambridge University Press, 1999.
———. "Nationhood and the National Question in the Soviet Union and Post-Soviet Eurasia: An Institutionalist Account." *Theory and Society* 23/1 (1994): 47–78.
Buber, Martin. *I and Thou.* New York: Charles Scribner's Sons, 1958.
Cohn, Norman. *Warrant for Genocide: The Myth of the Jewish World-Conspiracy and the Protocols of the Elders of Zion.* New York: Harper & Row, 1967.
Confino, Michael. "On Intellectuals and Intellectual Traditions in Eighteenth- and Nineteenth-Century Russia." *Daedalus* 101 (1972): 117–149.
Coser, Lewis A. *Men of Ideas: A Sociologist's View.* New York: Free Press, 1997.
Dahrendorf, Sir Ralf. *Reflections on the Revolution in Europe.* New York: Random House, 1990.
Donskis, Leonidas. *The End of Ideology and Utopia? Moral Imagination and Cultural Criticism in the Twentieth Century.* New York: Peter Lang, 2000.
Dumont, Louis. "Collective Identities and Universalist Ideology: The Actual Interplay." *Theory, Culture & Society*, Vol. 3, No. 3 (1986): 25–33.
———. *Essays on Individualism: Modern Ideology in Anthropological Perspective.* London & Chicago, IL: University of Chicago Press, 1986.
———. *From Mandeville to Marx: The Genesis and Triumph of Economic Ideology.* London & Chicago, IL: University of Chicago Press, 1977.
———. "German Idealism in Comparative Perspective: Hierarchy in the Thought of Fichte" in E. V. Walter, Vytautas Kavolis, Edmund Leites, and Marie Coleman Nelson, eds. *Civilizations East and West: A Memorial Volume for Benjamin Nelson.* Atlantic Highlands, NJ: Humanities Press, 1985: 105–115.
———. *Homo Hierarchicus: The Caste System and its Implications.* Rev. Ed. London & Chicago, IL: University of Chicago Press, 1980.

———. "Interaction between Cultures: Herder's *Volk* and Fichte's *Nation*" in Joseph B. Maier and Chaim L. Waxman, eds. *Ethnicity, Identity, and History: Essays in Memory of Werner J. Cahnman.* New Brunswick, NJ: Transaction, 1983: 13–26.

———. "The Modern Conception of the Individual: Notes on Its Genesis and That of Concomitant Institutions." *Contributions to Indian Sociology* 8 (1965): 13–61.

———. "A Modified View of Our Origins: The Christian Beginnings of Modern Individualism." *Religion* 12 (1982): 1–27.

———. "On Value." *The Proceedings of the British Academy* 66 (1980): 207–241.

Eco, Umberto. *Serendipities: Language and Lunacy.* London: Phoenix, 2000.

———. "Tolerance and the Intolerable." *Index on Censorship* 1/2 (1994): 47–55.

Edie, James M., Scanlan, James P., Zeldin, Mary-Barbara, eds., with the collaboration of George L. Kline. *Russian Philosophy.* 3 vols. Knoxville, TN: University of Tennessee Press, 1994.

Eisenstadt, S. N. "The Axial Age: The Emergence of Transcendental Visions and the Rise of Clerics." *European Journal of Sociology* 23 (1982): 294–314.

———. "The Breakdown of Communist Regimes and the Vicissitudes of Modernity." *Daedalus* 121 (1992): 21–41.

———. "Cultural Traditions and Political Dynamics: The Origins and Modes of Ideological Politics." *British Journal of Sociology* 32 (1981): 155–181.

———. "Intellectuals and Tradition." *Daedalus* 101 (1972): 1–19.

———. *Jewish Civilization: The Jewish Historical Experience in a Comparative Perspective.* Albany, NY: State University of New York Press, 1992.

———. *Revolution and the Transformation of Societies: A Comparative Study of Civilizations.* New York: Free Press, 1978.

Elias, Norbert. *The Civilizing Process.* Oxford & Cambridge, MA: Blackwell, 1994.

Friedman, Jonathan. *Cultural Identity and Global Process.* London: Sage, 1995.

Furet, François. *Marx and the French Revolution.* Ed. Lucien Calvié. London & Chicago, IL: University of Chicago Press, 1988.

———. *The Passing of an Illusion: The Idea of Communism in the Twentieth Century.* London & Chicago, IL: University of Chicago Press, 1999.

———, ed. *Unanswered Questions: Nazi Germany and the Genocide of the Jews.* New York: Schocken Books, 1989.

Geertz, Clifford. *The Interpretation of Cultures.* New York: Basic Books, 1973.

Gellner, Ernest. *Conditions of Liberty: Civil Society and its Rivals*. London: Penguin Books, 1996.

———. "The Importance of Being Modular" in John A. Hall, ed. *Civil Society: Theory, History, Comparison*. Cambridge: Polity Press, 1995: 32–55.

———. "Nationalism and Politics in Eastern Europe." *New Left Review*, Vol. 18, No. 189 (1991): 127–134.

———. *Nations and Nationalism*. Ithaca, NY: Cornell University Press, 1994.

———. *Plough, Sword and Book: The Structure of Human History*. London & Chicago, IL: University of Chicago Press, 1990.

———. *Postmodernism, Reason and Religion*. London & New York: Routledge, 1992.

———. "The Rest of History." *Prospect* (May 1996): 34–38.

———. *Thought and Change*. London: Weidenfeld & Nicolson, 1964.

Gerner, Kristian, and Hedlund, Stefan. *The Baltic States and the End of the Soviet Empire*. London & New York: Routledge, 1997.

———. *Ideology and Rationality in the Soviet Model: A Legacy for Gorbachev*. London & New York: Routledge, 1989.

Gilman, Sander L. *Jewish Self-Hatred: Anti-Semitism and the Hidden Language of the Jews*. London & Baltimore, MD: The Johns Hopkins University Press, 1986.

Greenfeld, Liah. *Nationalism: Five Roads to Modernity*. London & Cambridge, MA: Harvard University Press, 1992.

Greenfeld, Liah, and Chirot, Daniel. "Nationalism and Aggression." *Theory and Society* 23/1 (1994): 79–130.

Hobsbawm, Eric J. *Nations and Nationalism since 1780: Programme, Myth, Reality*. Cambridge: Cambridge University Press, 1990.

Hughes, Stuart H. *Sophisticated Rebels: The Political Culture of European Dissent, 1968–1987*. London & Cambridge, MA: Harvard University Press, 1988.

Hutchinson, John, and Smith, Anthony D., eds. *Nationalism*. Oxford & New York: Oxford University Press, 1994.

Kamenka, Eugene, "Nationalism: Ambiguous Legacies and Contingent Futures" in Aleksandras Shtromas, ed. *The End of "Isms"? Reflections on the Fate of Ideological Politics after Communism's Collapse*. Oxford & Cambridge, MA: Blackwell, 1994: 127–141.

———, ed. *Nationalism: The Nature and Evolution of an Idea*. London: Edward Arnold, 1976.

Kant, Immanuel. "Idea of a Universal History from a Cosmopolitan Point of View" (1784) in Patrick Gardiner, ed. *Theories of History*. New York: Free Press, 1959: 22–34.

———. *Perpetual Peace and Other Essays on Politics, History, and Morals*. Indianapolis, IN: Hackett, 1985.
Kavolis, Vytautas. *Civilization Analysis as a Sociology of Culture*. Lewiston, NY: The Edwin Mellen Press, 1995.
———. "Civilizational Models of Evil" in Marie Coleman Nelson and Michael Eigen, eds. *Evil: Self and Culture*. New York: Human Sciences Press, 1984: 17–35.
———. "Civilizational Paradigms in Current Sociology: Dumont vs. Eisenstadt." *Current Perspectives in Social Theory*, Vol. 7 (1986): 125–140.
———. "Civilizational Processes in Contemporary Eastern Europe." *Revue Baltique*, Vol. 2, No. 1 (1991): 95–107.
———. "Contemporary Moral Cultures and 'The Return of the Sacred'." *Sociological Analysis* 49 (1988): 203–216.
———. "Gebser and the Theory of Socio-Cultural Change" in Eric Mark Kramer, ed. *Consciousness and Culture: An Introduction to the Thought of Jean Gebser*. Westport, CT: Greenwood Press, 1992: 163–177.
———. "History of Consciousness and Civilization Analysis." *Comparative Civilizations Review* 17 (1987): 1–19.
———. "Logics of Evil as Secular Moralities." *Soundings* 68 (1985): 189–211.
———. "Moral Cultures and Moral Logics." *Sociological Analysis* 38 (1977): 331–344.
———. *Moralizing Cultures*. Lanham, MD: University Press of America, 1993.
———. "Nationalism, Modernization, and the Polylogue of Civilizations." *Comparative Civilizations Review* 25 (1991): 124–143.
———. "Nelson's Legacy of Comparative Studies" in E. V. Walter *et al.*, eds. *Civilizations East and West: A Memorial Volume for Benjamin Nelson*. Atlantic Highlands, NJ: Humanities Press, 1985: 17–24.
———. "On the Deformations of Intellectual Culture" in Rimvydas Šilbajoris, ed. *Mind against the Wall: Essays on Lithuanian Culture under Soviet Occupation*. Chicago, IL: Institute of Lithuanian Studies Press, 1983: 34–56.
———. "Post-Modern Man: Psychocultural Responses to Social Trends." *Social Problems* 17 (1970): 435–448.
———. "A Reconsideration of Symbolic Authority." *Indian Journal of Social Research*, Vol. XV, Nos. 2 & 3 (1974): 128–136.
———. "Structure and Energy: Toward a Civilization-Analytic Perspective." *Comparative Civilizations Review* 1 (1979): 21–41.
Koestler, Arthur. *Darkness at Noon*. New York: Bantam Books, 1968.

Kohn, Hans. *The Idea of Nationalism: A Study in its Origins and Background.* New York: Macmillan, 1944.

———. *Nationalism: Its Meaning and History.* Princeton, NJ: Van Nostrand, 1955.

———. *Pan-Slavism: Its History and Ideology.* 2nd Rev. Ed. New York: Vintage Books, 1960.

———. *Prelude to Nation-States: The French and German Experience, 1789–1815.* Princeton, NJ: Van Nostrand, 1967.

———. *Prophets and Peoples: Studies in Nineteenth Century Nationalism.* New York: Macmillan, 1946.

Kundera, Milan. "The Tragedy of Central Europe." *The New York Review of Books,* Vol. XXXI, No. 7 (April 26, 1984): 33–38.

Le Bon, Gustave. *The Crowd: A Study of the Popular Mind.* New York: Ballantine Books, 1969.

Lieven, Anatol. *The Baltic Revolution: Estonia, Latvia, Lithuania and the Path to Independence.* London & New Haven, CT: Yale University Press, 1993.

Marx, Karl, and Engels, Friedrich. *The German Ideology* (1846). London: Lawrence & Wishart, 1967.

———. *The Marx-Engels Reader.* 2nd Ed. Ed. Robert C. Tucker. London & New York: Norton, 1978.

McDaniel, Tim. *The Agony of the Russian Idea.* Princeton, NJ: Princeton University Press, 1996.

Meinecke, Friedrich. *Cosmopolitanism and the National State.* Princeton, NJ: Princeton University Press, 1970.

Michnik, Adam. "Market, Religion and Nationalism: Fundamentalisms in the New European Order." *International Journal of Politics, Culture and Society,* Vol. 8, No. 4 (1995): 525–542.

———. "Nationalism." *Social Research,* Vol. 58, No. 4 (1991): 757–763.

Mickunas, Algis. "Two Philosophers of Lithuanian Origins: Emmanuel Lévinas and Alphonso Lingis." *Lituanus: The Lithuanian Quarterly,* Vol. 24, No. 1 (1978): 44–61.

Miller, David, ed. *The Blackwell Encyclopaedia of Political Thought.* Oxford & Cambridge, MA: Blackwell, 1991.

Miłosz, Czesław. *The Captive Mind.* New York: Vintage Books, 1990.

———. *Native Realm: A Search for Self-Definition.* Garden City, NY: Doubleday, 1968.

———. "On Nationalism." *Partisan Review,* Vol. LIX, No. 1 (1992): 14–20.

Misiunas, Romuald J., and Taagepera, Rein. *The Baltic States: Years of Dependence, 1940–1990.* Expanded Ed. Berkeley, CA: University of California Press, 1993.

Mosse, George L. *The Culture of Western Europe: The Nineteenth and Twentieth Centuries.* Chicago, IL: Rand McNally College Publishing Company, 1974.

Motyl, Alexander J. "The Modernity of Nationalism: Nations, States and Nation-States in the Contemporary World." *Journal of International Affairs*, Vol. 45, No. 2 (1992): 307–323.

———. *Sovietology, Rationality, Nationality: Coming to Grips with Nationalism in the USSR.* New York: Columbia University Press, 1990.

———. *Will the Non-Russians Rebel? State, Ethnicity and Stability in the USSR.* Ithaca, NY: Cornell University Press, 1987.

Orwell, George. *Animal Farm.* London, New York & San Diego, CA: Harcourt Brace & Company, 1995.

———. *1984.* New York: Signet Classic, 1992.

———. "Notes on Nationalism" in George Orwell, *Decline of the English Murder and Other Essays.* Harmondsworth, Middlesex: Penguin Books, 1970: 155–179.

Parekh, Bhikhu. "Discourses on National Identity." *Political Studies*, Vol. XLII, No. 3 (1994): 492–505.

Pomper, Philip. *The Russian Revolutionary Intelligentsia.* Arlington Heights, IL: AHM Publishing Corporation, 1970.

Rieff, Philip, ed. *On Intellectuals.* Garden City, NY: Anchor Books, 1970.

Roepke, Wilhelm. *The Moral Foundations of Civil Society.* New Brunswick, NJ: Transaction, 1996.

Rothberg, Abraham. *The Heirs of Stalin: Dissidence and the Soviet Regime, 1953–1970.* London & Ithaca, NY: Cornell University Press, 1972.

Schöpflin, George. *Politics in Eastern Europe, 1945–1992.* Oxford & Cambridge, MA: Blackwell, 1993.

Schwartz, Benjamin I. "Culture, Modernity, and Nationalism—Further Reflections." *Daedalus* 122 (1993): 206–226.

Senn, Alfred Erich. *The Emergence of Modern Lithuania.* New York: Columbus, 1959.

———. *Gorbachev's Failure in Lithuania.* New York: St. Martin's Press, 1995.

———. *Lithuania Awakening.* Berkeley, CA: University of California Press, 1990.

Shatz, Marshall S. *Soviet Dissent in Historical Perspective.* Cambridge: Cambridge University Press, 1980.

Sheehan, James J. *German Liberalism in the Nineteenth Century.* London & Chicago, IL: University of Chicago Press, 1978.

Shtromas, Aleksandras. "Ideological Politics and the Contemporary World: Have We Seen the Last of 'Isms'?" in Aleksandras Shtromas, ed. *The*

*End of "Isms"? Reflections on the Fate of Ideological Politics after Communism's Collapse.* Oxford & Cambridge, MA: Blackwell, 1994: 183–225.

———. *The Jewish and Gentile Experience of the Holocaust: A Personal Perspective.* Worcester, MA: Assumption College, 1989.

———. "Official Soviet Ideology and the Lithuanian People" in Rimvydas Šilbajoris, ed. *Mind against the Wall: Essays on Lithuanian Culture under Soviet Occupation.* Chicago, IL: Institute of Lithuanian Studies Press, 1983: 57–73.

———. "To Fight Communism: Why and How?" *International Journal on World Peace*, Vol. 1, No. 1 (1984): 20–44.

———. *Who Are the Soviet Dissidents?* Bradford: University of Bradford, 1977.

Smith, Anthony D. "Culture, Community and Territory: The Politics of Ethnicity and Nationalism." *International Affairs*, Vol. 72, No. 3 (1996): 445–458.

———. *The Ethnic Origins of Nations.* Oxford & Cambridge, MA: Blackwell, 1986.

———. *The Ethnic Revival in the Modern World.* Cambridge: Cambridge University Press, 1981.

———. *Nationalism in the Twentieth Century.* Oxford: Martin Robertson, 1979.

———. *Theories of Nationalism.* New York: Harper & Row, 1971.

Snyder, Tim. "National Myths and International Relations: Poland and Lithuania, 1989–1994." *East European Politics and Societies*, Vol. 9, No. 2 (1995): 317–343.

Stern, Fritz. *The Politics of Despair: A Study in the Rise of the Germanic Ideology.* Berkeley, CA: University of California Press, 1963.

Sternhell, Zeev. *Neither Right nor Left: Fascist Ideology in France.* Berkeley, CA: University of California Press, 1986.

Talmon, J. L. *Political Messianism: The Romantic Phase.* New York: Frederick A. Praeger, 1960.

Tismaneanu, Vladimir, and Pavel, Dan. "Romania's Mystical Revolutionaries: The Generation of Angst and Adventure Revisited." *East European Politics and Societies*, Vol.8, No. 3 (1994): 402–438.

Trilling, Lionel. *Beyond Culture: Essays on Literature and Learning.* Harmondsworth, Middlesex: Penguin Books, 1967.

Venclova, Tomas. "Ethnic Identity and the Nationality Issue in Contemporary Soviet Literature." *Studies in Comparative Communism* 21 (1988): 319–329.

———. "A Fifth Year of Independence: Lithuania, 1922 and 1994." *East European Politics and Societies*, Vol. 9, No. 2 (1995): 344–367.
———. *Forms of Hope: Essays*. Riverdale-on-Hudson, NY: The Sheep Meadow Press, 1999.
———. "Prison as Communicative Phenomenon: The Literature of Gulag." *Comparative Civilizations Review* 2 (1979): 65–73.
———. "The Reception of World Literature in Contemporary Lithuania" in Rimvydas Šilbajoris, ed. *Mind against the Wall: Essays on Lithuanian Culture under Soviet Occupation*. Chicago, IL: Institute of Lithuanian Studies Press, 1983: 107–129.
Verdery, Katherine. "The Production and Defense of 'the Romanian Nation,' 1900 to World War II" in Richard G. Fox, ed. *Nationalist Ideologies and the Production of National Cultures*. Washington, D.C.: American Ethnological Society Monograph Series 2, 1990: 81–111.
Walzer, Michael. *The Company of Critics: Social Criticism and Political Commitment in the Twentieth Century*. New York: Basic Books, 1988.
Williams, Raymond. *Keywords: A Vocabulary of Culture and Society*. Oxford & New York: Oxford University Press, 1976.
Wittgenstein, Ludwig. *Culture and Value*. Ed. G. H. von Wright in collaboration with Heikki Nyman. London & Chicago, IL: University of Chicago Press, 1984.
Wolf, Larry. "A Heating of the Blood: From Early Modern Patriotism to Modern Polish Nationalism in the Age of the Partitions." *Ethnic Groups*, Vol. 10, No. 1–3 (1993): 85–99.
———. *Inventing Eastern Europe: Map of Civilization on the Mind of the Enlightenment*. Stanford, CA: Stanford University Press, 1994.
Zingeris, Markas. "Jewish Identity in a non-Jewish Environment after the Holocaust." *Vilnius: Lithuanian Literature, Culture, History* (Summer 2000): 186–195.

# Index

## A

Adamkus, Valdas, 73, 79
Aksyonov, Vassily, 126
Alantas, Vytautas, 18
Anderson, Benedict, 2, 67, 72
Antonescu, Ion, 21
Arbitblatas, Neemija, 23
Arendt, Hannah, 9, 79
Ariès, Philippe, 16, 45
Aristotle, 102
Aron, Raymond, 9, 49, 79, 82
Ash, Timothy Garton, 88, 118, 144, 161–162
Augustine, Saint, 19, 35
Aykhenvald, Yuri, 86

## B

Bakhtin, Mikhail, 47
Barrès, Maurice, 21, 26
Barry, Brian, 31, 36
Basanavičius, Jonas, 22–23, 52, 54
Baudrillard, Jean, 39, 104
Bauman, Zygmunt, 1, 9, 12, 104
Bayle, Pierre, 56
Bentham, Jeremy, 28
Berdyaev, Nikolai, 18–20, 35, 81, 128–129, 137
Berenson, Bernard, 23
Bergson, Henri, 105
Berlin, Sir Isaiah, 35, 114
Besançon, Alain, 79
Blaga, Lucian, 21
Błoński, Jan, 111–112
Bonald, Louis-Gabriel-Ambroise, Vicomte de, 19
Bonner, Elena, 75

Bordonaitė, Mira, 74
Bradbury, Ray, 155
Brahms, Johannes, 119
Brazauskas, Algirdas, 85
Brezhnev, Leonid, 124
Brodsky, Joseph, 121, 128–129, 141
Buber, Martin, 108, 128, 136–137
Bukovsky, Vladimir, 75, 91, 128, 147
Bulgakov, Sergei, 81
Bush, George, 34

## C

Carlyle, Thomas, 26
Chaadayev, Peter, 137–141, 161
Cioran, Emil, 20
Condorcet, Marie-Jean, Marquis de, 56
Conquest, Robert, 76
Coser, Lewis A., 110
Curie-Skłodowska, Maria (Marie), 127

## D

Daniel, Prophet, 19
Daniel, Yuli, 75, 86, 91
Danilevsky, Nikolai, 17
Darwin, Charles, 52, 135
Daudet, Léon, 21
Destutt de Tracy, Antoine Louis Claude, Comte 95
Dostoevsky, Fyodor, 18, 158
Dumont, Louis, 14–16, 31, 35, 37, 45–47, 50
Durkheim, Émile, 22

## E

Eco, Umberto, 104
Edwards, Ted, 76
Ehret, Joseph, 158
Eisenstadt, S. N., 45–47, 50
Eliade, Mircea, 20
Elias, Norbert, 14, 35, 45

## F

Faulkner, Robert, 76
Feuerbach, Ludwig, 48, 118
Fichte, Johann Gottlieb, 32
Fiore, Joachim de, 19
Flewelling, Ralph Tyler, 129, 137
Foucault, Michel, 16, 45
Frank, Semyon, 81
Frobenius, Leo, 17, 22, 32
Freud, Sigmund, 47, 59
Fukuyama, Francis, 95

## G

Galanskov, Yuri, 124
Galich, Alexander, 75
Gandhi, Mohandas Karamchand (Mahatma), 54
Garibaldi, Giuseppe, 92
Gediminas, Grand Duke of Lithuania, 55, 127
Gellner, Ernest, 2, 6, 9, 33, 37, 49–50, 67, 79, 82, 102
Genghis Khan, 142
Gimbutas, Marija, 127
Ginzburg, Alexander, 75, 124, 126
Girnius, Juozas, 21
Gobineau, Joseph-Arthur, Comte de, 87
Goethe, Johann Wolfgang von, 142
Gogol, Nikolai, 158
Gombrowicz, Witold, 151
Gurwitsch, Aron, 23
Gustainis, Valentinas, 22

## H

Havel, Václav, 3, 67, 121, 141, 144
Hegel, G. W. F., 17, 32, 142
Heidegger, Martin, 22, 100, 142
Heifetz, Jascha, 23
Helvétius, Claude-Adrien, 56
Herder, Johann Gottfried von, 15, 31–33, 55, 63, 99–100, 109, 137, 144
Herzen, Alexander, 125, 129, 137–138, 140
Hilckman, Anton, 22, 32
Hitler, Adolf, 80, 142, 153, 162
Hobsbawm, Eric J., 2, 6, 67
Hook, Sidney, 76
Hsu, Francis L. K., 46
Hughes, H. Stuart, 90, 118
Huntington, Samuel, 95

## I

Ionesco, Eugène, 20
Ionescu, Nae, 20

## J

Jagiełło (Władysław II), Grand Duke of Lithuania and King of Poland, 127
Jaspers, Karl, 9, 15, 79, 136–137

Jenkins, Roy, 76
John XXIII, 50
Juozaitis, Arvydas, 29

## K

Kafka, Franz, 88
Kagan, Lady Margaret, xiii, 74–76
Kamenka, Eugene, 30–31
Kant, Immanuel, 31–32, 37, 99–100
Kaplan, Morton, 76, 78
Karsavin, Lev, 18, 158
Kavolis, Vytautas, ix, xi, xiv, 3–6, 8–9, 12, 16, 20, 24, 35–36, 39–73, 78–79, 82, 84, 93, 103–105, 108–109, 115–116, 125, 128–129, 133–134, 137–138, 140, 145–146, 148, 157, 160–161
Khrushchev, Nikita, 75, 92
Klages, Ludwig, 22
Klein, Joseph, Rabbi, 105, 115
Koestler, Arthur, 9–10, 79
Kołakowski, Leszek, 49, 76, 79
Konrád, György, 141, 144
Kościuszko, Tadeusz, 92
Kozin-Štromienė, Eugenia, 74
Krėvė-Mickevičius, Vincas, 23, 151
Kudirka, Vincas, 22, 51–52, 54, 71
Kundera, Milan, 3, 35–36, 67, 79, 121, 141, 161

## L

Lamennais, Félicité Robert de, 27
Landsbergis, Vytautas, 80
Lebra, Takie Sugiyama, 46
Lenin, Vladimir, 85
Leonas, Petras, 35
Leontyev, Konstantin, 18
Lessing, Theodor, 114
Lévinas, Emmanuel, 23, 136–137, 142, 161
Lieven, Anatol, 5, 12
Lipchitz, Jacques, 23
Locke, John, 23, 28
Lotman, Yuri, 81–82, 123
Lukacs, John, 30

## M

Maceina, Antanas, 14, 18–21, 26–28, 35
Macenavičienė, Marija, 74
Macenavičius, Antanas, 74
Mackus, Algimantas, 41, 152
Maistre, Joseph, Comte de, 19–20, 96
Mandelstam, Osip, 158
Mandeville, Bernard, 28, 35
Mann, Thomas, 144
Mannheim, Karl, 5, 94
Maritain, Jacques, 129, 137
Marquand, David, 76
Marx, Karl, 32, 35, 48, 59, 95, 98, 114, 118, 142
Masaryk, Tomáš, 144
Maurras, Charles, 21, 26
Mauss, Marcel, 45
Mazzini, Giuseppe, 17, 51, 68, 92, 129, 140
McDaniel, Tim, 81–82, 118
McKinlay, Robert, 76
Mendelssohn, Felix, 119
Meras, Icchokas, 155, 158

Michelet, Jules, 17, 140
Michnik, Adam, 3, 121, 144, 149
Mickiewicz, Adam, 17, 51, 91, 125, 129
Mickunas, Algis, 142–143, 162
Mill, John Stuart, 22, 28, 52, 56, 99–100
Miłosz, Czesław, 3, 5, 8–10, 49, 67–68, 79, 84, 86–88, 109, 118, 121, 126–129, 140, 149–150
Miłosz, Oscar, 17
Minogue, Kenneth, 76
Modigliani, Amedeo, 23
Montesquieu, Charles-Louis de Secondat, Baron de la Brede et de, 56
Motyl, Alexander J., 33, 37
Mounier, Emmanuel, 129, 137
Mumford, Lewis, 15, 73
Mykolaitis-Putinas, Vincas, 18

## N

Nabokov, Vladimir, 141
Napoléon, Bonaparte, 19
Nekrasov, Viktor, 86
Nelson, Benjamin, 45, 71
Nietzsche, Friedrich, 106
Noica, Constantin, 20

## O

O'Brien, Conor Cruise, 33
Orlov, Yuri, 126
Orwell, George, 9–10, 79, 86, 88–89, 93, 118
Osipov, Vladimir, 90
Ovid, 125

Ozolas, Romualdas, 29, 36

## P

Paine, Thomas, 28
Parekh, Bhikhu, 76
Parsons, Talcott, 40
Paul VI, 50
Péguy, Charles, 108
Peter I (Peter the Great), 17, 90
Petkus, Viktoras, 126
Pinsky, Leonid, 75
Plato, 59, 142
Pomerantz, Grigory, 75
Popper, Sir Karl R., 79, 105
Pushkin, Alexander, 137

## Q

Quinet, Edgar, 140

## R

Račkauskas, Merkelis, 122
Radishchev, Alexander, 137
Rathenau, Walther, 114
Renan, Joseph-Ernest, 31–32, 55, 99–100
Ricardo, David, 28
Römeris, Mykolas, 22, 35
Rostropovich, Mstislav, 126
Rozanov, Vassily, 18
Rückert, Heinrich, 17, 32

## S

Sakharov, Andrei, 75, 86, 91, 141, 147, 149

Šalkauskis, Stasys, 14, 17–19, 21, 151
Šapoka, Adolfas, 25
Sartre, Jean-Paul, 142
Sauerwein, Georg Julius Justus, 52
Sauka, Donatas, 37
Schelling, Friedrich Wilhelm Joseph von, 137, 141
Schöpflin, George, 30, 36
Senn, Alfred Erich, xiii, 16
Sezemanas, Vosylius, 21
Shafarevich, Igor, 90
Shakespeare, William, 59, 75, 125
Sharansky, Natan (Anatoly), 126
Shtromas (Štromas), Aleksandras, ix, xi–xiv, 3–5, 8–10, 30, 32–33, 36–37, 73–89, 91–119, 121–122, 128–131, 135, 137, 140, 146, 148, 151, 153, 157, 159, 160–161
Singer, David, 76
Singer, Isaac Bashevis, 114
Sinyavsky, Andrei, 75, 86, 91
Škirpa, Kazys, 27, 36
Šliūpas, Jonas, 22, 52, 54
Smetona, Antanas, 25
Smith, Adam, 28
Smith, Anthony D., 2, 67
Šmulkštys, Julius, 73
Sniečkus, Antanas, 74–75
Socrates, 54, 125
Solovyov, Vladimir, 18
Solzhenitsyn, Aleksandr, 85–86, 90, 94, 126, 141, 147, 162
Sombart, Werner, 27
Sorel, Georges, 26
Sorokin, Pitirim A., 40, 45–46
Soutine, Chaïm, 23

Spengler, Oswald, 17, 20, 22, 32, 46
Spiwak, Pawel, 111–112
Spranger, Eduard, 22
Stahl, Henri, 21
Stalin, Joseph, 75, 86, 101, 106, 124, 133, 142, 153
Stočkus, Bronius, 21
Štromas, Jurgis, 74
Struve, Peter, 81

T

Taagepera, Rein, 77
Talmon, J. L., 16, 35
Tawney, R. H., 28
Tönnies, Ferdinand, 23
Trebitsch, Arthur, 114
Treitschke, Heinrich von, 27, 100
Trilling, Lionel, 121
Trotsky, Leon, 4
Trumpa, Vincas, 14–15, 35, 125
Tumas-Vaižgantas, Juozas, 23, 151
Turner, Victor, 47

V

Vairas-Račkauskas, Karolis, 122
Venclova, Antanas, 121–122, 124
Venclova, Tomas, ix, xi, xiv, 3–10, 12, 13, 24, 67, 75, 79, 85, 91, 103, 107–108, 111–112, 115, 119, 121–162
Vico, Giambattista, 20
Voegelin, Eric, 58
Voinovich, Vladimir, 86
Voltaire, 56
Vulcănescu, Mircea, 20

## W

Weber, Max, 22, 28, 45, 50, 59, 82, 96, 98
Weininger, Otto, 114
White, Hayden, 16, 45
Williams, Raymond, 20
Wittgenstein, Ludwig, 114, 119

## Z

Zamyatin, Yevgeny, 79
Zinkevičius, Zigmas, 36